QUIZ
QUEST
2
3-30-2010
Happy Birthday
Daniel!
Mrs Peters-Lambert
Principal
Kennedy Middle School
Kankakee, Illinois

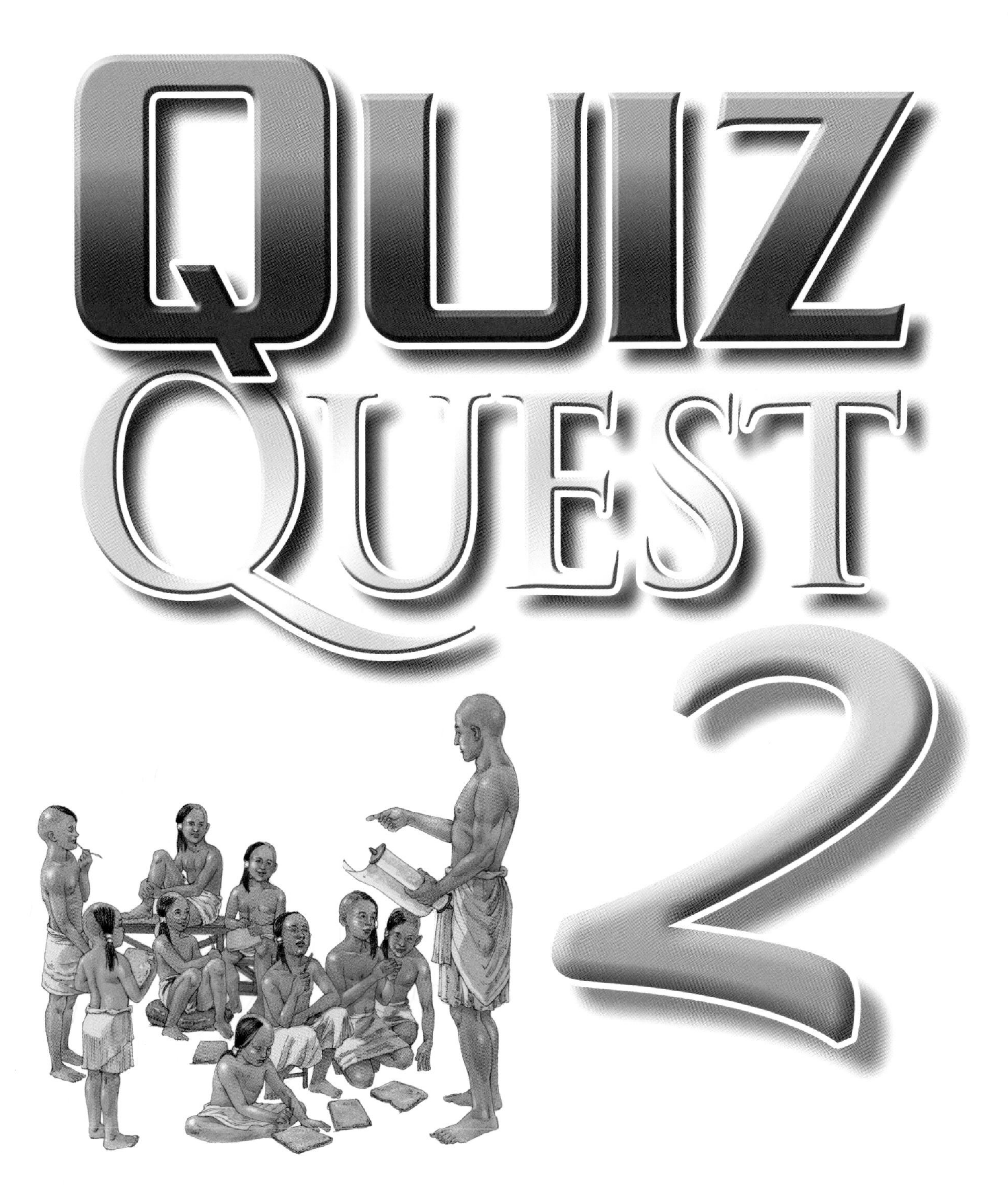
QUIZ
QUEST
2

KINGFISHER
BOSTON

KINGFISHER
a Houghton Mifflin Company imprint
222 Berkeley Street
Boston, Massachusetts 02116
www.houghtonmifflinbooks.com

First published in 2007
2 4 6 8 10 9 7 5 3 1
1TR/0107LFG/PICA(PICA)/140MA/C

Senior editor: Theresa Bebbington
Editor: Conrad Mason
Coordinating editor: Caitlin Doyle
Senior designers: Leah Germann, Steve Woosnam-Savage
Picture research manager: Cee Weston-Baker
Artwork archivist: Gina Weston-Baker
Senior production controller: Jessamy Oldfield
DTP coordinator: Catherine Hibbert

LIBRARY OF CONGRESS CATALOGING-IN-PUBLICATION DATA
has been applied for.

ISBN 978-0-7534-6078-8

Printed in China

Contents

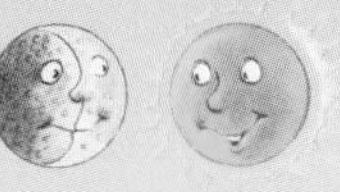

SCIENCE AND INVENTIONS 59

HISTORY 93

SPORTS AND ART 111

ANSWERS 128

INDEX 156

How this book works

It's as easy as one, two, three! Option one: Use the question panels to quiz yourself. Option two: Turn the page to read all about the topic—numbered circles show you where to look to figure out the answer for yourself. Option three: Look up the answers at the back of the book. These are the three ways that you can use *Quiz Quest 2*. Or you can just read the book all of the way through!

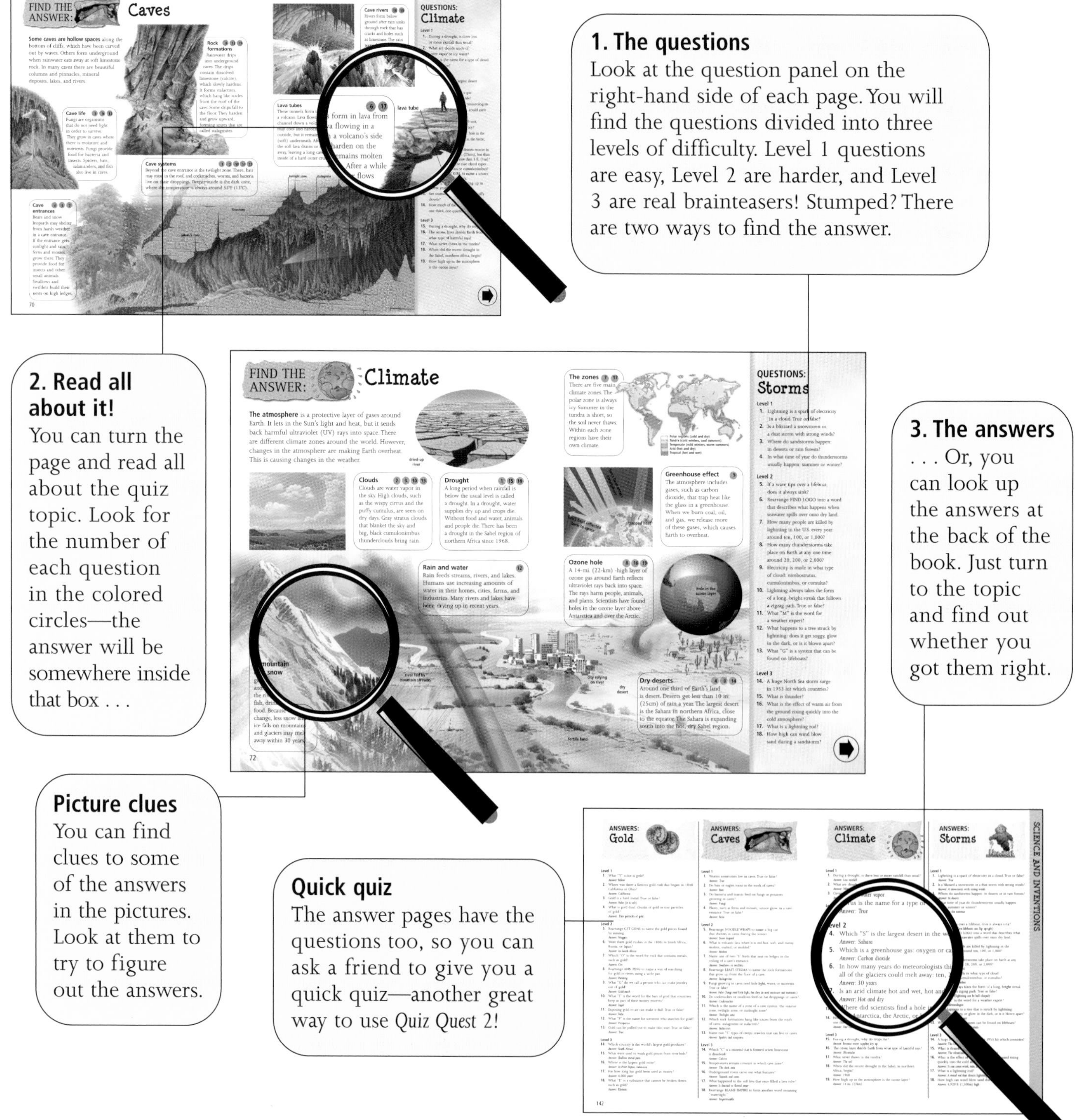

1. The questions
Look at the question panel on the right-hand side of each page. You will find the questions divided into three levels of difficulty. Level 1 questions are easy, Level 2 are harder, and Level 3 are real brainteasers! Stumped? There are two ways to find the answer.

2. Read all about it!
You can turn the page and read all about the quiz topic. Look for the number of each question in the colored circles—the answer will be somewhere inside that box . . .

3. The answers
. . . Or, you can look up the answers at the back of the book. Just turn to the topic and find out whether you got them right.

Picture clues
You can find clues to some of the answers in the pictures. Look at them to try to figure out the answers.

Quick quiz
The answer pages have the questions too, so you can ask a friend to give you a quick quiz—another great way to use *Quiz Quest 2*!

QUIZ ONE

Nature

Desert creatures

Spiders

Bees

Deadly creatures

Frogs

Coral reef creatures

Dolphins and porpoise

Killer whales

Baleen whales

Birds of prey

Rats and mice

Bats

Big cats

Great apes

Bears

Pets

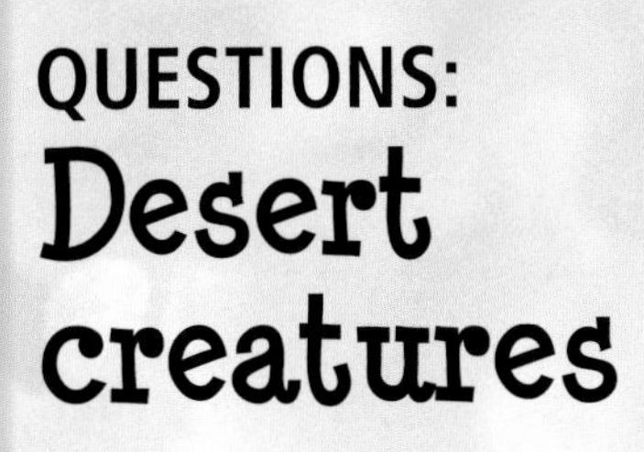

QUESTIONS:

Desert creatures

Level 1

1. What is a coyote: a wild dog or a wild cat?
2. What are the thorny devil and the Gila monster: reptiles, birds, or insects?
3. Desert foxes have large ears to help keep them cool. True or false?

Level 2

4. Some desert birds build their nests in cacti. True or false?
5. Desert birds of prey eat prickly plants. True or false?
6. Which desert lizard is poisonous: the Gila monster or the chameleon?
7. Which bird is not a desert bird of prey: the turkey vulture, lappet-faced vulture, or kestrel?
8. What kind of fox lives in the desert: red fox, arctic fox, or fennec fox?
9. Does the thorny devil collect dew on its body or from plants?
10. Which characteristics help desert hunters: swift movement, good eyesight, claws, or all of the above?
11. Does the Peruvian fox live in the Atacama Desert in South America or the Sahara in north Africa?
12. Which animal does the bobcat eat: rodents or coyotes?

Level 3

13. Which type of lizard lives its entire life in a decaying cactus?
14. Does the desert coyote weigh more or less than a coyote that lives in the mountains?
15. Which feature of a bobcat helps its hearing?
16. Which "B" is a flying creature that eats the nectar found in cactus flowers?
17. What is another name for the Peruvian fox?
18. Which "G" lizard can live for months without food?

FIND THE ANSWER:

Desert creatures

Deserts are harsh places to live, but many animals have adapted to life there. The biggest problems are finding water and staying cool in hot temperatures. Many desert animals, such as the camel, can live for days without drinking and get their water from the food that they eat such as insects, reptiles, and plants. To stay cool, animals such as the meerkat and the kangaroo rat make burrows underground.

Desert plant life
4 13 16

Animals use desert plants for shelter, food, and water. Bats eat their nectar, and some birds build nests on cacti. The yucca night lizard spends its entire life under a decaying cactus.

Bobcats
12 15

The bobcat lives in North America and preys on wild rabbits, hares, and rodents. It lives in deserts and scrublands (dry areas with stunted plants) and mountainous regions. The hairs on its ears help improve the bobcat's already excellent hearing.

Birds of prey
5 7

The lappet-faced vulture of Africa, the turkey vulture of the U.S., eagles, and other birds of prey eat rodents, rabbits, and snakes.

cactus

eagle

coyote

hare

kangaroo rat

scorpion

rattlesnake

Hunting
10

Desert hunters run or fly swiftly, have good eyesight, and have claws and sharp teeth to catch their prey. Many, such as the desert night lizard, hunt at night when it is cooler.

Foxes

3 8 11 17

Desert foxes have large ears to keep cool. Fennec foxes are the smallest foxes. They live in the Sahara in north Africa. The Peruvian, or Sechuran, fox lives in the Atacama Desert, in South America.

Lizards

2 6 9 18

Scaly-skinned lizards are reptiles that have adapted to life in dry desert climates. The thorny devil of Australia is covered in spikes that collect dew for drinking. The poisonous Gila monster lives for months without food by storing fat in its tail.

Gila monster

Coyotes

1 14

Like other wild dogs, the coyote communicates using barks and yaps. Its howl tells other coyotes where it is. Desert coyotes weigh less than half the weight of coyotes that live in the mountains.

QUESTIONS: Spiders

Level 1

1. Is the spider's body made up of two, three, or eight parts?
2. How many wings do spiders have: one pair, two pairs, or none?
3. Spiders spin silk to make spider webs. True or false?
4. Most spiders have no eyes. True or false?

Level 2

5. The trapdoor spider catches its prey in a web. True or false?
6. What shape does an orb weaver spin after it makes a frame: "X," "Y," or "Z"?
7. A spider's silk-making organs are in its abdomen. True or false?
8. Are a spider's legs attached to the front part of its body or its abdomen?
9. Can some spiders only see shadows and light?
10. How does a spider eat its prey: by chewing it, by turning its insides into liquid and sucking them out, or by eating it whole?
11. In what "A" part of the body are the organs that a spider uses for digesting food?
12. Which spider is the largest in the world?
13. The Goliath bird-eating spider only eats birds. True or false?

Level 3

14. A dry silk thread stays on the web when a spider finishes spinning. True or false?
15. What type of spiders are the wolf spider and tarantula?
16. What do a spider's hollow fangs hold?
17. Is it believed that jumping spiders have good or bad eyesight?
18. How does a bird-eating spider detect movement?
19. How does a spider turn its prey's insides into liquid?

FIND THE ANSWER: Spiders

garden cross spider

Spiders are not insects. They belong to a group of animals called arachnids. This group of more than 75,000 species (types) also includes scorpions, mites, and ticks. All spiders can make silk with glands in their bodies, but not all spiders spin webs. All spiders have venom glands, but only a few, such as the funnel-web spider, are harmful to people.

Anatomy 1 2 8

The spider's body is made up of two parts: the front part (the head and thorax together) and the back part (called the abdomen). The back part is protected by a special plate. Unlike insects, spiders have eight legs. These legs are attached to the front part of the spider's body. Spiders do not have wings or antennae.

abdomen

head and thorax

Inside 7 11 16

The front part of the spider is packed with muscles that are used to move its jaws and legs. Its jaws have hollow fangs, which contain poison that is made in special venom glands. The spider's abdomen holds the organs for digesting food and making silk, as well as the spider's heart and blood.

Eyes 4 9 17

Most spiders have six or eight eyes. The majority of spiders can only see shadows and light. However, some spiders, such as jumping spiders, are believed to have good eyesight.

Spinning webs 3 6 14

To form an orb web, a spider uses silk that comes out of small openings, called spinnerets, at the end of its body. It spins a frame of strong, dry threads, beginning with a "bridge" thread and a "Y" shape. After the frame is made, a temporary spiral is spun with the same dry silk. Finally, the spider spins sticky thread in a spiral and removes the dry silk.

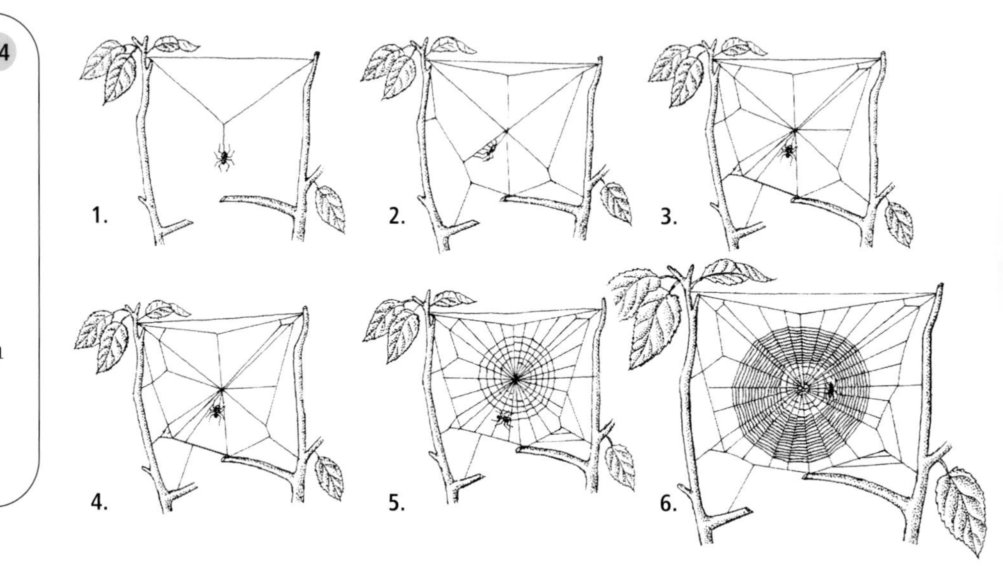

Catching prey

5 15

Web-spinning spiders wait for prey close to the center of their web or hide nearby. They catch their prey on the sticky, silk thread. Others, such as the trapdoor spider, lure their prey with a trap. The wolf spider and the tarantula are hunting spiders.

fly

Eating prey

10 19

Spiders bite their prey and inject them with venom, or they trap them in silk thread to stop them from moving. The spider then injects special juices to turn the insides of the prey into liquid. This allows the spider to eat by sucking out the liquid.

dragonfly

Bird eater

12 13 18

The Goliath bird-eating spider is the largest spider in the world. It is around the size of a dinner plate and has hairs on its body that it uses to detect movement. It lives in the rain forests of South America and usually eats insects, mice, or lizards, rather than birds.

QUESTIONS: Bees

Level 1

1. Honey comes from which creatures: bats, bees, or bears?
2. What "D" are male honeybees called?
3. Wild honeybees build their own nest, called a hive. True or false?
4. Bees do not have an abdomen. True or false?

Level 2

5. Are a bee's wings attached to its thorax (the middle section of its body) or to its head?
6. Worker bees collect pollen and nectar. True or false?
7. What "N" is honey made from?
8. What "H" shape is a cell in a beehive?
9. Does a honeybee have two or three types of wings?
10. Do bees' eggs hatch in three days, one week, or one month?
11. Bees have special glands that produce what: wax, oil, or fat?
12. Some bees have a special "honey stomach" for storing nectar. True or false?
13. What is the average number of flowers that a bee will visit in a single trip: 5–10, 50–100, or 500–1,000?

Level 3

14. Where do honeybees store pollen when they are collecting it?
15. Name the special tube that bees use to suck out nectar.
16. On average, how many eggs might a queen bee lay in one month?
17. How is honey removed from a honeybee?
18. Name a substance made by worker bees that is fed to future queen bees.
19. What does a honeybee do when it finds a new supply of food?

Bees

Bees are flying insects that are related to wasps and ants. Honeybees are well known because they pollinate food crops and produce honey and wax. They live in huge colonies. Each colony has a queen and many female worker bees. Male honeybees only enter the hive to mate with the queen.

abdomen

thorax

head

honey stomach

proboscis

Flying

9 19

Bees have two types of wings—a pair of forewings and a smaller pair of hind wings. They work together to help the bee fly. When a honeybee finds a new supply of food, it flies home and does a special "dance" to tell the other bees about it.

Feeding

15

Bees have a proboscis—a part of the mouth that is formed into a long, flexible tube. It works like a bendable straw and allows bees to suck sweet nectar from flowers. When a bee does not need its proboscis, the bee can pull it up and fold it beneath its head.

Anatomy

2 4 5 11

Bees have three main body parts: the abdomen, the thorax, and the head. The abdomen has special glands for producing wax (which is used to make honeycomb). The thorax, the middle section of the bee, is where the legs and wings are attached. Unlike male bees, or drones, female bees have stingers at the end of the abdomen that can inject venom. If the stinger breaks off, the bee will die.

Pollen

6 13 14

Worker honeybees leave the nest in the summer to visit flowers and gather nectar and pollen. Bees store pollen in pollen "baskets" on their hind legs. Worker bees will visit between 50 and 100 flowers in a single trip.

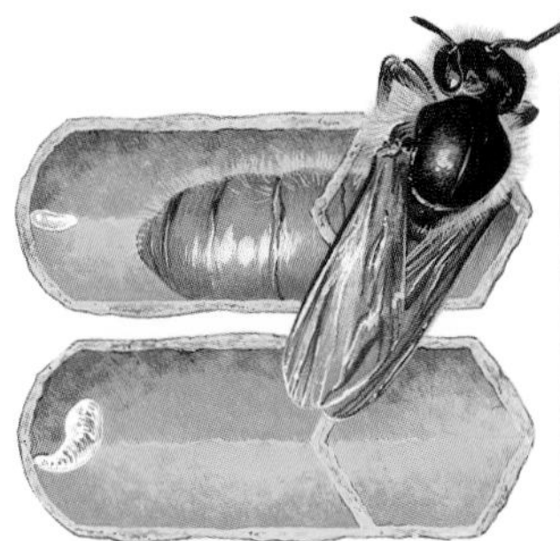

Eggs

10 16 18

The queen bee lays eggs in individual wax cells—as many as 200,000 in a year. The eggs hatch in three days, and the larvae are fed pollen and nectar by worker bees. Future queen bees are fed royal jelly, a substance made by worker bees.

Hive

3 8

In the wild, honeybees build their nest, or hive, in the hollow of a tree or in a cave. Beekeepers build a wooden hive. The hive is made from a waxy material, which is shaped into hexagonal, or six-sided, cells called honeycomb. A hive can last for 50 years or more.

Honey

1 7 12 17

Only honeybees can make honey. The ones that make it have a special "honey stomach" in which they hold nectar. In the hive, other worker bees suck out the nectar and mix it with special enzymes in their bodies. This mixture is spread onto the honeycombs. As it dries out, it becomes honey.

QUESTIONS: Deadly creatures

Level 1

1. Some snakes are poisonous. True or false?
2. What do great white sharks hunt: seals, porpoise, or both?
3. Female black widow spiders are dangerous to people. True or false?
4. Which creature wraps its body around its victim to kill it: the boa constrictor or the jellyfish?

Level 2

5. What "T" do jellyfish have?
6. How does a crocodile kill its prey: by tossing it into the air or by drowning it?
7. The cobra kills its prey by wrapping its body around it. True or false?
8. How do sharks find prey: by smell, by using special cells that sense movement, or both?
9. What does a jellyfish eat: small fish, worms, or both?
10. How heavy is a great white shark: 440 lbs. (200kg), 2,200 lbs. (1,000kg), or 4,400 lbs. (2,000kg)?
11. Is the tiger shark considered to be safe or dangerous to people?
12. Does the crocodile hide from its prey?

Level 3

13. What is another name for a box jellyfish?
14. How many clusters of tentacles does a box jellyfish have?
15. Which piranha is the most dangerous?
16. Which spider is the most dangerous?
17. The crocodile has what type of special feature to stay underwater?
18. What "B" does a piranha detect with a special sensory system?

FIND THE ANSWER:

Deadly creatures

Many animals have special features that can help them kill or harm other creatures. Some have venomous bites or stings, while others have razor-sharp teeth or claws.

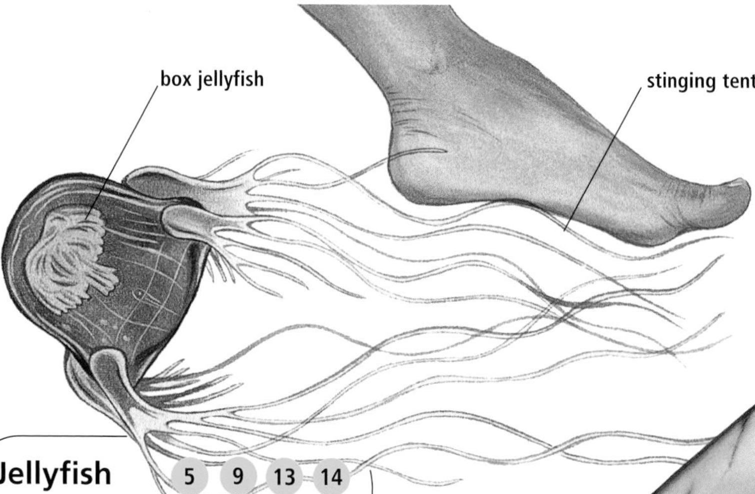

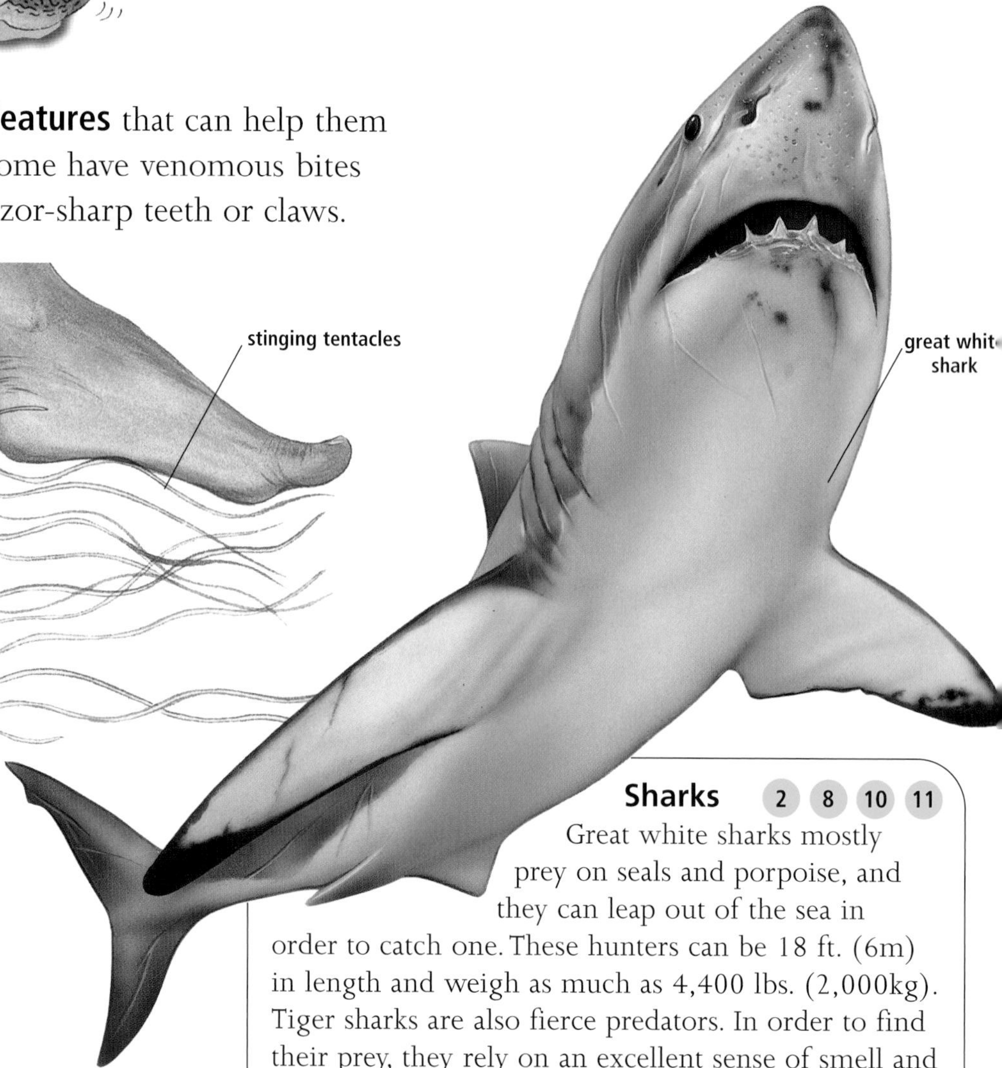

box jellyfish
stinging tentacles
great white shark

Jellyfish
5 9 13 14

Although many jellyfish are not deadly, the Australian box jellyfish, or sea wasp, can kill within minutes. Its four clusters of 15 tentacles are covered with thousands of stinging cells. They can stretch out to around 10 ft. (3m) when the jellyfish is hunting for small fish and other prey.

Sharks
2 8 10 11

Great white sharks mostly prey on seals and porpoise, and they can leap out of the sea in order to catch one. These hunters can be 18 ft. (6m) in length and weigh as much as 4,400 lbs. (2,000kg). Tiger sharks are also fierce predators. In order to find their prey, they rely on an excellent sense of smell and special cells that can sense movement in the water.

Crocodiles
6 12 17

To catch its meal, the crocodile has waterproof flaps to seal its eyes, ears, nostrils, and throat while it hides underwater. An animal that comes to the water for a drink cannot see or smell the crocodile that will suddenly explode from the water to snatch and drown its prey.

Spiders

3 16

All spiders have poisonous bites. Around 30 species are dangerous to people, including the female black widow, the Australian funnel-web spider, and the deadliest: the Brazilian wandering spider.

Snakes

1 4 7

Several snakes have poisonous bites such as the rattlesnake, the cobra, and the brown tree snake. Others, such as pythons and boa constrictors, wrap their bodies around their prey and crush it.

Piranhas

15 18

The piranha lives in rivers in South America. It has sharp teeth and strong jaws for eating meat. It can find its prey by using a special sensory system that can detect the smell of blood. Out of the 1,200 species of piranhas, the red-bellied piranha is the most dangerous. Piranhas rarely eat anything that is larger than themselves.

QUESTIONS: Frogs

Level 1

1. A baby frog is called a tadpole. True or false?
2. Do flying frogs have feathers, like birds, or flaps of skin?
3. Adult frogs have tails. True or false?
4. Do frogs lay their eggs in water or in nests made in trees?

Level 2

5. Tadpoles have tails, gills, and legs. True or false?
6. How often do most frogs shed their skin: once a week, once a year, or never?
7. How far can a flying frog glide: 6 ft. (2m), 40 ft. (12m), or 70 ft. (22m)?
8. All frogs catch food with their tongues. True or false?
9. How many days does it take for a frog's eggs to hatch: 3–5 days, 3–25 days, or 25–35 days?
10. FRET LOG can be rearranged to give the name of what stage of a frog before it becomes an adult?
11. Are frogs' ears specially tuned in to hear the calls of predators or to hear the calls of their own species?
12. Would a frog puff out its throat to call another frog, to scare a predator, or both?
13. What "A" do tadpoles eat?

Level 3

14. Where do poison dart frogs live?
15. Can a cricket frog jump twice its body length, ten times its body length, or more than 30 times its body length?
16. What "M" is the term that is used to describe the changes that a tadpole undergoes?
17. Name a species of frog that guards its eggs from predators.
18. The poison from the poison dart frog is used by some tribespeople to do what?
19. Give a reason why frogs need to keep their skin wet.

FIND THE ANSWER: Frogs

A frog is an amphibian without a tail. It is at home on land and in the water and can hop and swim. Some frogs climb trees. Frogs have lived on Earth for around 190 million years, and they live on every continent, except for Antarctica. Both frogs and toads are part of the same animal group, but toads often have drier, rougher skin.

frog's eggs

tadpole

froglet

adult

1. Eggs (4) (9) (17)

Females lay thousands of eggs in freshwater such as rivers and ponds. The eggs hatch 3 to 25 days later. Some species of frogs, such as the Darwin's frog and the poison dart frog, guard their eggs against predators.

2. Tadpole (1) (5) (13)

Baby frogs, called tadpoles, have gills for breathing and a tail for swimming, but they have no front or back legs. They eat plants such as algae. Many tadpoles are poisonous, so birds and beetles don't eat them.

3. Froglet (10) (16)

After several weeks, tadpoles undergo a metamorphosis (a change in form). They develop lungs and lose their gills. Their tail also begins to disappear. Froglets develop back and front legs and begin to eat insects instead of plants.

4. Adult (3) (6) (19)

Fully grown frogs do not have tails. They breathe through their skin as well as through their lungs, and they keep their skin wet so that they can get oxygen from the water. Once a week, frogs shed their skin.

Tongue (8)

Some frogs have long, sticky tongues to catch insects or spiders—often in less than one second. Other frogs catch prey with their front legs.

Jumping (15)

A frog's legs are made for leaping. The powerful hind legs have long ankle bones that help them jump. The tiny cricket frog is only around 1 in. (30mm) long, but it is a great jumper, leaping more than 3 ft. (1m). A frog's front legs are used for balance when it is sitting.

Puffing

11 12

A frog puffs out its throat when it is calling or trying to scare a predator. When making croaks and other sounds, the frog's vocal sacs expand to create a louder call. Frogs' ears are specially tuned in so that they can hear the calls of their own species.

flying frog

Feet

2 7

Flying frogs don't really fly, but they have webbed feet and flattened bodies with skin flaps so that they can glide as far as 40 ft. (12m) from tree to tree. They steer themselves by moving their feet.

Poisonous frogs

14 18

Poison dart frogs have brightly colored and patterned bodies to warn predators that they are poisonous. They live in the tropical rain forests of Central and South America. Some tribespeople use the frogs' poison on the tips of their blow darts for hunting.

QUESTIONS: Coral reef creatures

Level 1

1. Do most corals like warm, shallow water?
2. Is the anemone fish one of the many species of fish that live in the coral reef?
3. Starfish are not really fish. True or false?
4. Do jellyfish have brains?

Level 2

5. Some fish are colorful or patterned so that they can recognize each other. True or false?
6. CLEAT NETS can be rearranged to give the name of what part of a jellyfish?
7. What does a jellyfish's nerve net detect: touch or light?
8. How many species of fish inhabit the coral reef: more than 3,000, more than 4,000, or more than 5,000?
9. Which coral reef creature looks as harmless as a rock?
10. Are brain coral and elkhorn types of hard corals or soft corals?
11. What do corals use their tentacles for: to walk along the seabed, to feed themselves, or to swim?
12. Do sea anemones protect anemone fish or eat them?

Level 3

13. What "P" do corals eat?
14. What "S" means "life together"?
15. What is the name for a large group of jellyfish?
16. How many tentacles do soft corals have?
17. What part of their body do most fish move in order to swim?
18. Which "S" creature is an echinoderm?

FIND THE ANSWER:

Coral reef creatures

Coral reefs are teeming with life, and the coral itself is made up of billions of tiny creatures, called polyps. Polyps attach themselves to the reef and leave their skeletons behind when they die, building up hard limestone. New polyps attach to the limestone, and the reef grows larger. The Great Barrier Reef, one of several coral reefs around the world, stretches for almost 1,240 mi. (2,000km) along Australia.

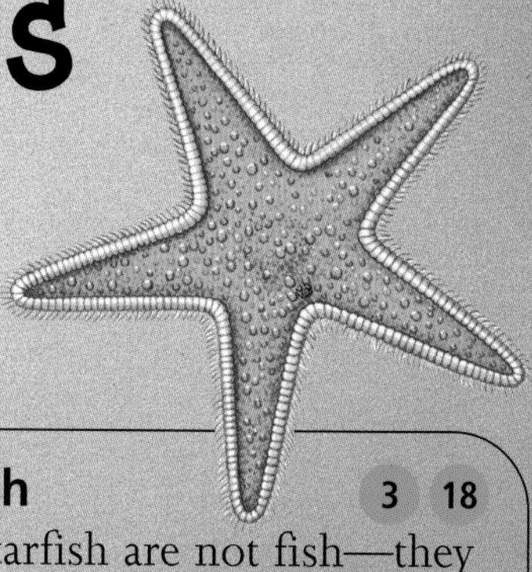

Starfish

3 18

Spiny starfish are not fish—they are echinoderms that eat corals, fish, and dead animals. Most starfish have five arms with eyespots, or light sensors, on the tips.

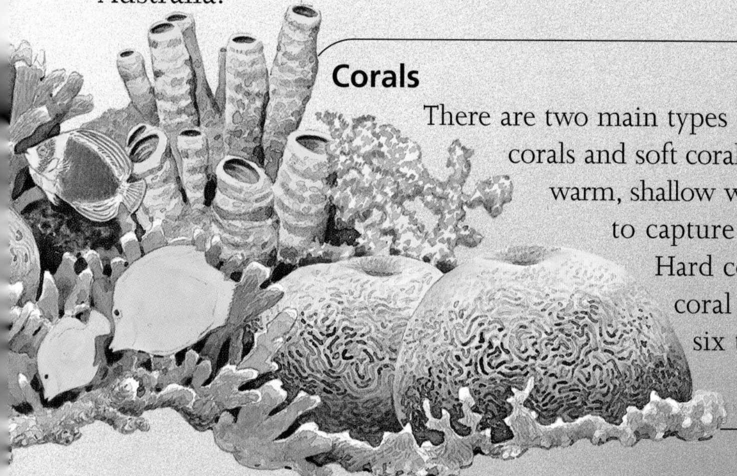

Corals

1 10 11 13 16

There are two main types of corals: hard corals and soft corals. Most corals like warm, shallow water and use tentacles to capture plankton for food. Hard corals, such as brain coral and elkhorn, have six tentacles. Soft corals have eight tentacles.

grouper

Jellyfish

4 6 7 15

To defend themselves or catch prey, jellyfish, such as the common moon jelly, use their stinging tentacles. Jellyfish do not have brains. Instead, they have a "nerve net." This is a nervous system that senses touch. A group of jellyfish is called a "smack," and large masses are "blooms."

butterfly fish

moray

Fish colors

5 9

The poisonous stonefish looks like a rock. This is a type of camouflage that is used to hide from prey. Other fish are colorful or patterned so that they can recognize each other.

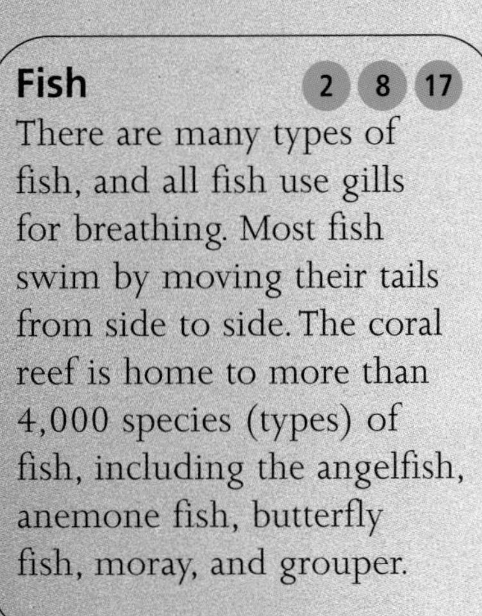

Fish 2 8 17

There are many types of fish, and all fish use gills for breathing. Most fish swim by moving their tails from side to side. The coral reef is home to more than 4,000 species (types) of fish, including the angelfish, anemone fish, butterfly fish, moray, and grouper.

Living together 12 14

Some fish have a symbiotic relationship with other animals. Symbiosis means "life together" and refers to two creatures relying on each other in a special way. Anemone fish are able to live among the stinging tentacles of sea anemones, which protect them from predators.

QUESTIONS:

Dolphins and porpoise

Level 1

1. Is the bottle-nosed a type of dolphin, crab, or lobster?
2. Most porpoise are smaller than dolphins. True or false?
3. What game do dolphins like to play: soccer, tennis, or bow riding?
4. Which type of animal is a dolphin: a mammal or a reptile?

Level 2

5. Dolphins have a "melon" in their head to help them find fish. True or false?
6. Do dolphins make clicks, whistles, or both to communicate with each other?
7. Why do porpoise swim upside down: to attract a mate or to eat their food?
8. How fast does a Dall's porpoise swim?
9. What "S" do dolphins like to play with?
10. Does a porpoise or a dolphin have a triangular dorsal fin?
11. Where do female dolphins give birth to their babies: close to the seabed or just below the surface of the water?
12. How many games are dolphins believed to play: more than three, more than 30, or more than 300?
13. What is the function of a "babysitter" dolphin?
14. Do female dolphins give birth to calves, kittens, or pups?

Level 3

15. How many species of porpoise are there?
16. Which species is the smallest porpoise?
17. What is a dolphin's beak called?
18. What is bow riding?
19. What "C" sound do dolphins use to learn about their surroundings and find fish?

FIND THE ANSWER:

Dolphins and porpoise

Dolphins are familiar to people as the playful mammals that swim alongside boats and ships. They are intelligent animals and have rescued drowning people by using their noses to push them back to shore. Porpoise are related to dolphins, but they are shy creatures and do not approach people like dolphins do.

Communication

1 6

The bottle-nosed dolphin can make up to 10,000 clicking noises per second to communicate with other dolphins. Whistles are used to call other members of a group or to warn of a shark. Some dolphins can identify themselves by using "signature whistles."

Dolphins

5 17 19

Unlike porpoise, dolphins have a beak called a rostrum. Dolphins have a "melon" above their upper jaw for echolocation, which is a way to learn about their surroundings and find fish by using clicking sounds. There are many sea dolphins, but there are only five species of freshwater dolphins.

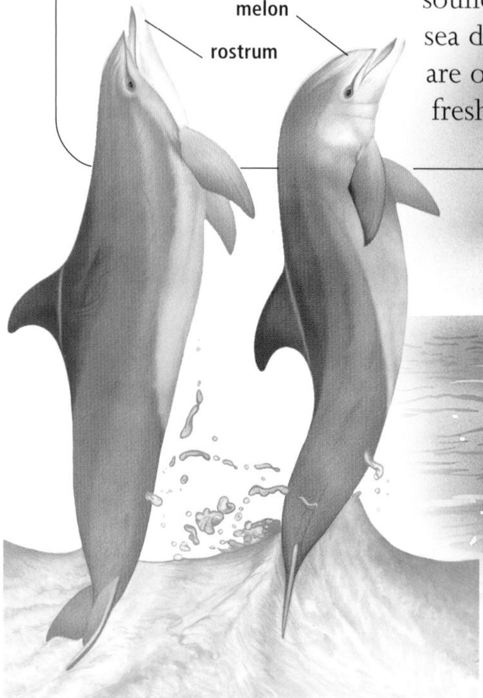

melon

rostrum

dolphins at play

Play

3 9 12 18

Dolphins have been observed playing more than 300 different games, including pretend fighting, jumping, playing with seaweed, and playing catch. They also like to surf on the waves and go "bow-riding" on the waves that are created by boats. Another favorite game is to create rings of bubbles that the dolphin then tries to bite.

Mothers and calves

4 11 13 14

Female dolphins give birth to their calves just below the surface of the water. Like other mammals, dolphins feed milk to their young, often for around 18 months. Other female dolphins act like aunts or babysitters. They help the mother teach the baby feeding and social skills such as playing and communicating.

Porpoise

8 15

There are six species of porpoise, including the harbor porpoise and Burmeister's porpoise. At 34 mph (55km/h), Dall's porpoise is one of the fastest swimmers among porpoise, dolphins, and whales.

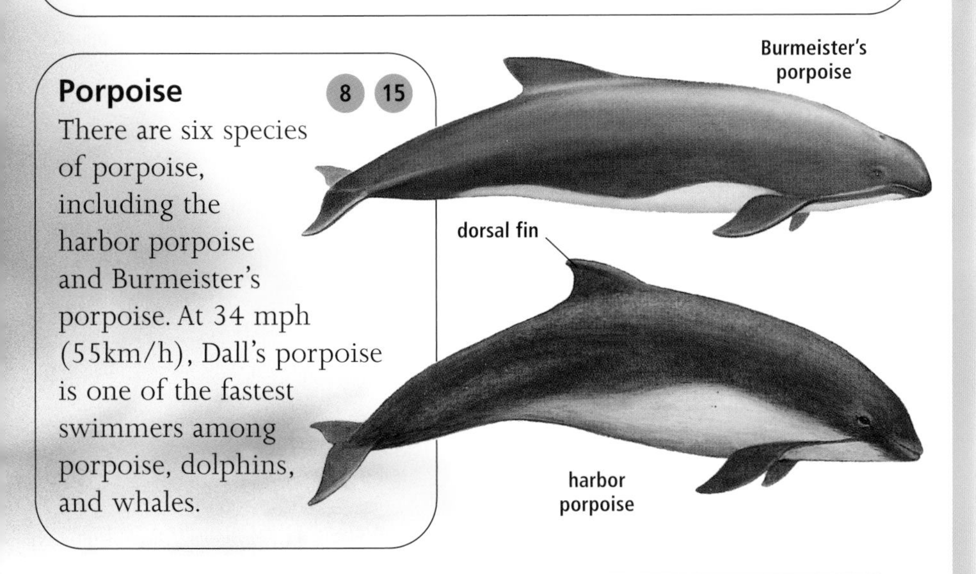

Anatomy

2 7 10 16

Most porpoise are smaller than dolphins and have blunt noses. They also have spadelike teeth and triangular-shaped dorsal fins. Some swim upside down to attract a mate. At only 60 in. (150cm) long, the smallest porpoise is the endangered Vaquita.

blunt nose

Dall's porpoise

QUESTIONS: Killer whales

Level 1

1. Do killer whales live in a family group called a pod?
2. Another name for the killer whale is the orca. True or false?
3. Do adult killer whales take care of their young, or do they let their young take care of themselves?
4. What is a whale jump called: a breach, hop, or bungee?

Level 2

5. Is a killer whale also called a shark of the ocean or a wolf of the sea?
6. How long is a male killer whale: up to 12 ft. (4m), 20 ft. (6m), or 32 ft. (10m)?
7. Killer whales sometimes hunt young blue whales. True or false?
8. Why would a whale breach: to scare prey, warn of danger, attract a mate, or all of the above?
9. What "C" and "W" noises will a whale use to send messages to another whale?
10. A clan is made up of several pods. True or false?
11. Does a killer whale poke its tail or its head out of the water when it is spyhopping?
12. Are killer whales mammals or large fish?
13. Do killer whales protect injured and sick members of their pod, attack them, or chase them away?

Level 3

14. What is a killer whale's cruising speed?
15. What is a lobtail?
16. How much faster does a killer whale swim when it's hunting and not cruising?
17. LEAD CIT can be rearranged to give what name for the common calls that are shared by a whale pod?
18. For how long can a whale hold itself up while it is spyhopping?

FIND THE ANSWER: Killer whales

The killer whale, or orca, belongs to the same family as the dolphin. It is a fierce, toothed hunter that eats fish, sea lions, and other whales. The killer whale is found in all of the oceans, but most of them are found in the cooler waters of the Arctic and Antarctic oceans. It can be identified by its tall dorsal fin and its coloring: black back, white chest, and white patches close to its eyes.

killer whale breaching

Orca 2 5

The killer whale, or orca, was first identified as a mammal by Aristotle (384–322 B.C.). Sailors called it "whale killer" because it kills other whales. It eventually became commonly known as the killer whale. It is also called "wolf of the sea" because it hunts in packs like wolves.

Behavior 4 8 15

A whale's jump is called a breach, and orcas can breach completely out of the water. Breaching may be done to scare prey, warn of danger, or attract a mate. A whale also lobtails, or smacks its tail on the water, possibly to communicate.

Spyhopping 11 18

Killer whales can poke their heads out of the sea to spyhop for as long as 30 seconds. They may be looking for things above the water such as seals.

dorsal fin

white patch close to eye

flipper

pod of whales

The family (1) (3) (13)

Betweeen 5 and 40 whales form a pod, often with several generations from the same family. They stay together for their whole lives, and members of the pod protect the young, injured, and sick.

Communication (9) (10) (17)

Whales that belong to the same pod share a dialect that is made up of a set of underwater calls, using whistles and clicking sounds to send messages to each other. Other pods with similar dialects are part of the whale's clan.

Hunting in packs (7)

Killer whales hunt together in packs, attacking larger prey from different angles. They have even been known to attack young blue whales and other large whales.

Speedy swimmers (6) (12) (14) (16)

Killer whales are large, fast mammals. Males can be up to 35 ft. (10m) long and swim at 30 mph (48km/h) when hunting. They cruise at 6 mph (10km/h).

QUESTIONS: Baleen whales

Level 1

1. Is the blue whale the largest mammal on Earth?
2. What do baleen whales eat: birds or shrimplike krill?
3. Whales never migrate with their young. True or false?
4. The blue whale is the loudest animal, much louder than humans. True or false?

Level 2

5. Only the blue whale has two blowholes. True or false?
6. The bowhead likes the warm waters of the Mediterranean Sea. True or false?
7. The gray whale migrates along which coast of the U.S.: the eastern or the western coast?
8. What are baleen plates used for: tossing fish, trapping krill, or swimming?
9. Do humpback whales use bubbles to trap krill?
10. Name one of two reasons why baleen whales migrate.
11. Why does the bowhead have a thick layer of blubber?
12. How far can the gray whale migrate: 600 mi. (1,000km), 3,000 mi. (5,000km), or 6,000 mi. (10,000km)?
13. Rearrange FREET FIELDS to describe how a baleen whale eats.

Level 3

14. How loud is a blue whale's call?
15. Do humpback whales eat the food that they catch by bubble netting on the seabed or at the surface?
16. What percentage of its total length is the head of the bowhead?
17. How many krill can a blue whale eat in a single day?

FIND THE ANSWER:

Baleen whales

Baleen whales, such as humpback whales and blue whales, have baleen instead of teeth. Baleen, or whalebone, is made out of keratin—the same material found in human hair and nails. Baleen plates run along the top of the whale's mouth and look like thick hair, but they are stiffer. Most baleen whales are larger than toothed whales.

blue whale

Blue whale

1 5

The largest mammal ever to live on Earth, the blue whale can grow up to 105 ft. (32m) in length and weigh 145 tons. At birth a blue whale calf weighs 2,970 lbs. (1,350kg). Like other baleen whales, blue whales have two blowholes.

Bowhead

6 11 16

The endangered bowhead lives in Arctic waters. Its large head makes up 40 percent of its body length. The bowhead has a covering of blubber, up to 30 in. (70cm) thick, to keep it warm.

Feeding

2 8 13 17

A baleen whale "filter feeds" by taking in water containing food such as shrimplike krill. The whale forces the water out and traps the krill behind its baleen plates. A blue whale can eat four million krill in a single day.

water taken in

baleen plate

krill

water forced out

Bubble netting

The humpback whale uses bubbles to catch fish and krill. The whale circles beneath them and blows air out of its blowhole. A net of air bubbles rises up and traps the fish or krill, which the whale eats at the surface.

feeding at the surface

Migration

3 7 10 12

Most baleen whales travel long distances to breed and feed, either alone or in small groups. A gray whale can travel 6,000 mi. (10,000km) with its young along the western coast of the U.S., from Mexico to the Bering Strait.

Calls

4 14

Blue whales are the loudest animals, with calls up to 188 decibels. A human's shout is 70 decibels. The blue whale's calls can last up to 35 seconds and can travel hundreds of miles.

QUESTIONS: Birds of prey

Level 1

1. Which bird is the national bird of the U.S.: the golden eagle, harpy eagle, or bald eagle?
2. Does the osprey live close to water or in the mountains?
3. The peregrine falcon is faster than any other creature in the world. True or false?
4. What are talons: claws, wings, or legs?

Level 2

5. How many species of falcons are there: around five, 35, or 75?
6. What type of eagle is the South American harpy: a snake eagle, buzzardlike eagle, or sea eagle?
7. How fast can a peregrine falcon dive: 14 mph (23km/h), 140 mph (230km/h), or 200 mph (320km/h)?
8. Which birds of prey have longer talons: those that catch rabbits or those that catch fish?
9. How many species of eagles are there: around 20, 40, or 60?
10. Which bird of prey has the largest wingspan?
11. What is the world's largest eagle?
12. What does the bald eagle eat: small animals, fish, or both?
13. What type of wings enable eagles and buzzards to soar for long periods: broad wings or long, tapered wings?
14. Is the kestrel a type of falcon or eagle?

Level 3

15. Which wing shape allows birds to maneuver easily?
16. The golden eagle is which type of eagle?
17. What is unusual about the bottom of an osprey's feet?
18. What happens to a bald eagle at three or four years of age?

FIND THE ANSWER:

Birds of prey

Most birds of prey are diurnal, or daytime, hunters that kill other creatures for food. However, vultures are scavengers that feed on creatures that are already dead. All birds of prey have sharp claws, strong beaks, and excellent eyesight.

Eagles

6 9 11 16

There are around 60 species of eagles. The main eagle groups are snake eagles, buzzardlike eagles, booted eagles (the golden eagle is one), and sea eagles. The largest eagle is the buzzardlike South American harpy. Some eagles can spot prey, such as a rabbit, from 2 mi. (3km) away.

golden eagle catching a rabbit

kestrel

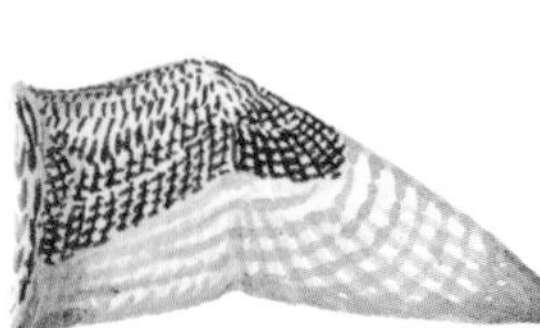

peregrine falcon

buzzard

Wings

10 13 15

Broad wings enable eagles and buzzards to soar for long periods, while hawks and kestrels have short, rounded wings that are ideal for easy maneuvering. Long, tapered wings, such as those of the peregrine falcon, are designed for speed. The Andean condor has the largest wingspan of all birds of prey, at up to 10 ft. (3m) wide.

Bald eagle

1 12 18

The bald eagle, the national bird of the U.S. since 1782, lives close to water and eats fish and small animals. Its white head and yellow beak do not appear until the bird is three or four years old. Its nest is the largest bird's nest and can be more than 20 ft. (6m) deep and 8 ft. (2.5m) wide.

Falcons

3 5 7 14

There are around 35 species of falcons such as the prairie falcon, kestrel, and peregrine falcon. The prairie falcon flies fast and low to catch its prey. The peregrine falcon dives up to 250 mph (320km/h)—faster than any other creature in the world.

Talons

4 8

The claws on birds of prey are called talons. All birds of prey have powerful, curved talons to catch—and kill—their prey. Fish-killing birds of prey have the longest and most curved talons. The osprey's outer toe is reversible, which enables it to grip its prey with two talons in front and two in back.

Osprey

2 17

The osprey is similar to an eagle and lives in most parts of the world. It feeds on fish, so it lives close to fresh water or salt water. The bottoms of the osprey's feet are covered with spiny scales, which are designed to help the bird grip and carry its slippery prey.

QUESTIONS: Rats and mice

Level 1

1. To what animal group do rats and mice belong: rodents, insects, or reptiles?
2. Is the Swiss albino mouse the most common pet mouse?
3. The Norway rat is the most common rat in the world. True or false?
4. What disease were rats blamed for spreading: the Plague, flu, or colds?

Level 2

5. A mouse has a lot of fur when it is born. True or false?
6. The Norway rat killed off many black rats when it arrived in Europe. True or false?
7. Do some rats live in houses and other buildings?
8. Do dormice build nests or live in caves?
9. Where did the Norway rat originate: Europe, Asia, or Africa?
10. What "I" are teeth that both rats and mice have?
11. How many species of mice are there: less than ten, between ten and 100, or more than 100?
12. What is another name for the Norway rat?
13. What "H" do dormice do during the winter?

Level 3

14. What "H" is one of the smallest types of mice?
15. In which areas is the black rat more common than the brown rat?
16. What does the Latin word *rodere* mean?
17. How did the Norway rat arrive in North America?
18. How fast can a mouse run?
19. How many baby mice might a female mouse give birth to in a year?

FIND THE ANSWER: Rats and mice

Rats and mice are rodents. All rodents have two large front teeth. These continue to grow throughout the animal's life, and gnawing on food and other objects keeps them from growing too long. There are around 900 species of rats and mice living in different areas around the world.

Norway rat
3 9 12

Also called the brown rat, the Norway rat is the most common rat in the world. It spread from Asia across the world in the 1700s. It is a disease carrier.

Types of rats
7 15 17

Norway rats and black rats started living in people's homes and other buildings thousands of years ago. Norway rats arrived in North America in 1755 on the ships of the new settlers. Black rats are more common in tropical areas.

Norway rat

Sharp teeth
1 10 16

The word "rodent" comes from the Latin word *rodere* (meaning "to gnaw"), and rats and mice can chew through very tough materials such as wires. Rats have molars and incisors. Mice have large incisors.

Brown rat vs. black rat
6

Most black rats were killed off in Europe when their relative the Norway rat arrived. The black rat is darker and has a longer tail than the Norway rat.

Plague-infested house

The Plague
4

Rats were blamed for spreading the Plague—a deadly disease that struck Europe in the 1600s. The Plague was spread by fleas that passed from rats to people.

Mice

14 18

Mice are small, nocturnal (active at night) rodents. They are quick runners (up to 8 mph, or 13km/h), but many animals prey on them. The harvest mouse is one of the world's smallest mice.

Swiss albino mouse

Types of mice

2 11

There are hundreds of species of mice. The most common is the house mouse, which lives close to humans all over the world. The Swiss albino mouse is the most popular pet mouse.

house mouse

Mothers and babies

5 19

A mouse gives birth to as many as eight young at a time and up to five times a year. At birth, baby mice, called kittens, have no fur and they cannot see or hear. At three weeks old, mice leave the nest. Female mice can give birth when they are as young as seven weeks old.

baby mice

Dormice

8 13

The bushy-tailed dormouse can spend up to three quarters of its life asleep. When food is scarce, it hibernates—it sleeps for several months during the winter. The dormouse will build a nest to keep itself warm and protected.

QUESTIONS: Bats

Level 1

1. Bats are flying mammals. True or false?
2. Vampire bats drink the blood of which animals: cattle, lizards, or snails?
3. Are a bat's bones light in weight to make flying easier?

Level 2

4. What are fruit bats sometimes called: flying cats, flying foxes, or flying monkeys?
5. All bats use echolocation to help them find food. True or false?
6. Some baby bats can fly when they are only two weeks old. True or false?
7. What do bats use the clawed fingers on their wings for: climbing or hanging upside down?
8. How many squeaks per second might a bat use during echolocation: two, 200, or two million?
9. Which part of its body does a vampire bat use to detect heat?
10. TURF BAITS can be rearranged to name which bats found in Asia, Africa, and Oceania?
11. Do bats have strong legs or weak legs?
12. What is the wingspan of the largest bat: 5 ft. (1.5m), 7 ft. (1.8m), or 8 ft. (2.5m)?

Level 3

13. Why does the vampire bat have less teeth than other bats?
14. What is another name for the bumblebee bat?
15. How do the fingers of fruit bats differ from other bats?
16. What is the difference in wingspan between the smallest bat and the largest bat?
17. How do some bats find fruits and nectar?
18. Where can a flap of skin be found on a bat?

Bats

Bats are small flying mammals that are nocturnal, or active at night. There are around 1,000 species of bats around the world. Many bats eat insects, but there are also fruit-eating bats, fish-eating bats, and vampire bats, which feed on blood. During the day colonies of bats sleep in caves, hanging upside down by their feet.

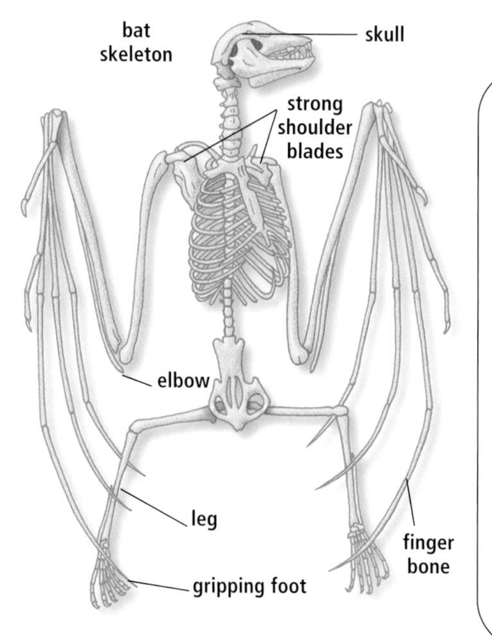

Bones 3 7 11

A bat's bones are light for easier flying. Finger bones form the wings, but the first finger has a claw for climbing and is not part of the wing. Only one muscle opens and extends the wings. Because bats have weak legs, they do not walk very well.

Fruit bats 4 10 15

Types of fruit bats live in tropical parts of Asia, Africa, and Oceania. Fruit bats are often called flying foxes because of their foxlike faces. Unlike other bats, fruit bats have claws on both their first and second fingers. Most fruit bats feed on fruits, but some drink flower nectar. They spread seeds and help pollinate the plants that they visit.

fruit bat

Rare breed 14

Kitti's hog-nosed bat, also called the bumblebee bat, lives in Thailand and was discovered in 1973. It is the smallest mammal in the world—it is only around 1.25 in. (3.1cm) long and weighs around 0.07 oz. (2g). Its skull is only 0.4 in. (11mm) long.

Echolocation 5 8 17

Some bats find their prey, such as insects and small animals, by using echolocation. These bats make up to 200 high-pitched squeaks per second. These bounce, or echo, off their prey, telling the bats where to find them. Other bats use their sense of smell to find fruits and nectar.

large ears for hearing echoes

sound waves

prey

Flying mammal

1 6 12 16 18

Bats are the only flying mammals. Their wings are formed from double-sided, leathery skin. A flap of skin also joins the legs and the tail. Baby bats can fly at only two to five weeks old. The wingspan of the smallest bat is 6 in. (15cm), while the largest bat has a wingspan of 7 ft. (1.8m).

strong arm

leathery wing

flap of skin

Vampire bats

2 9 13

Vampire bats—which are named because of their diet of blood—are only found in Central and South America. These bats drink the blood of mammals such as cattle. A heat sensor on its nose helps the bat locate warm blood. Vampire bats have less teeth than most bats because they do not need to chew their food.

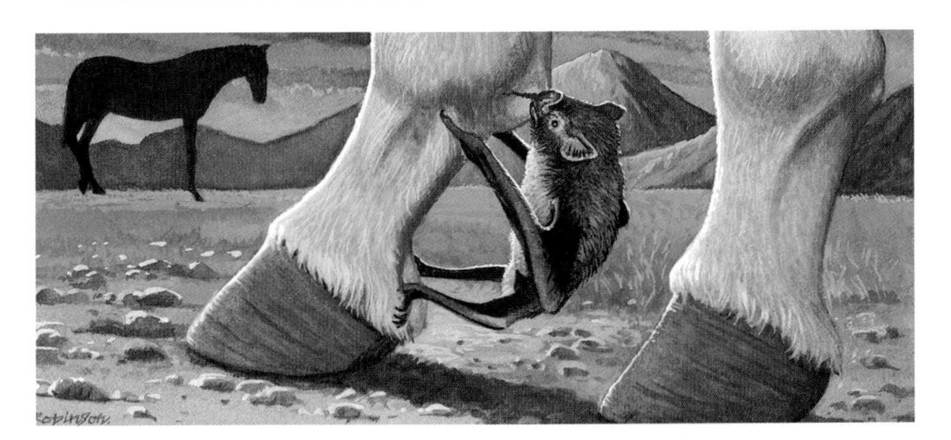

QUESTIONS: Big cats

Level 1

1. Lions hunt their prey in a group. True or false?
2. What is a group of lions called: a pride or a school?
3. Do lions and tigers both roar?
4. All big cats are mammals. True or false?
5. What does a lion eat: zebras, penguins, or lobsters?

Level 2

6. The tiger, leopard, jaguar, and lynx are all big cats. True or false?
7. How much can a tiger eat in one meal: 22 lbs. (10kg), 88 lbs. (40kg), or 176 lbs. (80kg) of meat?
8. Which animal is the fastest on land: the jaguar, lion, or cheetah?
9. Which cat is the largest: the lion, tiger, or cheetah?
10. Rearrange ROD LEAP to name a big cat that feeds on impalas, hares, and birds.
11. Each tiger has the same pattern of stripes on both sides of its body. True or false?
12. Which cat will hide its kill in a tree: a lion, tiger, or leopard?
13. Which is the only big cat that lives in the Americas: the cheetah, jaguar, or ocelot?
14. Which "S" describes the way that lions and tigers hunt?

Level 3

15. Which small tiger is native to Asia?
16. Which mammal group includes lions, tigers, leopards, and jaguars?
17. What two things help hide a big cat when it is hunting?
18. How far can a cheetah travel in just three strides?
19. Which is the only big cat that cannot fully retract its claws?

Big cats

The big cat family is a group of large mammals. Their numbers have been seriously threatened by hunting and by their habitat being destroyed. The Caspian tiger and Javan tiger have both become extinct within the last 50 years. Even now, big cats, such as the snow leopard, are hunted for fur. Of all the continents, only Australia and Antarctica do not have native cats.

Types of cats 3 4 6 13 16

The mammal group *Panthera* includes lions, tigers, leopards, and jaguars. Only the jaguar is found in the Americas. All of these cats can roar. The cheetah and the puma are not true big cats because they cannot roar. Neither can medium-sized cats such as the lynx and the ocelot.

Tigers 7 9 11 15

As the largest of the big cats, tigers can eat around 88 lbs. (40kg) of meat in one meal. Each tiger's pattern of stripes is unique, and it is also different on each side of the tiger. The Siberian tiger is the largest, and the Sumatran tiger, from Indonesia, is the smallest. Tigers are strong swimmers.

Lions 1 2 5

A group of lions, or a pride, hunts together. Females, or lionesses, do most of the hunting for prey such as zebras and wildebeests.

Stalking

14 17

Big cats will spend hours watching their prey and waiting for the right moment to pounce. Tall grass and the color of their fur can camouflage, or hide, the cats.

The chase

8 18 19

Cheetahs are the fastest land animals. They can reach 60mph (100km/h) in three seconds and cover 20 ft. (6m) in one stride. They are the only cats that cannot fully retract their claws.

Hiding the kill

10 12

Tigers and leopards will hide their kill from other meat-eating animals. The leopard may hide its meal in a tree. It has a varied diet, eating large and small prey such as impalas, hares, and birds.

QUESTIONS:
Great apes

Level 1

1. Do chimps live together in groups?
2. What is an adult male gorilla called: a silverback, grayfront, or bluetop?
3. Chimps have calls to communicate with each other. True or false?
4. Because rain forests are being destroyed, are all of the great apes in danger of becoming extinct?

Level 2

5. Gorillas and chimps live in both Africa and Asia. True or false?
6. At what age do gorillas learn to "knuckle walk": three weeks, nine months, or nine years?
7. The orangutan is a sociable creature. True or false?
8. Is blackback another name for a young male gorilla, a young male orangutan, or a young male chimpanzee?
9. Which is an enemy of the gorilla: the leopard, tiger, or jaguar?
10. How long will a juvenile male gorilla stay with his family: until he is three years old, eight years old, or 11 years old?
11. How many gorillas do the largest wild groups contain: ten, 30, or 200?
12. What feature identifies an adult male gorilla: a silver, black, or brown patch of fur along its back?
13. What is a gorilla group called: a clan, troop, or family?
14. Where do orangutans live: in trees, caves, or tall grass?

Level 3

15. Bonobo is another name for what type of chimp?
16. How many nests can an orangutan make in seven days?
17. What do opposable thumbs allow a great ape to do?
18. Which member of a gorilla group decides when it is time to move on?
19. What do gorillas eat?

FIND THE ANSWER:

Great apes

Great apes are primates. They include humans, gorillas, chimpanzees, orangutans, and bonobos—the smallest of the great apes. All of these animals are intelligent. Chimps share 98.4 percent of our DNA. Apes are not monkeys—they are larger, more intelligent, and spend more time raising their young.

gorilla with baby in a tree nest

Habitat
4 5

Africa and Asia are home to wild great apes, but gorillas and chimps only live in Africa. All of the wild great apes are in danger of becoming extinct because the rain forests in which they live are being destroyed.

Gorilla groups
8 11 13

Up to 30 gorillas live in a group, called a troop. Each troop has a male leader, a few juvenile blackback males, many females, and their young. Mature males may form a "bachelor" group before females join them.

adult male

grooming

Young gorillas
6 10

Gorillas learn to "knuckle walk" by nine months old, but they travel on their mothers' backs until they are two or three years old. They leave the group at around 11 years old.

female and baby

Gorilla leader
2 9 12 18 19

An adult male gorilla is called a silverback because of the silver patch of fur on his back. The dominant silverback decides where the group lives, protects it from enemies, such as leopards, and decides what the gorillas will eat. Gorillas are mostly vegetarian and eat plants, but they will also eat insects.

chimpanzee mother and baby

Chimpanzees (1) (3) (15)

Chimps live in groups called communities. They have around 30 calls for communicating. Bonobos, or pygmy chimps, live in the Congo, in Africa.

Orangutans (7) (14) (16)

The word "orangutan" is from the Indonesian and Malaysian words for person (*orang*) and forest (*hutan*). The tree-dwelling orangutan is not a social animal. It lives alone after it leaves its mother at the age of around eight. An orangutan can make up to 14 nests in seven days.

orangutan with a palm leaf umbrella

Using tools (17)

Great apes, like humans, have opposable thumbs, which means that they can grasp things. These creatures have the intelligence to use tools to help them with everyday tasks. Gorillas, for example, use sticks to find out the depth of water. When it is raining hard, an orangutan will keep itself dry by making an umbrella out of a large palm leaf.

QUESTIONS: Bears

Level 1

1. Bears hibernate by going into a long sleep. True or false?
2. Where do polar bears live: the Arctic, the Antarctic, or South America?
3. Are baby bears called kittens, pups, or cubs?
4. Where do mother bears give birth: underwater, by a lake, or in a den?
5. Bears are sometimes scavengers. True or false?

Level 2

6. The grizzly bear is a type of brown bear. True or false?
7. For how long can a black bear hibernate: 50, 100, or 200 days?
8. Is the sun bear, Kodiak bear, or spectacled bear the smallest bear?
9. Does a polar bear have a 1 in. (2.5cm), 4 in. (10cm), or 20 in. (50cm) layer of fat around its body?
10. At what age does a bear cub leave its mother: one year old, two years old, or three years old?
11. What "S" do Alaskan brown bears love to eat?
12. Where does the spectacled bear live: in mountains, deserts, or tundra?

Level 3

13. If a black bear weighs 400 lbs. (180kg) in the spring, how much would it weigh at hibernation?
14. What "S" is a marine animal that is eaten by polar bears?
15. Name one of two main things that cubs learn from their mothers.
16. What is an omnivore?
17. Which is the largest bear?
18. Which bear eats bromeliad plants?
19. In the fall how many hours a week, on average, does a bear spend eating?

FIND THE ANSWER: Bears

Bears are large mammals with furry bodies and short tails. They usually have small, rounded ears and a good sense of smell. Although they walk on all fours, bears can stand on their hind legs. Most bears are fast runners and good swimmers. Only mothers and their babies, called cubs, live together.

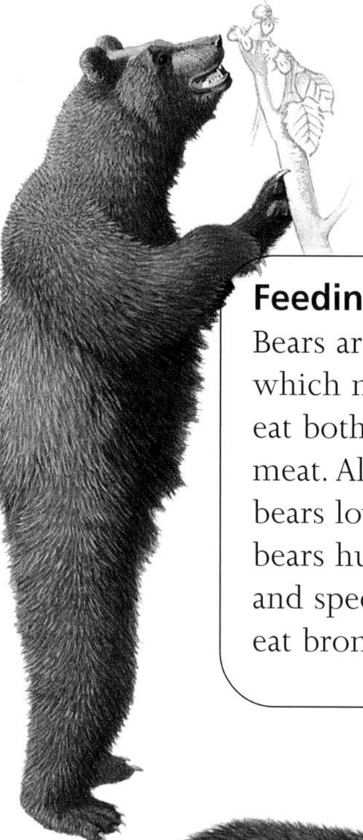

grizzly bear

Bears 6 8 12

Brown bears include the large grizzly bear (it can weigh 990 lbs., or 450kg), the Kodiak bear of North America, and the European brown bear. The sun bear of southeast Asia is the smallest of the bears. The mountain-dwelling spectacled bear builds platforms in the tops of trees for feeding and resting.

Feeding 11 16 18

Bears are omnivores, which means that they eat both plants and meat. Alaskan brown bears love salmon, sun bears hunt for termites, and spectacled bears eat bromeliad plants.

Young 3 4 10 15

Female bears make dens in which to have their cubs. Bear cubs stay close to their mothers for up to three years, while they learn how to hunt and make shelters.

black bear

polar bear

European brown bear

Hibernation

1 7 13

Many bears go into a winter sleep called hibernation. The black bear can sleep for 100 days without eating or drinking. Before this long sleep, bears can increase their weight by 400lbs. (180kg).

Scavenging

5 19

Bears eat for 20 hours a day in the summer and fall. They are great scavengers and will eat whatever food is available. Black bears sometimes raid garbage cans.

Polar bears

2 9 14 17

The largest bear is the polar bear. It lives in the Arctic, where it preys on seals. Its fur looks white because it reflects the light, but, in fact, it is translucent. The bear's skin is black to attract heat from the Sun. The bear has a 4 in. (10cm) layer of fat under its skin to keep warm.

QUESTIONS: Pets

Level 1

1. Pet fish are kept in a tank called an aquarium. True or false?
2. Cats use their whiskers to find their way around at night. True or false?
3. Are rabbits fast runners or slow animals?
4. Is a cat happy or unhappy if it holds its tail high?

Level 2

5. Cavies are also called guinea pigs. True or false?
6. Do domestic cats have short hair, long hair, or either type?
7. Are dogs most closely related to rabbits, foxes, or wolves?
8. Can a rabbit see almost 90 degrees, 180 degrees, or 360 degrees?
9. Which is not a type of parrot: macaw, parakeet, or quetzal?
10. What "H" means an animal that eats plants?
11. The Abyssinian guinea pig has smooth, short hair. True or false?
12. Which animal is also known as a desert rat: the guinea pig, gerbil, or rabbit?
13. Rearrange DEER BURP to spell a word used to describe cats of a particular type.

Level 3

14. What must a hamster do because its teeth grow all the time?
15. What ability is the African gray parrot known for?
16. What "S" is another name for the golden hamster?
17. Pet fish owners need to make sure that what "T" in an aquarium is properly controlled to suit the type of fish?
18. How many breeds of dogs are there?
19. Rabbits are most active during which times of the day?
20. In which states is it illegal to keep gerbils?

FIND THE ANSWER: Pets

Pets are animals that are kept by people for companionship or amusement. Dogs are often called "man's best friend" because of their loyal nature. Cats, guinea pigs, and hamsters are also favorite pets. Horses are kept in stables. People also keep all types of exotic fish and birds, reptiles, and insects.

Bernese mountain dog

Dogs

There are more than 400 breeds of dogs that are divided into seven groups: sporting, hounds, working, toy, terriers, nonsporting, and herding. Dogs are related to wolves and have a good sense of smell. Dogs are the most dependent pets, relying on their owners for company.

Cats

2 4 6 13

Although there are only a few purebred cats, there are many more domestic short- or long-haired cats. Cats use their whiskers to help them move around at night. A cat's tail can show how it is feeling: a high tail means that the cat is happy, while a low tail means that the cat is unhappy.

Labrador

Yorkshire terrier

Guinea pigs

5 11

Cavies, or guinea pigs, are rodents. The American guinea pig has smooth, short hair. The Abyssinian has a rough coat of swirls.

Hamsters

14 16

The Syrian, or golden, hamster is a popular pet, but dwarf hamsters, including the Roborovski, are also common. Like other rodents, a hamster's teeth grow all the time, so they gnaw on whatever is available.

domestic cat

guinea pig

hamster

gerbil

Gerbils

12 20

"Desert rats," or gerbils, are native to desert regions. They live between two and four years and are sociable. It is illegal to keep them in California and in Hawaii.

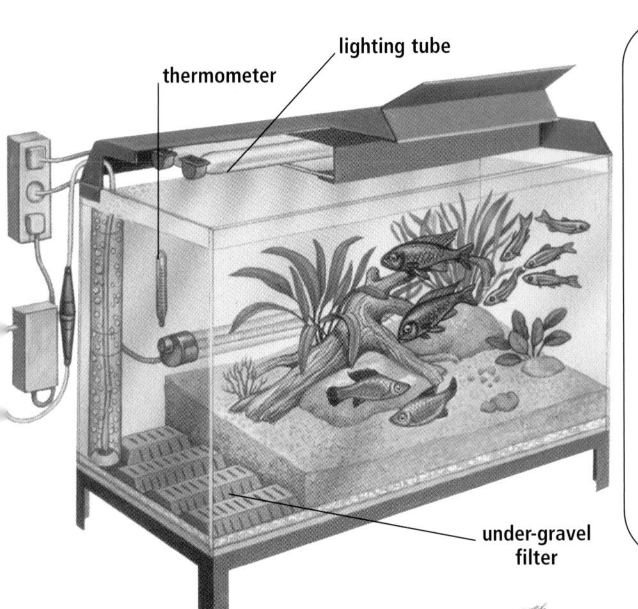

Fish 1 17

Aquariums, or tanks, with filtered fresh water or salt water are homes for pet fish. The water temperature is controlled to suit the type of fish. Goldfish like cold water, but tropical fish need heated water in order to survive.

Rabbits 3 8 10 19

Because rabbits are herbivores, they eat plants. Their powerful back legs make rabbits fast-moving animals. They are at their most active at dawn and dusk. Their eyes are on the sides of their heads, which allows them to see almost 360 degrees.

parakeets

Parrots 9 15

There are more than 300 species of parrots, including macaws, cockatoos, parakeets, budgerigars, and lovebirds. One of the best mimics is the African gray parrot. Parrots are native to tropical and subtropical areas and feed on fruits and nuts. Parrots taken from their natural habitat in the wild make bad pets.

QUESTIONS: Where in the world?

Level 1

1. The giant panda lives in Asia. True or false?
2. Do lions live in North America or Africa?
3. The polar bear lives in Antarctica. True or false?

Level 2

4. Where does the sloth live: in South America, Africa, or Asia?
5. Which type of animal lives in Europe: bats, weasels, deer, or all of the above?
6. Do most Asian elephants live in the wild, or are most of them used to help people do their work?
7. Which animal lives in the Midwest region of North America: the polar bear, jaguar, or prairie dog?

Level 3

8. What type of animal is a wallaby?
9. Which animal rules the African savanna?
10. Where does the kangaroo carry her young?

Where in the world?

All mammals are warm-blooded creatures and produce milk to feed their young. They live on every continent except for Antarctica, and some, such as whales, even live in the oceans. Some groups of mammals, such as the big cats, can be found on most continents, but many that live in Australia, such as the platypus, cannot be found anywhere else.

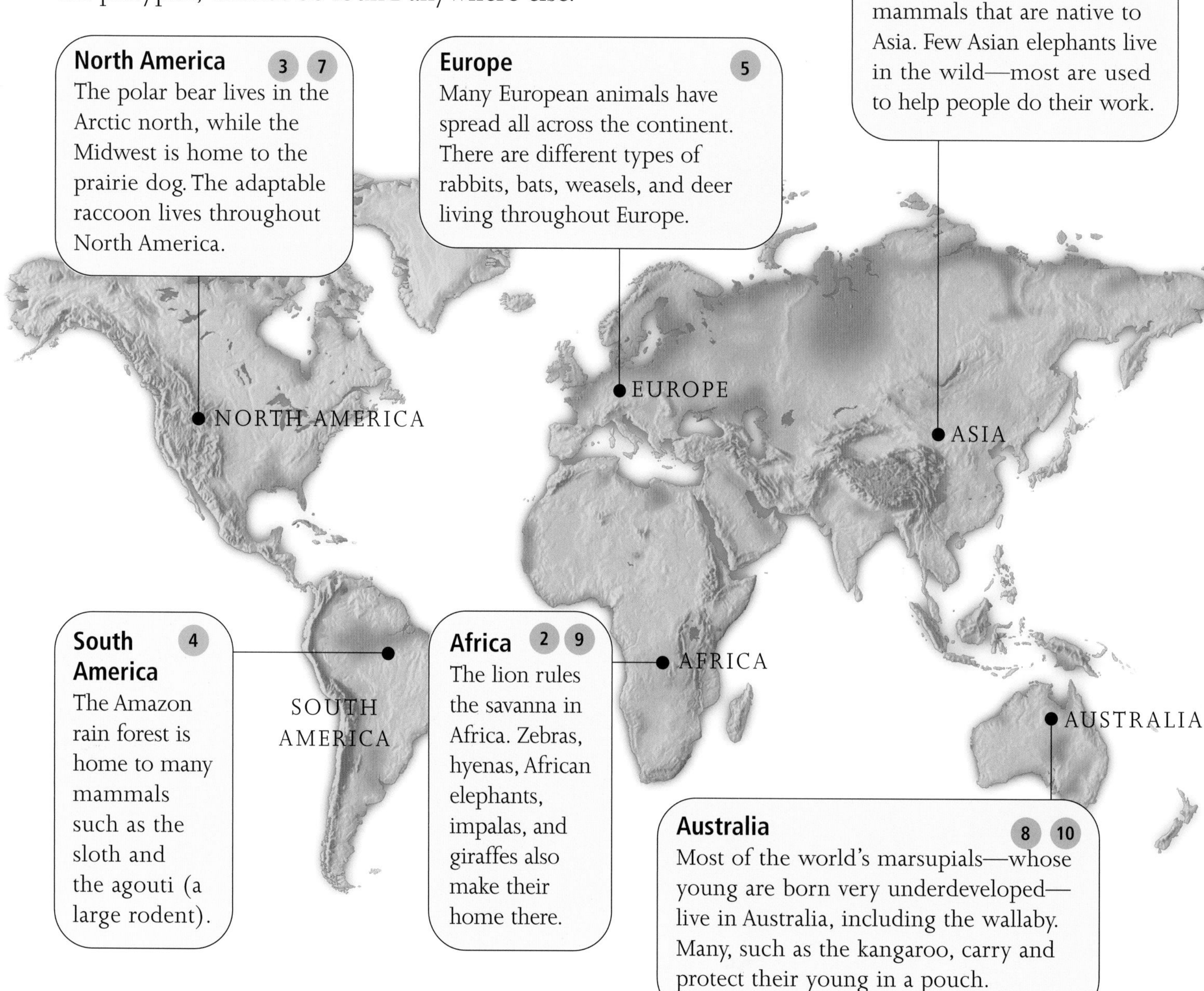

Asia 1 6
The giant panda, Siberian tiger, and sun bear are mammals that are native to Asia. Few Asian elephants live in the wild—most are used to help people do their work.

North America 3 7
The polar bear lives in the Arctic north, while the Midwest is home to the prairie dog. The adaptable raccoon lives throughout North America.

Europe 5
Many European animals have spread all across the continent. There are different types of rabbits, bats, weasels, and deer living throughout Europe.

South America 4
The Amazon rain forest is home to many mammals such as the sloth and the agouti (a large rodent).

Africa 2 9
The lion rules the savanna in Africa. Zebras, hyenas, African elephants, impalas, and giraffes also make their home there.

Australia 8 10
Most of the world's marsupials—whose young are born very underdeveloped—live in Australia, including the wallaby. Many, such as the kangaroo, carry and protect their young in a pouch.

Answers 1) True **2)** Africa **3)** False (the Arctic) **4)** South America **5)** All of the above **6)** Most are used to help people do their work **7)** Prairie dog **8)** Marsupial **9)** The lion **10)** In her pouch

QUIZ TWO

Geography

Africa

The Middle East

Asia

Europe

North America

South America

Australia and Oceania

Antarctica

QUESTIONS: Africa

Level 1

1. Is Mount Kilimanjaro Africa's highest point?
2. The Sahara is the largest desert in the world. True or false?
3. Which "N" in Africa is the longest river in the world?
4. Who built the pyramids: the ancient Europeans, ancient Egyptians, or ancient Americans?

Level 2

5. The Serengeti is a sandy desert. True or false?
6. Lake Tanganyika is the longest lake in the world. Is it also the deepest in Africa?
7. Where does the Nile river flow to: the Mediterranean Sea, Red Sea, or Atlantic Ocean?
8. Is the Serengeti in Tanzania and Kenya or Botswana and South Africa?
9. What happens every year along the Nile river: does the river dry up, stay the same, or flood its banks?
10. How many blocks of stone make up the Great Pyramid: 23,000, 230,000, or 2,300,000?
11. What "N" are people who live in the Sahara?
12. How many animals migrate in the Serengeti each year: almost 200,000, two million, or five million?
13. Rearrange MAIN GOLF to name a bird that migrates to Lake Tanganyika.

Level 3

14. How long is Lake Tanganyika?
15. Name the highest point on Mount Kilimanjaro.
16. For which "C" pharaoh was the Great Pyramid built?
17. What is a stratovolcano?
18. How large is the Sahara?

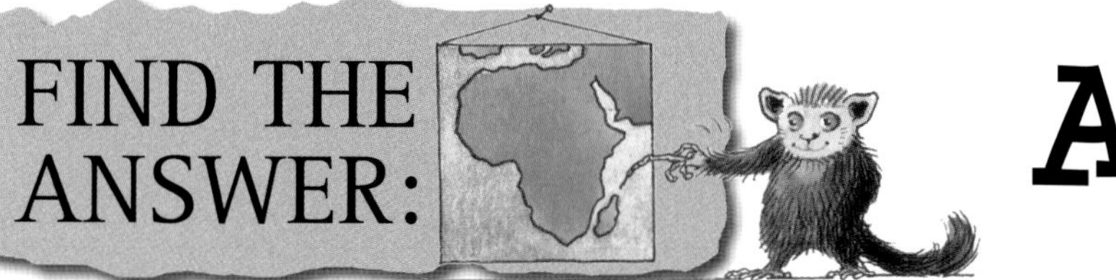

Africa

The African continent is the second-largest continent in the world (Asia is the largest). It is a land with different habitats, including mountains, grasslands, and deserts. Archaeologists believe that humans have lived in Africa for more than seven million years. Few people live in the Sahara, which makes up around one quarter of Africa.

Pyramids

4 10 16

The ancient Egyptians built pyramids as tombs for pharaohs and queens. Three pyramids were built in Giza, close to Cairo. The Great Pyramid was built for Pharaoh Cheops. Workers used 2,300,000 stone blocks and built it in 20 years.

The Nile river

3 7 9

The world's longest river is the Nile river. It starts in mountains and flows downhill, north into the Mediterranean Sea. It has two main branches: the White Nile and the Blue Nile. Every year the Nile river floods its banks and deposits rich soil that is ideal for farming.

Grassland migration

5 8 12

In Tanzania and Kenya the grassland "Serengeti" (meaning "the place where the land moves on forever") is home to almost two million animals. These include elephants, wildebeests, giraffes, and zebras. They go on a circular migration, traveling in search of fresh pastures.

Sahara

2 11 18

The Sahara is the largest desert in the world, covering 3,500,000 sq. mi. (9,000,000km^2). The few people who live there are mostly nomads, which means that they travel from place to place. They must carry all their food, relying on their camels and sheep for meat.

Lake Tanganyika 6 13 14

The longest lake in the world, at 415 mi. (670km), is Lake Tanganyika in the Great Rift Valley. It is also the deepest lake in Africa, at 4,820 ft. (1,470m). Flamingoes are one of the many birds that migrate to the lake.

pink flamingoes

Kilimanjaro 1 15 17

Mount Kilimanjaro in Tanzania is a large, inactive stratovolcano—a volcano that is made of hardened lava and volcanic ash. Mount Kilimanjaro is 19,650 ft. (5,895m) high and has three summits. Kibo, which is Africa's highest peak, is the youngest of the three.

QUESTIONS:
The Middle East

Level 1

1. The Blue Mosque is in Istanbul. True or false?
2. Do Muslims make pilgrimages to Mecca?
3. Is the tallest hotel in the world in Dubai or in Antarctica?
4. Minarets are tiny Islamic dancers. True or false?

Level 2

5. Diriyah was once the capital of which country: Saudi Arabia, Greece, or Spain?
6. How many blue tiles are inside of the Blue Mosque: more than 200, more than 2,000, or more than 20,000?
7. Was the Blue Mosque completed in 3600 B.C. or A.D. 1616?
8. Was Diriyah destroyed by a flood or an Egyptian-led army?
9. Which is a servant in an Islamic mosque: the muezzin or the serf?
10. In which "S" country was the Krak des Chevaliers built?
11. The Blue Mosque is also known as the Sultan Ahmed Mosque. True or false?
12. What is a caliph: an Islamic leader or a Jewish leader?
13. What "G" once covered the Dome of the Rock?

Level 3

14. Who ordered the building of the Dome of the Rock?
15. Mecca is in which country?
16. What does Krak des Chevaliers mean?
17. Around how much higher than the Burj al-Arab will the Burj Dubai be?
18. When were the Crusades?

The Middle East

Southwest Asia and parts of northern Africa make up the Middle East. The countries in this region include Egypt, Iran, Iraq, Israel, Lebanon, Saudi Arabia, and Syria. Islam is one of the most important religions in the region. Muslims who follow this religion study the Koran and believe that Muhammad is God's prophet.

Dome of the Rock 12 13 14

The ninth caliph, or Islamic leader, Abd al-Malik, built the Dome of the Rock in Jerusalem, in Israel. It was built between A.D. 687 and 691 on a holy site, where Muslims believe that Muhammad ascended to heaven from the rock in the dome. The dome was once covered in gold.

Inside 6

The Blue Mosque is named after the 20,000 blue tiles that are inside of the building.

minaret

tiled walls

Minarets 4 9

The towers on mosques are called minarets. The muezzin, a type of servant, announces the adhan, or call to prayer, from a minaret.

balcony

Mecca 2 15

Mecca, in Saudi Arabia, is the sacred city of Islam. Every year thousands of Muslims make pilgrimages to Mecca to pray at the Sacred Mosque.

Blue Mosque 1 7 11

The Blue Mosque in Istanbul, Turkey, is also called the Sultan Ahmed Mosque after Ahmed I. He had the mosque built between A.D. 1609 and 1616.

Blue Mosque

Saudi Arabia (5) (8)

Diriyah was the capital of Saudi Arabia until 1818. At that time, an Egyptian-led army destroyed the buildings and palm groves to make Diriyah uninhabitable.

Syria (10) (16) (18)

Krak des Chevaliers ("Fortress of the Knights"), in Syria, is a castle that was built between the 1000s and 1200s. It was used during the Crusades—a series of wars between European Christians and Arab Muslims.

Dubai (3) (17)

Dubai is one of seven small countries that make up the United Arab Emirates, or U.A.E. The Burj al-Arab, built in the shape of a sail, is the tallest hotel in the world, at 1,053 ft. (321m). When it is completed in 2008, the Burj Dubai will be the world's tallest skyscraper, at around 2,660 ft. (810m).

QUESTIONS: Asia

Level 1

1. Mount Everest is the tallest mountain in the world. True or false?
2. Is the Taj Mahal in India, Croatia, or Spain?
3. In building the Taj Mahal, more than 1,000 elephants were used to haul marble. True or false?
4. Mount Fuji in Japan is a dormant volcano. True or false?

Level 2

5. Shah Jahan built the Taj Mahal for his favorite daughter. True or false?
6. What "T" does "wat" mean?
7. Where is the Potala Palace: in Japan, Malaysia, or Tibet?
8. Which building was built in Kuala Lumpur, the capital of Malaysia: Angkor Wat, the Great Wall, or Petronas Twin Towers?
9. How many people climb Mount Fuji's summit to pray each year: 5,000, 50,000, or 500,000?
10. When was Angkor Wat built: in the 1000s, 1100s, or 1200s?
11. The Sarawak Chamber is the world's largest cave chamber. True or false?
12. Name one of the first two people to reach the summit of Mount Everest.
13. During which dynasty did the building of the Great Wall begin?

Level 3

14. For how many years did the Dalai Lamas use the Potala Palace as their winter home?
15. Where can the Sarawak Chamber be found?
16. If Mount Fuji is 12,385 ft. (3,776m) high, how much higher is Mount Everest than Mount Fuji?
17. If the Petronas Twin Towers' skybridge is 558 ft. (170m) high, how much taller are the towers themselves?
18. How long is the Great Wall of China?

FIND THE ANSWER:

Asia

Mount Fuji

Asia is the largest of Earth's seven continents. It is divided from Europe by the Ural Mountains along Asia's western borders. Asia contains the world's two most populated countries: China and India.

Mount Fuji

4 9

Japan's Mount Fuji is the country's highest peak, at 12,385 ft. (3,776m). It is a dormant volcano that last erupted in 1708. Mount Fuji is sacred to the Japanese—more than 500,000 people climb it every year to pray on its summit.

Potala Palace

Tibet

7 14

The Potala Palace in Lhasa, Tibet, was built in the Himalayas on a hill with a sacred cave. It was the winter home of the Dalai Lama from 1648 until 1959, when Tibet was occupied by China. Unlike many other Tibetan religious buildings, the palace was not destroyed.

Taj Mahal

2 3 5

When his wife died in 1631, Shah Jahan employed more than 20,000 workers to build the Taj Mahal, close to Agra, India, in her memory. More than 1,000 elephants were used to haul marble from faraway quarries.

Himalayas

1 12 16

The tallest mountain in the world is Mount Everest in the Himalayas, at 29,021 ft. (8,848m) high. Since Edmund Hillary and Tenzing Norgay first reached the top in 1953, other people have climbed Mount Everest.

mountain climbers

Big cave

11 15

Sarawak Chamber, or Lubang Nasib Bagus, is the world's largest cave chamber, at around 230 ft. (70m) high, 2,300 ft. (700m) long, and 984 ft. (300m) wide. It is in Borneo, Malaysia.

Petronas Twin Towers

8 17

Kuala Lumpur, the capital of Malaysia, is the home of the Petronas Twin Towers. It is one of the tallest buildings in the world, at 1,483 ft. (452m) high. There are 88 stories in each one of the towers. A double-decker skybridge, which weighs around 750 tons, connects the two towers on the 41st and 42nd floors.

fort

Great Wall

13 18

The Great Wall of China, the world's longest man-made structure, stretches for 3,900 mi. (6,300km), but it may be even longer. The wall was built over a period of 2,000 years. Work began during the Qin dynasty, around 221 B.C., when China's first emperor ordered several existing walls to be connected and this continued until the early 1600s.

Angkor Wat

6 10

More than 100 wats, or temples, were built in Angkor Wat, Cambodia, between the 800s and 1200s. The largest is Angkor Wat, built for the Hindu god Vishnu in the 1100s.

Angkor Wat

QUESTIONS: Europe

Level 1

1. Where is Red Square: in Paris, France, or Moscow, Russia?
2. Does the Channel Tunnel go under or over the English Channel?
3. The Leaning Tower of Pisa was designed to lean. True or false?
4. How many tracks are in the Channel Tunnel: one, two, or three?

Level 2

5. The Eisriesenwelt ice cave is the largest ice cave in the world. True or false?
6. Is the Guggenheim Museum in Paris, Bilbao, or Salzburg?
7. Was the Eiffel Tower built in Paris, France, to celebrate Bastille Day, the end of the Hundred Years' War, or the Universal Exhibition?
8. Who commissioned the building of Saint Basil's Cathedral: Ivan the Terrible, Rasputin, or Catherine the Great?
9. What does "Eisriesenwelt" mean: tiny ice world, giant cave, or giant ice world?
10. Which famous Alpine mountain is pyramid-shaped?
11. What features appear on the top of Saint Basil's Cathedral?
12. How high is Mont Blanc: 15,770 ft. (4,808m), 19,050 ft. (5,808m), or 25,610 ft. (7,808m)?
13. What is a campanile: a bell tower, dome, or steeple?
14. How much does the Eiffel Tower's structure weigh: around 5,330, 7,300, or 10,300 tons?

Level 3

15. How long is the Channel Tunnel?
16. How long did it take to construct the Leaning Tower of Pisa?
17. What forms the bottom of the Eiffel Tower?
18. What material covers the curved panels of the Guggenheim Museum?

Europe

Europe is the world's second-smallest continent. It lies west of the Ural Mountains, which divide it from Asia. Europe consists of many countries and several microstates. Despite being small, these microstates are independent states. Vatican City is the smallest microstate in the world. This tiny state lies within Rome, Italy.

Pisa

3 13 16

The Leaning Tower of Pisa, in Pisa, Italy, is the city's campanile, or bell tower. The tower started leaning during its construction, which began in 1173 and ended in 1370. There are 294 steps to the bell tower, which has seven bells.

Moscow

1 8 11

Ivan the Terrible ordered Saint Basil's Cathedral in Moscow's Red Square to be built. The cathedral was built between 1555 and 1561. Each one of the towers has a unique onion-shaped dome.

Channel Tunnel

2 4 15

Eleven giant tunnel-boring machines were used to dig the Channel Tunnel under the English Channel, between Great Britain and France. The tunnel was completed in 1994 after seven years of work. It is 31 mi. (50km) long, with 24 mi. (39km) running under the sea. The tunnel contains three tracks: two tracks for trains, and one that is used as a service track.

Eiffel Tower
(7) (14) (17)

The Eiffel Tower, in Paris, France, was built in 1889 for the Universal Exhibition. Its structure weighs around 7,300 tons. It is 1,063 ft. (324m) high and stands on a base that is held up by four pillars.

Modern museum
(6) (18)

The architect Frank O. Gehry designed the Guggenheim Museum in Bilbao, Spain. It opened in 1997. The curved panels are covered in titanium.

The Alps
(10) (12)

This mountain range is in Germany, Austria, France, Italy, Liechtenstein, Slovenia, and Switzerland. Mont Blanc is the highest peak, at 15,770 ft. (4,808m) high. The Matterhorn is known for its pyramid shape.

Ice cave
(5) (9)

The largest ice cave in the world is the Eisriesenwelt, or "giant ice world," close to Salzburg, Austria. It is part of a cave system that is around 26 mi. (42km) in length, with 0.6 mi. (1km) of the cave covered in ice. Although local hunters knew about the cave, Eisriesenwelt was officially "discovered" in 1879 by Anton Posselt.

QUESTIONS: North America

Level 1

1. The Statue of Liberty is in Washington, D.C. True or false?
2. How many waterfalls make up Niagara Falls?
3. The Grand Canyon is in Arizona. True or false?
4. Which is the world's tallest tree: the coast redwood or the Scots pine?
5. Does the Golden Gate Bridge cross the San Francisco Bay?

Level 2

6. Which U.S. president's face is not carved on Mount Rushmore: Lincoln, Kennedy, or Theodore Roosevelt?
7. How many main sections make up the Grand Canyon: three, five, or seven?
8. How many faces of U.S. presidents were carved into Mount Rushmore: three, four, or five?
9. How high is the Statue of Liberty: 271 ft. (82.5m), 307 ft. (93.5m), or 312 ft. (95m)?
10. How old is the oldest giant sequoia: 1,000, 3,200, or 5,500 years old?
11. Do the vertical ribs on the Golden Gate Bridge stand out on a sunny day?
12. What "S" on the Statue of Liberty's crown represent the world's seven seas and continents?
13. Rearrange COWES TOAST to name where redwoods grow.

Level 3

14. Why do the towers on the Golden Gate Bridge appear taller than they are?
15. How do the plants change as you go farther down into the Grand Canyon?
16. How much wider is Horseshoe Falls than American Falls?
17. How long did it take to carve the monument at Mount Rushmore?
18. How long is the Golden Gate Bridge?

FIND THE ANSWER: North America

The continent of North America includes Greenland and dozens of small islands in the Caribbean, as well as the United States, Canada, Mexico, and the Central American countries. The name "America" is probably in honor of Amerigo Vespucci, who first wrote about it as a separate "New World."

Statue of Liberty

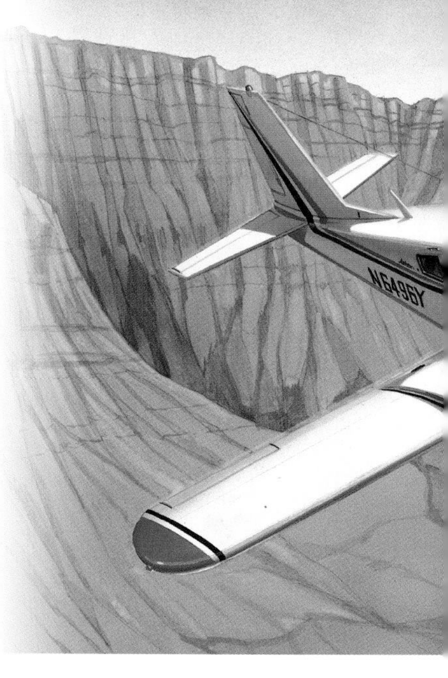

Liberty 1 9 12

The 307-ft.-tall (93.5m) Statue of Liberty, in New York Harbor, was a gift from France in 1884. It was designed by Gustave Eiffel. The seven spikes in the crown represent the world's seven seas and continents.

Redwoods 4 10 13

The west coast of the U.S. is home to impressive redwood trees. The coast redwood is the tallest tree, at 367 ft. (112m) tall. The oldest giant sequoia is 3,200 years old.

Golden Gate Bridge 5 11 14 18

The San Francisco Bay in California can be crossed by the Golden Gate Bridge, which is 8,977 ft. (2,737m) long. The longest span between the main posts is 4,198 ft. (1,280m). The towers are smaller at the top than at the base to make the towers appear taller. The vertical ribs stand out on a sunny day when the Sun's rays light up the bridge.

coast redwood

Grand Canyon

3 7 15

There are three main sections of the Grand Canyon in Arizona: the South Rim, the North Rim, and the Inner Canyon. Each section has a different climate and plant life. Plants become shorter and sparser as they grow farther down the canyon, and desert scrub lives on the canyon floor.

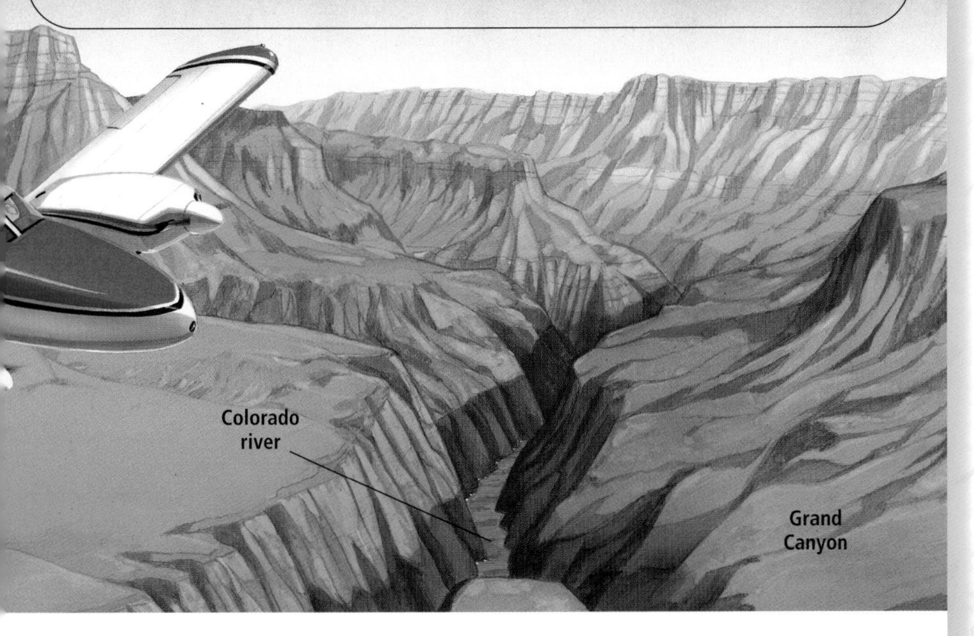

Niagara Falls

2 16

There are three waterfalls that together form Niagara Falls: American Falls (1,059 ft., or 323m, wide), Horseshoe Falls (2,598 ft., or 792m, wide), and Bridal Veils Falls (56 ft., or 17m, wide). The waterfalls and the Niagara river flow between Ontario, Canada, and New York.

Mount Rushmore

6 8 17

The faces of four U.S. presidents—Lincoln, Jefferson, Washington, and Theodore Roosevelt—were carved into Mount Rushmore, in South Dakota, by Gutzon Borglum and 400 workers from 1927 to 1941.

George Washington

Thomas Jefferson

Theodore Roosevelt

Abraham Lincoln

QUESTIONS: South America

Level 1

1. Did the Incas build Machu Picchu in the Andes?
2. Angel Falls is the highest waterfall in the world. True or false?
3. The Amazon is the world's largest river, but not the longest. True or false?
4. Which city is famous for its beaches: Lima or Rio de Janeiro?
5. The llama is a type of wild cat. True or false?

Level 2

6. Can a statue of Jesus be found at the top or the base of Sugar Loaf Mountain in Brazil?
7. What percentage of Earth's oxygen does the Amazon rain forest produce: two percent, ten percent, or 20 percent?
8. Angel Falls is named after which American pilot?
9. Machu Picchu was built in which century: the 1200s, 1300s, or 1400s?
10. Is Lake Titicaca a freshwater lake or a saltwater lake?
11. How many structures made up Machu Picchu: around ten, 100, or 200?
12. What "A" in Argentina has fine fleece?
13. In the Quechua language does Machu Picchu mean "high mountain," "old mountain," or "young mountain"?
14. Can the source for the Amazon river be found in the Andes, Himalayas, or Rocky Mountains?

Level 3

15. How long is the Amazon river?
16. Where can most of the remaining rain forests be found?
17. What are the artificial islands in Lake Titicaca made from?
18. What material did the Incas use to build their structures?

FIND THE ANSWER:

South America

The continent of South America is divided into 12 countries, the largest of which is Brazil. It is connected to North America by the Isthmus of Panama—a tiny strip of land. As well as Spanish and Portuguese, many native languages are spoken in South America such as Aymara, Guarani, and Quechua—the language that was used by the Incas.

tropical rain forest

Rain forest 7 16

More than half of the world's remaining rain forests can be found in the Amazon basin. The Amazon rain forest contains more species than any other rain forest. It also produces around 20 percent of Earth's oxygen.

Rio 4 6

Rio de Janeiro, in Brazil, is set at the foot of Sugar Loaf Mountain. It is famous for its Copacabana Beach and the statue of Jesus, known as Christ the Redeemer. The statue is on the top of the mountain.

Copacabana Beach

Amazon 3 14 15

The Amazon river is the world's largest river by volume of water. At 3,960 mi. (6,387km), it is the second-longest river, after the Nile river. The source of the Amazon is a stream on Nevado Mismi, high up in the Andes.

Angel Falls 2 8

The world's highest waterfall, at 3,211 ft. (979m) high, is Angel Falls in Venezuela. It is 15 times higher than Niagara Falls. It is named after James Crawford Angel, an American pilot who flew over the falls in 1933.

Machu Picchu 1 9 13

In around 1450 the Incas built Machu Picchu in the Andes in Peru, on a site that was probably a sacred place. Machu Picchu means "Old Mountain" in the Quechua language. Its ruins were rediscovered by Hiram Bingham in 1911.

Lake Titicaca (10) (17)

South America's largest freshwater lake is Lake Titicaca. It lies in the Andes of Peru and Bolivia. The Uros are the people who live on the artificial islands in the lake. The islands are made from reeds that grow in the lake, and they last around 30 years.

Pampas (5) (12)

The Argentinian pampas extends from the Atlantic Ocean to the Andes. Llamas graze the grasslands. The Incas used this camelid for its wool and its meat. Its cousin, the alpaca, has finer fleece.

Structure (11) (18)

The Incas built Machu Picchu using ashlar blocks (polished rectangular stones). The city had around 200 structures, including temples to the Sun god, Inti.

remains of Inca structure

QUESTIONS: Australia and Oceania

Level 1

1. Is Sydney Australia's largest city or one of its smaller cities?
2. Easter Island (or Rapa Nui) is the home of statues that were carved by Polynesian settlers. True or false?
3. Does the kangaroo live in Australia?
4. Road trains are really trucks that pull trailers. True or false?

Level 2

5. Uluru in Australia is also called Ayers Rock. True or false?
6. How many statues are there on Easter Island (or Rapa Nui): six, 60, or 600?
7. Uluru is sacred to: British convicts, Australian Aborigines, or marsupials?
8. What is attached to the front of an Australian road train: a roo bar, bull bar, or marsupial bar?
9. What can be found on New Zealand's North Island: volcanoes, geysers, hot springs, or all of the above?
10. How long was the longest road train: 13 trailers, 33 trailers, or 113 trailers?
11. What "F" are the Naracoorte Caves in Australia known for?
12. Was Sydney founded as a new colony for sheep farmers, for sugar plantations, or as a convict settlement?

Level 3

13. What is the name for the Easter Island (or Rapa Nui) statues?
14. What "M" is a type of animal group, with the largest one living in Australia?
15. In what year did paleontologists first visit Victoria Fossil Cave—one of the Naracoorte Caves in Australia?
16. Where was the Sydney Opera House built?
17. What is the Maori name for New Zealand?
18. How far is Easter Island from South America?

FIND THE ANSWER:

Australia and Oceania

The continent of Australia is an island that is surrounded by the Pacific and Indian oceans. It is the flattest continent, as well as one of the driest. Australia is also the name of the country on the island. Oceania is a term that is used for a region of more than 25,000 islands, including Australia, New Zealand, and the Polynesian islands, found in the Pacific Ocean and nearby seas.

Sydney 1 12 16

Captain Arthur Philip founded Sydney, Australia's largest city, in 1788 as a British convict settlement. It was built around Sydney Harbour. The famous Sydney Opera House was built on Bennelong Point in the harbor.

Uluru 5 7

The largest rock in the world is known as Uluru, or Ayers Rock. It is a sacred place for the Aborigines who live in central Australia. The rock is almost 1,141 ft. (348m) high and measures almost 6 mi. (9km) around its base.

Hot springs 9 17

New Zealand, called Aotearoa by the native Maori people, is made up of two islands: North Island and South Island. They lie on the edge of the Pacific Plate and the Indo-Australian plate. The area around Rotorua, on the North Island, has active volcanoes, geysers, hot springs, and mud pools.

hot springs

Naracoorte Caves 11 15

The small town of Naracoorte, in South Australia, has a series of 26 limestone caves. In 1969 paleontologists discovered thousands of fossils inside Victoria Fossil Cave. Holes had opened in the top of the caves, which are weak because they are just below the ground. The fossils are from animals that fell into the holes and were trapped.

Marsupials

3 14

Animals in the marsupial group give birth to young that are underdeveloped and are often carried in their mother's pouches. The largest marsupial, the kangaroo, lives in Australia, as do koalas and the sugar glider, which is a possum.

Easter Island statues

Easter Island

2 6 13 18

Chile's Easter Island, or Rapa Nui, is a Polynesian island in the Pacific Ocean, 2,480 mi. (4,000km) from South America. Early Polynesian settlers carved 600 statues, or *moai*, on the island around 1,000 years ago.

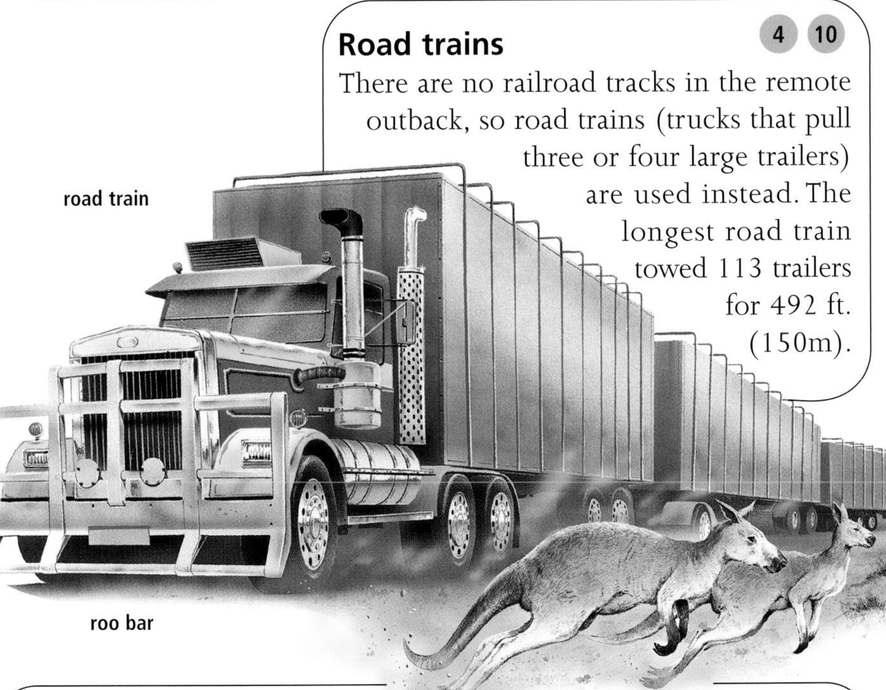

Road trains

4 10

There are no railroad tracks in the remote outback, so road trains (trucks that pull three or four large trailers) are used instead. The longest road train towed 113 trailers for 492 ft. (150m).

Roo bars

8

Because there are so many vehicle collisions with kangaroos in Australia, a "roo bar" is attached to the front of a road train to protect the vehicle and the driver. In areas where cattle roam, a "bull bar" is used.

QUESTIONS: Antarctica

Level 1

1. Penguins live in Antarctica. True or false?
2. How do people travel on the ice in Antarctica: by snowmobile, car, or bus?
3. There are permanent research stations in Antarctica. True or false?
4. What are groups of elephant seals called: harems or groupies?
5. A penguin is a bird. True or false?

Level 2

6. How many scientists live and work in Anatarctica during the summer: 400, 4,000, or 40,000?
7. What does the Global Positioning System link to: the Internet, cell phones, or satellites?
8. Is the Lambert Glacier Antarctica's largest, smallest, or youngest glacier?
9. How deep can an elephant seal dive: down to 50 ft. (15m), 500 ft. (150m), or 5,000 ft. (1,500m)?
10. Why do whales migrate north: to breed, feed, or follow ships?
11. When do whales migrate south: in the spring, summer, fall, or winter?
12. What is a Dornier 228: a plane, snowmobile, or bulldozer?
13. Ranulph Fiennes and Mike Stroud pulled their own sleds as they crossed Antarctica in 1993. True or false?

Level 3

14. What are rookeries?
15. What is the name of Earth's most southern point?
16. Which vehicle has tracks like a bulldozer?
17. What might a beachmaster have in his harem?
18. Why are special tents used by scientists?

FIND THE ANSWER: Antarctica

Antarctica measures 5.46 million sq. mi. (14 million km^2), almost one-and-a-half times the size of the U.S. Its landscape is made up of only two percent barren rock—the remaining 98 percent is ice. It is the coldest, windiest, and driest continent in the world. No one lives there all year-round, but scientists travel there to study, and they live in specially equipped research stations.

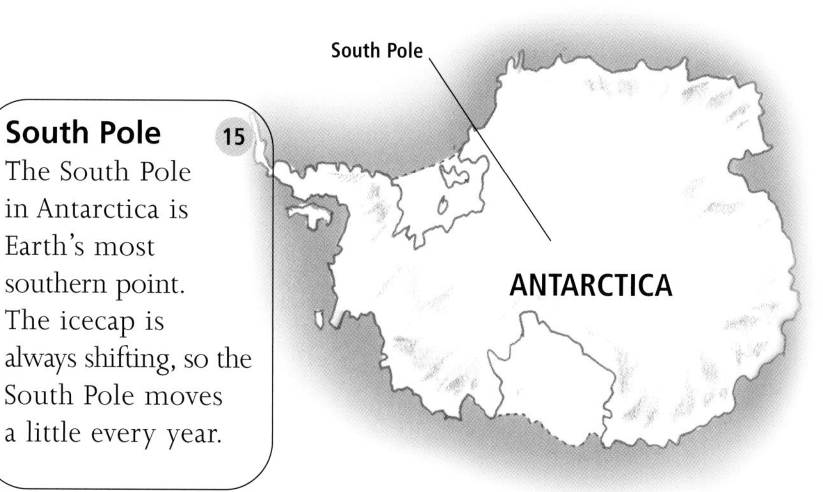

South Pole 15

The South Pole in Antarctica is Earth's most southern point. The icecap is always shifting, so the South Pole moves a little every year.

piked whale

Whales 10 11

Antarctic whales, such as the sperm whale, piked whale, and humpback whale, migrate to the southern oceans for the summer to feed on swarms of shrimplike krill. They then travel north to breed.

Transportation 2 12 16

The Dornier 228 plane is used to carry passengers and cargo. Land travel is by snowmobile or the Hagglund—it has tracks like a bulldozer.

Dornier 228

Explorers 13

Roald Amundsen was the first person to reach the South Pole, but in 1993 Ranulph Fiennes and Mike Stroud made the first unsupported walk across Antarctica, each man pulling a 495-lb. (225-kg) sled.

Penguins 1 5 14

Antarctica's penguins include the emperor, adélie, and gentoo. Penguins do not fly, but they are good swimmers and can leap to avoid predators. The birds breed in large colonies called rookeries.

Scientists 3 6

Permanent and summer research stations are run in Antarctica by 27 different countries. During the summer, around 4,000 scientists live and work there. Less than 1,000 people live in Antarctica during the winter.

Glaciers

8

Lambert Glacier is the largest glacier in the world, at 50 mi. (80km) wide and 310 mi. (500km) long. Fisher Massif is a 5,576-ft.-tall (1,700m) nunatak, or mountain, that runs along the western side of the glacier.

Seals

4 9 17

Elephant seals are powerful swimmers and can dive down to 5,000 ft. (1,500m). They live in breeding groups called harems. Bulls (males) fight over breeding rights. The winner, called the beachmaster, may have up to 50 cows (females) in his harem.

Scientific study

7 18

The Global Positioning System (GPS) links to satellites above Earth to give scientists an accurate reading of their position in Antarctica. Special tents are made to resist the strong icy winds that can reach 90 mph (145km/h).

QUESTIONS: Where in the world?

Level 1

1. The Great Rift Valley can be found on which continent: Asia, Africa, or Europe?
2. Can castles and cathedrals be found throughout Europe?
3. The Rocky Mountains stretch from Canada into South America. True or false?

Level 2

4. Where do most Australians live: along the coast or in the outback?
5. The Atacama Desert is the driest place on Earth. True or false?
6. Do China's large rivers flow east to west or west to east?
7. Is the Chang Jiang a river or a mountain in China?
8. Which continent is the driest inhabited continent: Africa, Australia, or Antarctica?

Level 3

9. How long is the Great Rift Valley?
10. Which continent has the least fertile soil?
11. Who built the Palace of Versailles?

FIND THE ANSWER: Where in the world?

Amazing sites are found all over the world. There are dramatic landscapes, such as the Grand Canyon and the Sahara, and bustling cities, such as London and Tokyo. With the exception of Antarctica, historic buildings can be found on every continent—evidence of the people living there over hundreds of years.

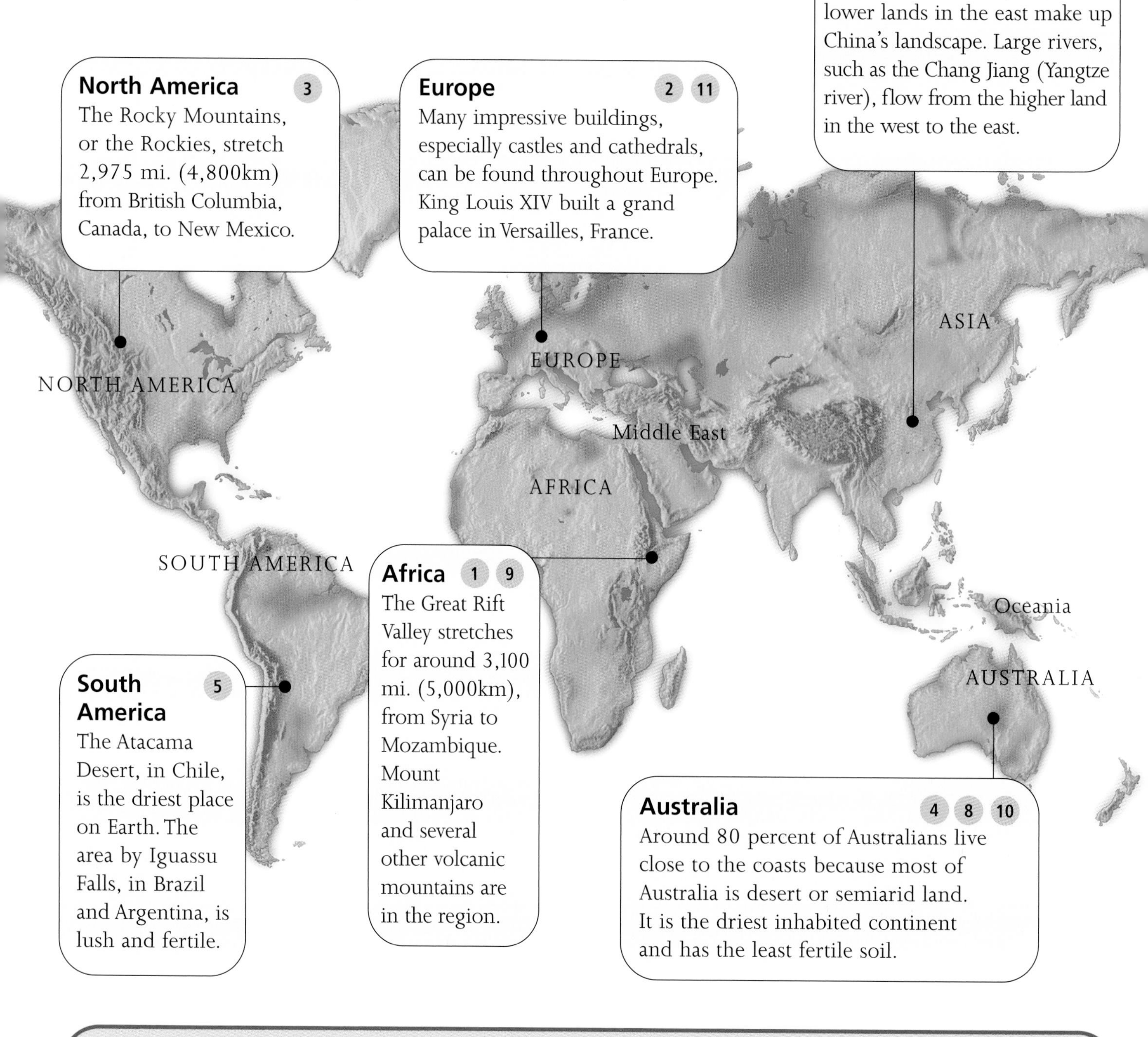

China 6 7
Mountains in the west and lower lands in the east make up China's landscape. Large rivers, such as the Chang Jiang (Yangtze river), flow from the higher land in the west to the east.

North America 3
The Rocky Mountains, or the Rockies, stretch 2,975 mi. (4,800km) from British Columbia, Canada, to New Mexico.

Europe 2 11
Many impressive buildings, especially castles and cathedrals, can be found throughout Europe. King Louis XIV built a grand palace in Versailles, France.

Africa 1 9
The Great Rift Valley stretches for around 3,100 mi. (5,000km), from Syria to Mozambique. Mount Kilimanjaro and several other volcanic mountains are in the region.

South America 5
The Atacama Desert, in Chile, is the driest place on Earth. The area by Iguassu Falls, in Brazil and Argentina, is lush and fertile.

Australia 4 8 10
Around 80 percent of Australians live close to the coasts because most of Australia is desert or semiarid land. It is the driest inhabited continent and has the least fertile soil.

Answers 1) Africa **2)** Yes **3)** False (only to New Mexico) **4)** Along the coast **5)** True **6)** West to east **7)** A river **8)** Australia **9)** Around 3,100 mi. (5,000km) **10)** Australia **11)** King Louis XIV of France

QUIZ THREE

Science and inventions

The Sun

The Moon

Constellations

Outer space

Gold

Caves

Climate

Storms

Hurricanes and tornadoes

Tsunamis

The senses

Digestion

Inventors

Cars

Motorcycles

Airplanes

QUESTIONS:

The Sun

Level 1

1. The Sun has a core. True or false?
2. While it is daytime in one part of Earth, can it be nighttime in another part of Earth?
3. What "S" is the name that we give to the different times of the year?
4. Rearrange RINSE US to spell the time of day when Earth turns toward the Sun and the Sun first appears above the horizon.

Level 2

5. Energy released from the Sun affects electronic systems, such as telephone networks, on Earth. True or false?
6. At sunset is Earth turning toward or away from the Sun?
7. Bright patches that appear in the Sun's corona are called solar prominences. True or false?
8. How long does a sunspot cycle usually last?
9. What comes between Earth and the Sun in a solar eclipse: the Moon, Mars, or Venus?
10. What "R" does Earth do as it orbits around the Sun?
11. What are magnetic storms on the Sun called: coronas, sunspots, or eclipses?
12. What "H" does the Sun seem to sink below at sunset?
13. What is visible during a solar eclipse: sunspots, the Sun's corona, or neither?
14. Do solstices occur when Earth is most or least tilted on its axis?

Level 3

15. How hot is the hottest part of the Sun?
16. What "T" is the dividing line between daytime and nighttime?
17. How large can sunspots be?
18. Name three things that are released from a buildup of energy in the Sun's corona.

FIND THE ANSWER: The Sun

The Sun is a medium-sized star that is made of a huge, rotating ball of hot gas. It is located in the galaxy (a group of star systems) called the Milky Way. The Sun is in the center of the solar system and an average of 93,000,000 mi. (150,000,000km) from Earth. Its powerful gravity keeps all of the planets in its solar system in orbit. Most life on Earth depends on heat and light from the Sun.

The core (1) (15)

The Sun's hottest part, its core, may be more than 59,000,000°F (15,000,000°C). Huge amounts of energy are released from the core and carried out.

sunspot

core

The seasons (3) (14)

Earth has seasons—spring, summer, fall, and winter—because its axis (an imaginary line through its center) tilts at an angle. This brings different areas of Earth closer to the Sun at various times during the year, which affects the weather. The solstices occur when Earth's axis is the most tilted.

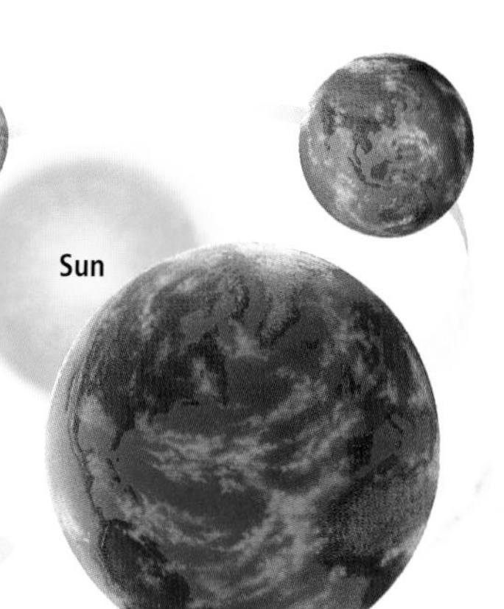

Night and day (2) (10) (16)

While Earth orbits (travels around) the Sun, it also rotates, or spins. The half of Earth that faces the Sun is in daylight, while the half that faces away from the Sun is in darkness. A line called the "terminator" separates daytime from nighttime. A supersonic jet can overtake it.

Sunset and sunrise (4) (6) (12)

The Sun seems to sink below the horizon at sunset. In fact, the sky darkens as Earth rotates away from the Sun. At sunrise, Earth is turning toward the Sun.

The corona 5 7 18

Temperatures in the Sun's outer atmosphere, called the corona, are more than 1,800,000°F (1,000,000°C). Streams of gas called solar prominences shoot out millions of miles into space. Huge bright patches called solar flares appear in the corona, caused by a buildup of energy. This is released into space as radio waves, ultraviolet light, and X-rays. These cause chaos in telephone networks on Earth.

solar prominence

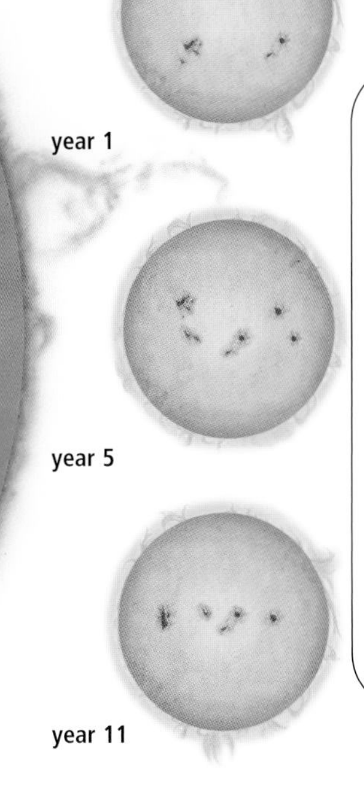

Sunspots 8 11 17

Dark patches seen in the Sun's photosphere (its outer surface) are called sunspots. These are magnetic storms that occur on the Sun. Although they look small from Earth, sunspots can be as large as 31,000 mi. (50,000km) in diameter. Their temperature of 7,363°F (4,073°C) is considered cool for the Sun. Sunspots regularly appear and disappear in 11-year cycles.

Eclipse of the Sun 9 13

During a solar eclipse, the Moon comes between Earth and the Sun. From Earth, the Moon blocks the Sun from view, and only the corona is seen. This plunges Earth into twilight. Because Earth is spinning, the eclipse is visible along a path that crosses the planet.

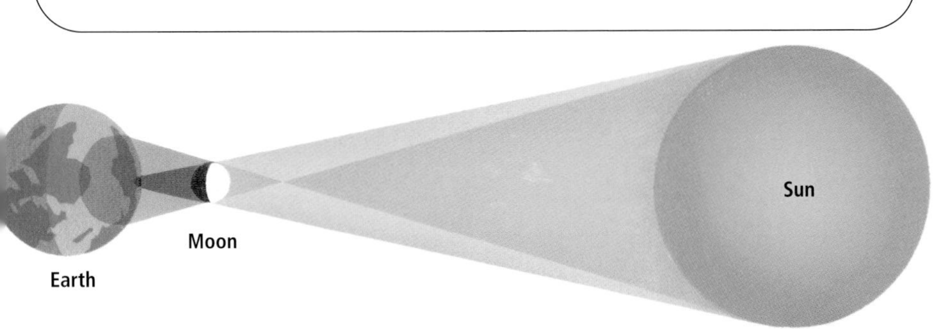

QUESTIONS: The Moon

Level 1

1. Does the Sun or Earth light up the Moon?
2. The Moon doesn't have any gravity. True or false?
3. Does the Moon orbit around Earth or the Sun?
4. When the sea falls away from the shore, it is low tide. True or false?

Level 2

5. The new moon is sunny on the side that we cannot see. True or false?
6. There is a face of the Moon that we never see. True or false?
7. What "G" causes tides?
8. Which type of tide occurs when the Moon is overhead: high tide or low tide?
9. How long does the Moon take to orbit Earth: 24 hours, 27.3 days, or 39.5 days?
10. Who was the first astronaut to set foot on the Moon: Al Shepard, Buzz Aldrin, or Neil Armstrong?
11. Does Earth's or the Sun's shadow pass over the Moon during a lunar eclipse?
12. Which "W" means that the Moon is getting thinner?
13. Are high tides higher or lower during spring tides?
14. Do neap tides occur when Earth, the Moon, and the Sun are in line?

Level 3

15. What is the diameter of the Moon?
16. How long does the Moon take to pass through all of its phases?
17. Where are the Sun and the Moon when there is a full moon?
18. When does a lunar eclipse occur?
19. What was the date of the first U.S. Moon landing?

The Moon

The Moon is a satellite that orbits around Earth. It is bigger than the dwarf planet Pluto, but it has no atmosphere. The "seas" that can be seen on the face of the Moon are craters made by asteroids that crashed there 3,000 to 4,000 years ago. The Moon's gravity causes the tides—the rising and falling of Earth's oceans and seas.

Tides (4) (7) (8)

When the Moon is overhead, its gravity pulls the sea up to the shore. This is high tide. As Earth turns the Moon's pull weakens, and the sea falls back to low tide.

high tide

low tide

The Moon (2) (15)

The diameter of the Moon is 2,155 mi. (3,476km), and its orbit is 238,328 mi. (384,400km) from Earth. Its gravity is only one sixth of the force of gravity produced by Earth.

Spring tides (13)

When Earth, the Sun, and the Moon are in line, high tides are higher and low tides are lower. These are called spring tides.

Neap tides (14)

When Earth, the Moon, and the Sun move apart, high tides are lower and low tides are higher. These are called neap tides.

Earth

The Moon's face (3) (6) (9)

The Moon rotates on its axis, but we only see one face. This is because Earth's pull always keeps one side of the Moon in sight. The Moon rotates and orbits Earth in the same amount of time: 27.3 days.

Moon orbiting around Earth

Phases of the Moon (1) (5) (16)

The Sun lights up the orbiting Moon from different directions. At new moon it lights up the side that we never see. The Moon passes through eight phases over 29.3 days. Six phases are shown here.

new moon
day 1

waxing crescent moon
day 4

first quarter
day 7

full moon
day 14

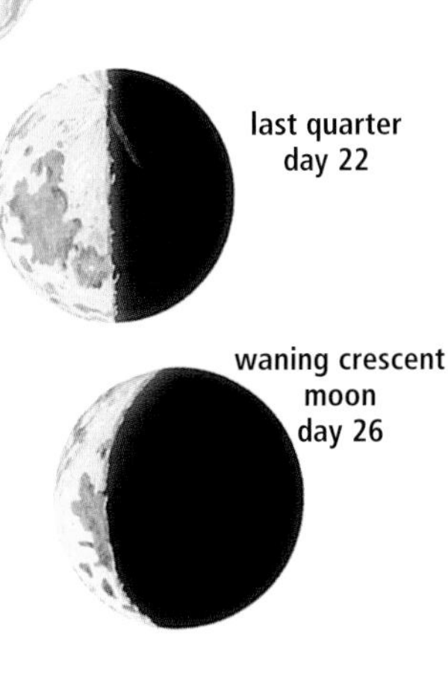

last quarter
day 22

waning crescent moon
day 26

Full moon (12) (17)

When a full moon occurs, the Sun and the Moon are on opposite sides of Earth. A new moon "waxes"—more of it is seen each day—until the full moon on day 14. Then it "wanes," or grows thinner each day.

Lunar eclipse (11) (18)

When a full moon passes exactly behind Earth, Earth blocks sunlight from reaching the Moon. We see Earth's shadow pass over the Moon. This is called a lunar eclipse.

On the Moon (10) (19)

U.S. space missions landed on the Moon six times between 1969 and 1972. Neil Armstrong was the first astronaut to walk on the Moon, on July 21, 1969. The Moon's gravitational force is less than Earth's, so the astronauts could easily jump across the landscape.

QUESTIONS: Constellations

Level 1

1. You must always use binoculars or a telescope to see stars. True or false?
2. The constellation Scorpius is also known as Scorpio. True or false?
3. How many halves can the celestial sky be split into: two or three?
4. Can the Southern Cross be seen in the Northern Hemisphere?
5. Centaurus is a constellation named after a creature from Greek mythology. True or false?

Level 2

6. Pegasus is named after which animal from Greek mythology: a winged horse, bull, or goat?
7. Columba is named after which bird sent from the Ark by Noah to look for land: a dove, pigeon, or eagle?
8. Which constellation did sailors use to navigate in the Southern Hemisphere?
9. Rearrange BRUIN COLAS to name an instrument that is used for stargazing.
10. Which star is the brightest: Sirius, Orion, or Cygnus?
11. Which "O" is the constellation with the largest number of bright stars?
12. Rearrange BEE GLUE SET to spell the name of the bright red star that marks Orion's shoulder.
13. Which "C" is a southern constellation that can be seen in the Northern Hemisphere in February?

Level 3

14. What object does the constellation Libra depict?
15. What is the name of the 13th-brightest star in the sky?
16. When in history do we know that the Southern Cross could be seen from the Middle East?
17. Name the bright star that marks the tail of Cygnus.

FIND THE ANSWER: Constellations

Constellations are groups of stars that form a shape, such as a creature from mythology. There are 88 constellations in total, and they can be seen the best on dark nights. Farmers and astronomers have used constellations for more than 6,000 years to identify the stars.

Centaurus (5)

This constellation is in the shape of a centaur—a creature from Greek mythology that is half man and half horse. It can be seen in the Southern Hemisphere.

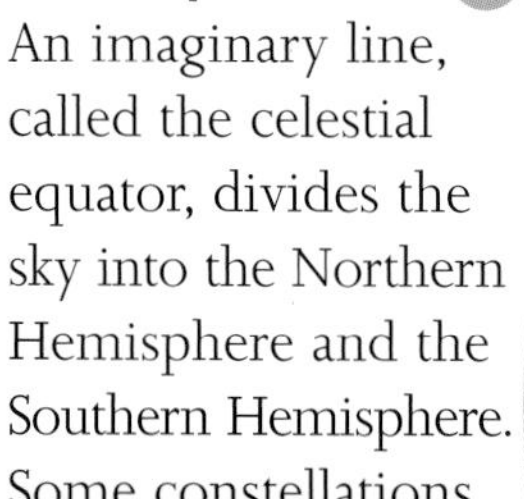

Hemispheres (3)

An imaginary line, called the celestial equator, divides the sky into the Northern Hemisphere and the Southern Hemisphere. Some constellations and stars appear to move between the hemispheres throughout the year.

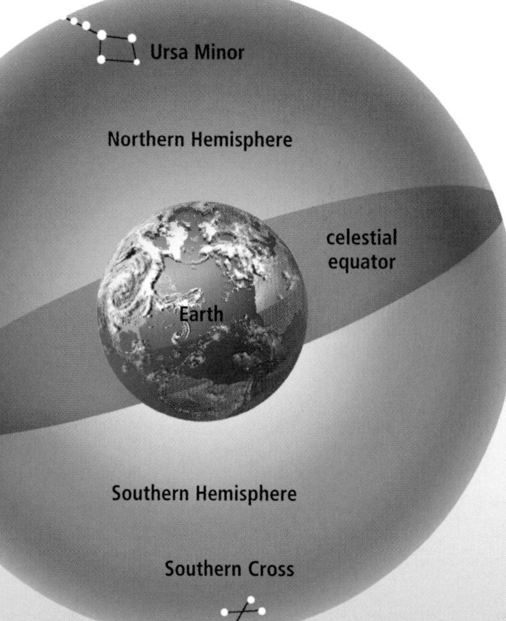

Southern Cross (4) (8) (16)

Sailors in the southern oceans use this constellation to navigate when they are sailing. In biblical times it could be seen in the Middle East, but now it can only be seen in the Southern Hemisphere.

looking into the celestial sky

Stargazing (1) (9) (10) (11)

Binoculars or a telescope are used for seeing faint stars, but some stars are bright enough to be seen with only your eyes. The brightest star in the night sky is Sirius. It is in the constellation of Canis Major. Orion is the constellation with the largest number of bright stars.

Libra (14)

The ancient Greeks saw Libra as the scales held by Virgo, the goddess of justice, whose constellation is nearby. Libra is in the Southern Hemisphere, and its stars are faint.

Cygnus (17)

The swan, or Cygnus, appears to fly south along the Milky Way. Deneb is the bright star in its tail. With binoculars, you can see millions of faint stars in Cygnus.

Scorpio (2) (15)

Scorpius, or Scorpio, rises close to the horizon as Orion sets in the summer sky. In its body is Antares—a giant red star and the 13th-brightest star in the sky.

Pegasus (6)

This Northern Hemisphere constellation is named after Pegasus—a winged horse in Greek mythology. It shares a star called Delta Pegasi with the constellation Andromeda.

Columba (7) (13)

Although it is a southern constellation, Columba moves into northern skies in February. It was named after the biblical dove that Noah sent to look for land.

Orion (12)

Four bright stars form the body of Orion—the hunter in Greek mythology. It is in the Northern Hemisphere, and Betelgeuse, a red supergiant star, marks his shoulder.

QUESTIONS: Outer space

Level 1

1. Which can you find in outer space: a green hole, black hole, or orange hole?
2. Who was a famous astronomer: Rubble, Bubble, or Hubble?
3. The galaxy that contains Earth is called the Creamy Way. True or false?
4. Does a star begin life in a nest or in a nebula?

Level 2

5. A galaxy is a large group of black holes. True or false?
6. Stars usually last for billions of years. True or false?
7. Which is an American space agency: LASA, MASA, or NASA?
8. When a nebula shrinks and condenses, does it heat up or cool down?
9. Does the Milky Way appear to be pale, colorful, or dark in the night sky?
10. Rearrange RAVEN SOUP to name a type of space explosion.
11. How many galaxies are in the Local Group: around three, around 30, or around 300?
12. A nebula is a large star. True or false?
13. Is the Milky Way a large galaxy or a small galaxy?
14. How many types of galaxies are there: four, five, or seven?
15. Which forms first: a red giant or a white dwarf?

Level 3

16. In which part of the Milky Way is Earth's solar system?
17. What do some scientists believe lies in the center of our galaxy?
18. What is the main gas that is found in the Eagle Nebula?

FIND THE ANSWER: Outer space

The universe is so huge that astronomers (scientists who study space) measure distances in light-years—the distance that light travels in one year. The solar system that includes Earth is only a tiny part of the universe. The area outside of the solar system is called outer space. Astronomers are always learning more about outer space as technology becomes more and more advanced.

The Milky Way (3) (9) (11) (13) (16)

Earth's solar system lies in one of the arms of the Milky Way, which is a large barred spiral galaxy. This galaxy gets its name from its pale appearance in the night sky. The Milky Way is part of a group of around 30 galaxies that is known as the Local Group.

Milky Way (barred spiral galaxy)

Types of galaxies (2) (5) (12) (14)

A huge group of stars is called a galaxy. Astronomer Edwin Hubble showed that galaxies conform to a set of basic shapes. The four main shapes are elliptical, spiral, barred spiral, and irregular. Each galaxy has billions of stars and nebulae—clouds of dust or gas.

irregular galaxy

spiral galaxy

elliptical galaxy

Eagle Nebula (7) (18)

American scientists from NASA (the National Aeronautics and Space Administration) study outer space using the Hubble Telescope, which orbits (travels around) Earth. They can see new stars forming within the clouds of hydrogen gas in the Eagle Nebula.

Life cycle of a star

4 6 8 15

A star begins life as part of a nebula, which shrinks and condenses. As this happens, the nebula heats up. When it is hot enough, a newborn star will begin to shine. Over billions of years, the star grows and swells into a red giant. At this point, the star will expel its outer layers, leaving the white-hot core. This is a white dwarf star.

Black hole

1 10 17

Sometimes an especially large star at the end of its life swells enough to become a supergiant and then explodes. This is a supernova. When this happens, the star collapses in on itself and creates a black hole—a bottomless pit that sucks in anything nearby, even light. Some scientists think that there is a giant black hole in the center of the Milky Way.

QUESTIONS: Gold

Level 1

1. What "Y" color is gold?
2. Where was there a famous gold rush that began in 1848: California or Ohio?
3. Gold is a hard metal. True or false?
4. What is gold dust: chunks of gold or tiny particles of gold?

Level 2

5. Rearrange GET GUNS to name the gold pieces that are found by mining.
6. Were there gold rushes in the 1800s in South Africa, Russia, or Japan?
7. Which "O" is the word for rock that contains metals such as gold?
8. Rearrange ANN PING to name a way of searching for gold in rivers using a wide pan.
9. What "G" do we call a person who can make jewelry out of gold?
10. What "I" is the word for the bars of gold that countries keep as part of their money reserves?
11. Exposing gold to air can make it dull. True or false?
12. What "P" is the name for someone who searches for gold?
13. Gold can be pulled out to make thin wire. True or false?

Level 3

14. Which country is the world's largest gold producer?
15. What were used to wash gold pieces from riverbeds?
16. Where is the largest gold mine?
17. For how long has gold been used as money?
18. What "E" is a substance that cannot be broken down such as gold?

FIND THE ANSWER: Gold

Pure gold is an orangey-yellow metal that forms underground in layers called lodes, or veins. Its purity is measured in carats, and pure gold is 24 carats. Because gold is soft, it is usually mixed with another metal. This mixture, called an alloy, becomes a paler yellow, reddish, or white.

Gold 11 18
Pure gold is a chemical element, which means that it cannot be broken down into other elements. Leaving it in water or exposed to air does not destroy it or dull its shine.

Gold rush 2 6
In the 1800s gold deposits were found in North America, Australia, and South Africa. People rushed to these places to "stake a claim." A famous gold rush began in 1848 in California.

Mining 7 12 15
Mines are sunk to dig up ore (rocks containing gold). Most 19th-century prospectors (searchers) mined gold that was carried to the surface by underground rivers or volcanic lava flows. Prospectors washed gravel from riverbeds in sluice boxes, which trapped gold pieces called nuggets.

Panning 4 5 8
Some miners put river mud into a shallow metal pan filled with water and swirled it around. Sand and pebbles were washed away, but the heavier gold sank to the bottom. Panning collected gold nuggets, flakes, and tiny particles of gold dust.

mud washed in large metal pans

Modern gold mining (14) (16)

Today miners blast and drill tunnels into rock to find veins of gold ore. The ore is refined to separate the gold from the rock. South Africa is the world's largest gold producer. The largest gold mine is in West Papua, Indonesia.

camp hut

Currency (10) (17)

Gold has been used as money for 4,000 years. Merchants paid for goods with gold bars called ingots. Today most countries store gold ingots as part of their reserve of money.

gold ingots

Jewelry (1) (3) (9) (13)

Gold is valued for its yellow color and its shine. Goldsmiths make jewelry from gold. Because gold is a soft metal, they can beat it into many shapes and pull it into thin wire.

gold ring

sluice box

QUESTIONS: Caves

Level 1

1. Worms sometimes live in caves. True or false?
2. Do bats or eagles roost in the roofs of caves?
3. Do bacteria and insects feed on fungi or potatoes growing in caves?
4. Plants, such as ferns and mosses, cannot grow in a cave entrance. True or false?

Level 2

5. Rearrange NOODLE WRAPS to name a big cat that shelters in caves in the winter.
6. What is volcanic lava when it is red-hot, soft, and runny: molten, malted, or molded?
7. Name one of two "S" birds that nest on ledges in the ceiling of a cave's entrance.
8. Rearrange LEAST STIGMA to name the rock formations that grow up from the floors of caves.
9. Fungi growing in caves need little light, water, or nutrients. True or false?
10. Do cockroaches or swallows feed on bat droppings in caves?
11. Which is the name of a zone of a cave system: the sunrise zone, twilight zone, or midnight zone?
12. Which rock formations hang like icicles from the roofs of caves: stalagmites or stalactites?
13. Name two "S" types of creatures that can live in caves.

Level 3

14. Which "C" is a mineral that is formed when limestone is dissolved?
15. Temperatures remain constant in which cave zone?
16. Underground rivers carve out what features?
17. What happened to the soft lava that once filled a lava tube?
18. Rearrange BLAME EMPIRE to form another word that means "watertight."

FIND THE ANSWER: Caves

Some caves are hollow spaces along the bottom of cliffs that have been carved out by waves. Others are formed underground when rainwater eats away at soft limestone rock. In many caves there are beautiful columns and pinnacles, mineral deposits, lakes, and rivers.

Rock formations

Rainwater drips into underground caves. The drips contain dissolved limestone (calcite), which slowly hardens. It forms stalactites, which hang like icicles from the roof of the cave. Some drips fall to the floor. They harden and grow upward, forming spires that are called stalagmites.

Cave life 3 9 13

Fungi are organisms that do not need light in order to survive. They grow in caves where there is moisture and nutrients. Fungi provide food for bacteria and insects. Spiders, bats, salamanders, and fish also live in caves.

Cave systems 1 2 10 11 1

Beyond the cave entrance is the twilight zone. There, ba may roost in the roof, and cockroaches, worms, and bacteri live on their droppings. Deeper inside is the dark zone, where the temperature is always around 55°F (13°C).

Cave entrances 4 5 7

Bears and snow leopards may shelter from harsh weather in a cave entrance. If the entrance gets sunlight and rain, ferns and mosses grow there. They provide food for insects and other small animals. Swallows and swiftlets build their nests on high ledges.

limestone

entrance zone

Cave rivers 16 18

Rivers form below ground after rain sinks through rock, such as limestone, that has cracks and holes. The rain seeps down until it reaches impermeable, or watertight, rock. A river forms and flows toward the sea, carving out tunnels and caves.

Lava tubes 6 17

These tunnels form in lava from a volcano. Lava flowing in a channel down a volcano's side may cool and harden on the outside, but it remains molten (soft) underneath. After a while the soft lava drains or flows away, leaving a long cave inside of a hard outer crust.

hard outer crust
lava tube

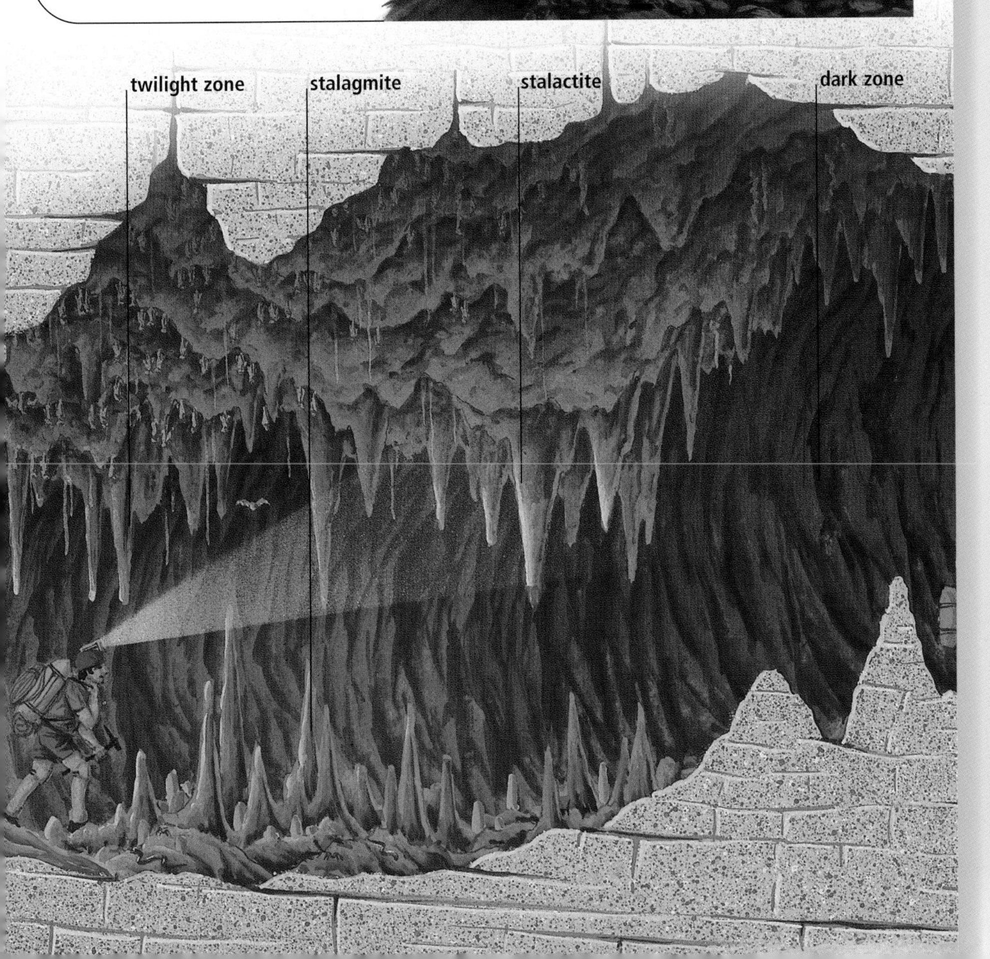

QUESTIONS: Climate

Level 1

1. During a drought, is there less or more rainfall than usual?
2. What are clouds made of: water vapor or icy water?
3. Cirrus is the name for a type of cloud. True or false?

Level 2

4. Which "S" is the largest desert in the world?
5. Which is a greenhouse gas: oxygen or carbon dioxide?
6. In how many years do meteorologists think that all of the glaciers could melt away: ten, 20, or 30?
7. Is an arid climate hot and wet, hot and dry, or cold and icy?
8. Where did scientists find a hole in the ozone layer: over Antarctica, the Arctic, or both?
9. How much rainfall do deserts receive in a year: less than 10 in. (25cm), less than 20 in. (50cm), or more than 3 ft. (1m)?
10. Which one of these two cloud types brings rain: cirrus or cumulonimbus?
11. Rearrange ACE GIRL to name a source of water entering rivers.
12. What "L"s have been drying up in recent years?
13. Are cumulus clouds wispy or puffy clouds?
14. How much of the land on Earth is desert: one third, one quarter, or one fifth?

Level 3

15. During a drought, why do crops die?
16. The ozone layer shields Earth from what type of harmful rays?
17. What never thaws in the tundra?
18. When did the recent drought in the Sahel, northern Africa, begin?
19. How high up in the atmosphere is the ozone layer?

FIND THE ANSWER: Climate

The atmosphere is a protective layer of gases around Earth. It lets in the Sun's light and heat, but it sends back harmful ultraviolet (UV) rays into space. There are different climate zones around the world. However, changes in the atmosphere are making Earth overheat. This is causing changes in the weather.

dried-up river

Clouds 2 3 10 13

Clouds are water vapor in the sky. High clouds, such as the wispy cirrus and the puffy cumulus, are seen on dry days. Gray stratus clouds that blanket the sky and big, black cumulonimbus thunderclouds bring rain.

Drought 1 15 18

A long period when rainfall is below the usual level is called a drought. In a drought, water supplies dry up and crops die. Without food and water, animals and people die. There has been a drought in the Sahel region of northern Africa since 1968.

Rain and water 12

Rain feeds streams, rivers, and lakes. Humans use increasing amounts of water in their homes, cities, farms, and industries. Many rivers and lakes have been drying up in recent years.

mountain snow

river fed by mountain streams

Mountains and glaciers 6 11

The springtime melting of mountain snow and glaciers (rivers of ice) and summer rains feed the rivers where people fish, drink, and grow food. Because of climate change, less snow and ice falls on mountains and glaciers may melt away within 30 years.

The zones 7 17

There are five main climate zones. The polar zone is always icy. Summer in the tundra is short, so the soil never thaws. Within each zone regions have their own climate.

Polar regions (cold and dry)
Tundra (cold winters, cool summers)
Temperate (mild winters, warm summers)
Arid (hot and dry)
Tropical (hot and wet)

Greenhouse effect 5

The atmosphere includes gases, such as carbon dioxide, that trap heat like the glass in a greenhouse. When we burn coal, oil, and gas, we release more of these gases, which causes Earth to overheat.

Ozone hole 8 16 19

A 14-mi.-high (22km) layer of ozone gas around Earth reflects ultraviolet rays back into space. The rays harm people, animals, and plants. Scientists have found holes in the ozone layer above Antarctica and over the Arctic.

hole in the ozone layer

city relying on river

dry desert

fertile land

Dry deserts 4 9 14

Around one third of Earth's land is desert. Deserts get less than 10 in. (25cm) of rain a year. The largest desert is the Sahara in northern Africa, close to the equator. The Sahara is expanding south into the hot, dry Sahel region.

QUESTIONS: Storms

Level 1

1. Lightning is a spark of electricity in a cloud. True or false?
2. Is a blizzard a snowstorm or a dust storm with strong winds?
3. Where do sandstorms happen: in deserts or rain forests?
4. What time of year do thunderstorms usually happen: in the summer or winter?

Level 2

5. If a wave tips over a lifeboat, does it always sink?
6. Rearrange FIND LOGO into a word that describes what happens when seawater spills over onto dry land.
7. How many people are killed by lightning in the U.S. every year: around ten, 100, or 1,000?
8. How many thunderstorms take place on Earth at any one time: around 20, 200, or 2,000?
9. Electricity is made in what type of cloud: nimbostratus, cumulonimbus, or cumulus?
10. Lightning always takes the form of a long, bright streak that follows a zigzag path. True or false?
11. What "M" is the word for a weather expert?
12. What happens to a tree that is struck by lightning: does it get soggy, glow in the dark, or is it blown apart?
13. What type of "G" system can be found on lifeboats?

Level 3

14. A huge North Sea storm surge in 1953 hit which countries?
15. What is thunder?
16. What is the effect of warm air from the ground rising quickly into the cold atmosphere?
17. What is a lightning rod?
18. How high can wind blow sand during a sandstorm?

Storms

Different types of storms occur, depending on the climate. Hot air along the equator rises, then colder air rushes in, causing strong winds. Across northern Europe and the U.S. rain and snowstorms occur in the winter when icy air from the North Pole meets warmer air from the south. The warm air chills, sinks, and blows outward as wind.

positive (+) charge

cumulonimbus (thundercloud)

negative (–) charge

lightning

How storms form (4) (8) (16)

Thunderstorms often occur in the summer, when warm air rises fast from ground level into the cold atmosphere. This causes rain, wind, lightning, and thunder. At any one time, around 2,000 thunderstorms are happening on Earth.

Thunder and lightning (1) (9) (15)

Lightning is a huge spark of electricity that is made in a cloud. Cumulonimbus clouds have a positive electrical charge above and a negative charge beneath them. This electricity builds up. The electricity heats up the air so fast that it vibrates, making thunder. Negatively charged electricity streams to the ground, and a positive charge rises up to meet it, making a channel for the lightning to streak through.

Lightning damage (7) (12) (17)

In addition to blowing trees apart, lightning kills around 100 people each year in the U.S. Tall buildings have metal lightning rods attached to the top. They conduct, or direct, the lightning down a cable to the ground, where it won't cause damage.

Ball lightning (10) (11)

Meteorologists (weather experts) cannot explain the ball-shaped lightning that is sometimes seen. It can be as small as a golf ball or as large as a basketball.

Sandstorms and snowstorms

2 3 18

In desert areas winds blow sand into clouds that are 4,920 ft. (1,500m) high. In cold northern regions the wind whips snow and ice into clouds that blot out the Sun. A large snowstorm with strong winds is called a blizzard.

Storm surges

6

High winds blowing across the ocean for many days can cause a storm surge. The winds whip up the waters above normal sea level, and high waves hit the coast, causing flooding. This often occurs when high tides pull the seas to their highest level.

Rescue at sea

5 13 14

A North Sea storm surge in 1953 drove waves up to 11 ft. (3.36m) higher than normal onto the U.K.'s and the Netherlands' coasts. Thousands died in the floods. Hundreds more died at sea when lifeboat crews could not find them in the storm. Today's lifeboats have Global Positioning System receivers and good communication. The boats can operate in wild weather. If a huge wave tips a lifeboat, it flips back upright.

QUESTIONS:

Hurricanes and tornadoes

Level 1

1. Are planes ever flown into the center of a hurricane?
2. There is torrential rain during a hurricane. True or false?
3. Do hurricanes usually happen during the warmer or colder months?
4. Are hurricanes strong enough to lift up boats and trucks?
5. What is the term for studying storms close up: storm chasing, storm checking, or storm charting?

Level 2

6. Tornadoes are not much more than 30 ft. (10m) in diameter. True or false?
7. What is the name of the truck that is used for studying storms close up?
8. Do hurricanes form over land or water?
9. Where is Tornado Alley: in China, India, or the U.S.?
10. What "D" is a type of radar that is used to investigate storms?
11. How many tornadoes can the U.S. have in a year: ten, 100, or more than 1,000?
12. What is the minimum water temperature needed for a hurricane to form: 72°F (22°C), 81°F (27°C), or 86°F (30°C)?
13. What "R" equipment can be found on a weather-tracking plane?
14. Do hurricanes move faster or slower as they get close to land?

Level 3

15. What two things do weather-tracking planes measure about a hurricane?
16. Inside what type of cloud do tornadoes form?
17. What are hurricane surges?

Hurricanes and tornadoes

Hurricanes are huge whirling storms that rise up over warm tropical oceans north and south of the equator. Tornadoes are powerful whirlwinds that are faster and more violent than hurricanes. Meteorologists use satellites, ships, air balloons, and aircraft to build up a picture of hurricanes and tornadoes and to broadcast warnings.

Tracking a hurricane (1) (13) (15)

Weather-tracking planes are equipped with radars and probes. They fly into the eye, or center, of hurricanes to measure the wind speed and pressure.

clouds spin in an upward spiral

warm ocean

Hurricanes (3) (8) (12)

In the warmer months hurricanes occur when two air masses meet over an ocean with a temperature that is above 81°F (27°C). Warm, moist air is pulled up from the ocean in a slow, circular motion. This is caused by Earth's spin.

The storm hits (2) (4) (14) (17)

Hurricanes can be more than 250 mi. (400km) in diameter, with wind speeds of 75–220 mph (120–350km/h). Many last for several days. At sea they can build up giant waves, causing surges that flood coasts. They often grow bigger and faster as they move toward land. When they hit the coast, they lift boats and trucks, rip up trees and roofs, and blow down buildings. They bring torrential rain, which can cause flooding.

Tornadoes (6) (16)

The inside of huge thunderclouds called supercells are where tornadoes form. They are fed by currents of warm air that rise up into the clouds from below. These currents start spinning and grow into a funnel shape, up to 1 mi. (1.5km) wide. As tornadoes grow they descend and touch land or water.

Storm chasing (5) (7) (10)

Scientists can use Doppler radar to investigate storms. Special "Dopplers on wheels" (trucks with satellite dishes) are used to closely follow tornadoes and hurricanes and study them. This dangerous job is called "storm chasing."

Tornado land (9) (11)

The U.S. has more than 1,000 tornadoes a year. Most hit Tornado Alley—between the Gulf of Mexico and the Great Lakes. Russia and eastern Asia also get tornadoes.

Doppler on wheels

QUESTIONS: Tsunamis

Level 1

1. A tsunami can travel thousands of miles. True or false?
2. A tsunami is only around 3 ft. (1m) high when it is traveling across the ocean. True or false?
3. Can ships pass over tsunamis before they reach the coast?
4. A tsunami is one massive wave. True or false?
5. Does a tsunami start on land or at sea?

Level 2

6. Rearrange HE ATE QUARK to name an undersea event that can cause a tsunami.
7. What "A" is a rock hurtling through space, which may crash into the sea and set off a tsunami?
8. Tsunamis can be formed by rock slides. True or false?
9. What is the average height above sea level of a tsunami wave as it hits a coast: 10 ft. (3m), 150 ft. (45m), or 1,640 ft. (500m)?
10. There is usually a two to four hour gap between two tsunami waves in a train. True or false?
11. How fast can a train of waves travel: 43 mph (70km/h), 105 mph (170km/h), or 434 mph (700km/h)?
12. Do waves from tsunamis look curved or square when they are seen from the side?
13. Are megatsunami waves less than 13 ft. (4m), 46 ft. (14m), or more than 130 ft. (40m) high?

Level 3

14. Name the parts of Earth's crust that move, causing an earthquake.
15. Why do tsunamis slow down as they approach a shore?
16. How many people were killed in the Indian Ocean tsunami?
17. Which volcano in Indonesia erupted in 1883, causing massive waves that killed 36,000 people?
18. What does the word "wavelength" mean?

FIND THE ANSWER: Tsunamis

A sign that a tsunami is coming is the sea sucking back from the shore. A huge wall of water then races to the shore, growing higher and higher. The wave floods inland, causing terrible damage. The Indian Ocean tsunami in 2004 was caused by earthquakes beneath the Indian Ocean. The Pacific Ocean, where 85 percent of tsunamis occur, has tsunami-warning systems.

Waves
2 3 12

Tsunamis racing across the ocean, around 3 ft. (1m) high, are so small that ships pass over them. When they pile up on the coast, they look square from the side. Waves that are made by hurricanes will look curved.

Megatsunamis
13 17

The waves of a megatsunami are 130 ft. (40m) high or more. In 1883 Krakatoa, a volcano close to Java, Indonesia, erupted. Its lava chamber emptied and collapsed. The sea then rushed in, creating massive waves that killed 36,000 people.

Trains
4 9 15

A tsunami is really a train, or series, of waves. The waves only grow when they reach land. A rising seabed close to the coast slows down the waves to around 60 mph (100km/h). They then pile up, one on top of another. They reach an average of 10 ft. (3m) above sea level, but they can be much higher. The sea pulls back from the shore before each wave in the train surges inland.

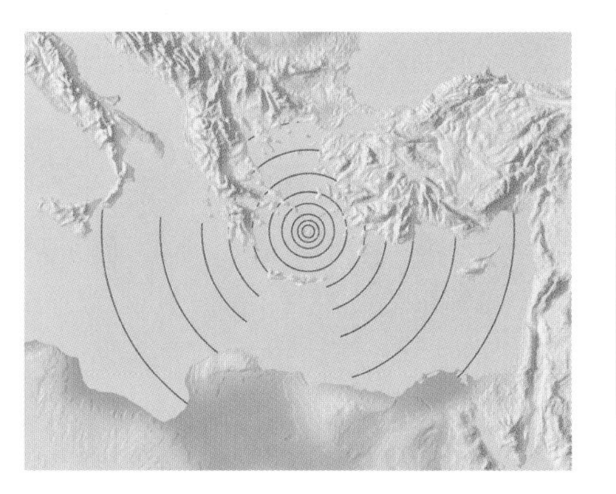

A tsunami's journey 1 5 6 11

An undersea earthquake pushes seawater up and out. A train of waves, around 3 ft. (1m) high, forms. They can race up to 434 mph (700km/h) across the ocean for thousands of miles.

How tsunamis form 7 8 14

Most tsunamis occur when two parts of Earth's crust—tectonic plates—move below the seabed. They jolt or go underneath each other. Tsunamis can also be formed by huge rock slides or asteroids falling into the sea.

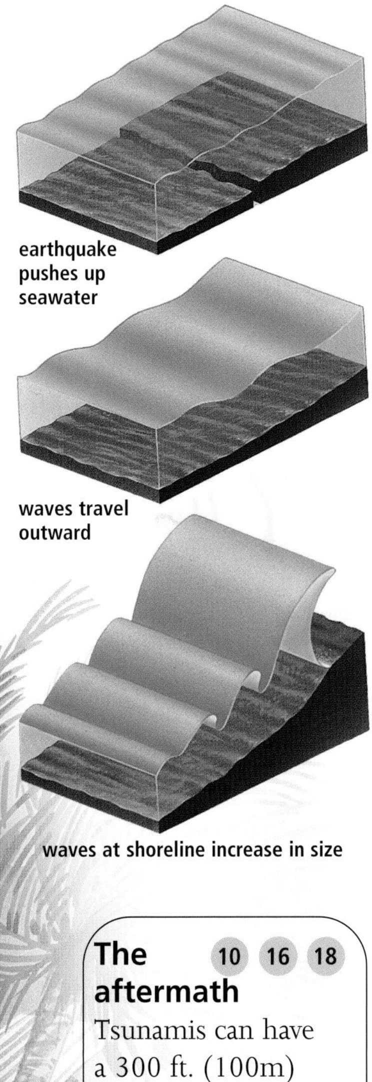

The aftermath 10 16 18

Tsunamis can have a 300 ft. (100m) wavelength (distance between waves). They surge onto the coast every 15–60 minutes and travel up to 0.6 mi. (1km) inland. They are very destructive. In the Indian Ocean tsunami in 2004 around 230,000 people were killed.

QUESTIONS: The senses

Level 1

1. Which "T" is the part of the mouth that you use to taste food?
2. To smell something, you have to breathe in the smell through your nose. True or false?
3. Do sensors in the ear send information about sound to the other ear or to the brain?
4. If a person needs glasses, are the objects that he or she sees without them focused or blurry?

Level 2

5. Rearrange FINEST GRIP to name a part of the body that is sensitive to touch.
6. Does light enter the eye through the pupil, lens, or retina?
7. Do sound waves first enter the ear through the outer ear, middle ear, or inner ear?
8. Rearrange LIBERAL to name a method that people can use to read with their fingertips.
9. Is the middle ear made up of tiny bones, cilia, or sensor cells?
10. Name four basic types of tastes that your tongue can detect.
11. Which "C" is the word for the tiny hairs in the nose?
12. How many taste buds can be found on your tongue and throat: less than 100, 1,000, or up to 10,000?
13. What "G" would you wear to correct blurry vision?
14. Which part of the ear vibrates: the eardrum, middle ear, or cochlea?

Level 3

15. Where on your body are the sensors that detect temperature?
16. Upside-down images form on which part of the eye?
17. Rearrange CHEER TOP TROOPS into a word for cells that are found in the retina.
18. Do the sounds made by flutes have long wavelengths?

FIND THE ANSWER:

The senses

We have five senses—hearing, sight, smell, taste, and touch—to communicate with the world around us. Millions of sensor cells all over the body send information about what we sense to the brain. The senses work together. Smell and taste are so closely linked that if you have a cold and cannot smell, food tastes bland.

Smell 2 11

When you smell something, you breathe in tiny chemical particles. They dissolve in the mucus in your nose and are sensed by tiny hairs in the nose, called cilia. The cilia are attached to smell receptor cells.

Touch 5 8 15

There are millions of touch sensors in your skin. People can read Braille by feeling the raised dots with their sensitive fingertips. Some sensors can detect temperature. If you move your hands from hot water into cold water, your brain will notice the difference.

lens
object
retina
pupil
optic nerve

Images 4 13 16

The lens bends light that passes through it. This turns the image upside down as it focuses on a point on the retina. The brain then turns the image the right way around. If the image does not reach the correct point on the retina, it is blurry. Glasses can correct this problem.

Sight 6 17

When you see an object, light streams from the object into your eye through your pupil. Your lens focuses it on photoreceptors—cells in your retina. They send details along your optic nerve to your brain, which creates an image of the object.

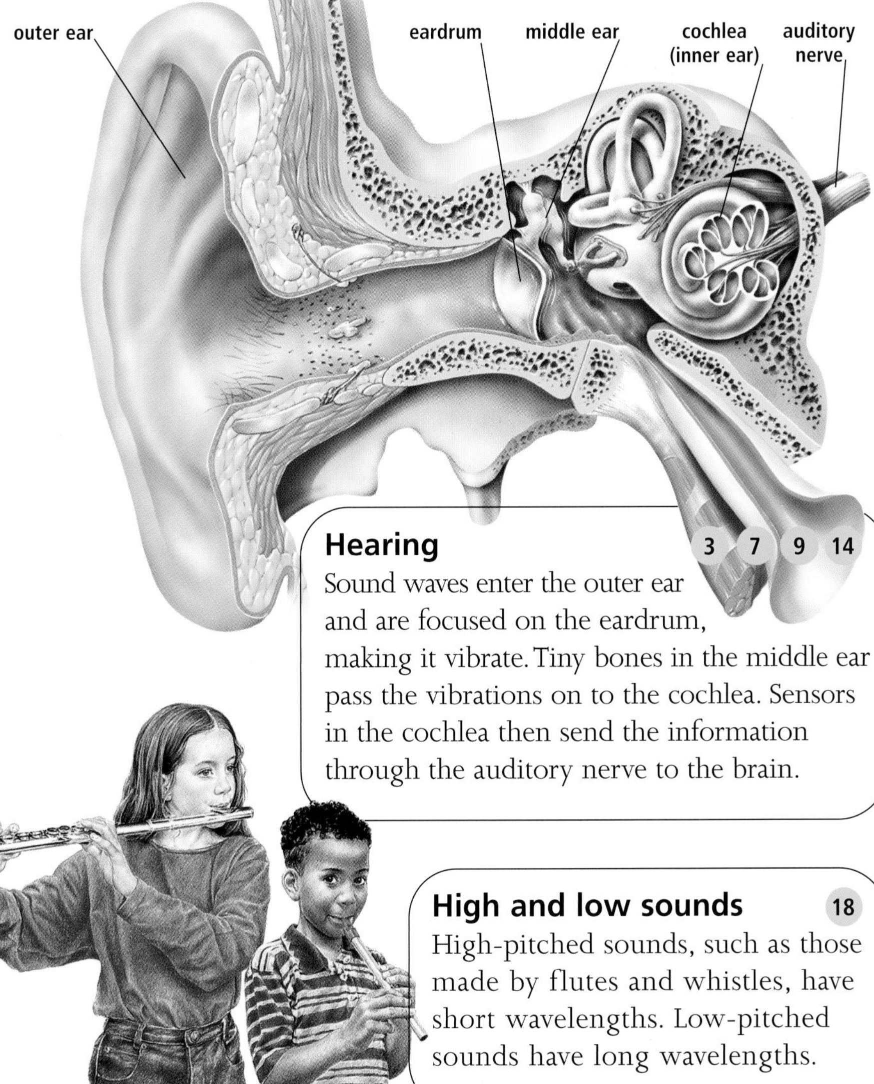

Hearing

3 7 9 14

Sound waves enter the outer ear and are focused on the eardrum, making it vibrate. Tiny bones in the middle ear pass the vibrations on to the cochlea. Sensors in the cochlea then send the information through the auditory nerve to the brain.

High and low sounds

18

High-pitched sounds, such as those made by flutes and whistles, have short wavelengths. Low-pitched sounds have long wavelengths.

Taste

1 10 12

We have up to 10,000 taste buds on our tongue and throat. Each contains 50–100 sensors. There are different taste areas on our tongue that are sensitive to sweetness, saltiness, bitterness, and sourness.

bitter
sour
salty
sweet

QUESTIONS: Digestion

Level 1

1. Waste passes from the large intestine to the anus. True or false?
2. What should you do when you feel thirsty: eat ice cream or drink water?
3. Where is saliva produced: in the mouth or the liver?
4. What "T" rolls food into a ball before swallowing?

Level 2

5. Most sugars and fats are broken down in the large intestine. True or false?
6. Are finger-shaped villi found in the small intestine?
7. Why do we need proteins: to prevent heart disease, provide energy, or for bodybuilding?
8. Rearrange BOTCHED ARRAYS to name something that is found in food.
9. Is urine held in the stomach, bladder, or lungs?
10. Where is bile stored: in the small intestine, stomach, or gallbladder?
11. Does digestion in the stomach take one, two, or four hours?
12. What "B" is the name of the ball of food that is pushed down to your stomach when you swallow?
13. How long does digestion usually take in the intestines: eight, 20, or 30 hours?
14. How much of our bodies is water: one third, two thirds, or four fifths?

Level 3

15. What role does saliva play in digestion?
16. What are enzymes?
17. What does bile do?
18. What "P" is the name for the muscle movements that push food down the esophagus?

FIND THE ANSWER:

Digestion

Digestion is what the body does to get the energy that it needs from food. As food travels from your mouth to your stomach and then to your intestines it is broken down by acids and digestive chemicals called enzymes. The body can use the proteins, sugars, fats, vitamins, and other nutrients that it contains. The body also needs water.

The mouth 3 15

The teeth chop food into small pieces. Glands inside the mouth make saliva. It starts to break down sugars.

Stomach 11 16

Food is churned in the stomach for at least four hours. It is mixed with an acid to kill germs. An enzyme (digestive chemical) begins to break down proteins.

Swallowing 4 12 18

The tongue moistens chewed food with saliva and rolls it into a bolus, or ball. Swallowing pushes the bolus into the esophagus. This tube has muscles that relax ahead of the bolus and tighten behind it. These movements, called peristalsis, push the bolus into the stomach in less than one minute.

muscle

esophagus

bolus

liver

stomach

small intestine

large intest

The intestines 1 5 6 13

Partially digested food travels by peristalsis along the small intestine. There, enzymes break down sugars and fats. Finger-shaped villi absorb these with water and pass them to the blood vessels. Waste passes into the large intestine and is pushed out of the anus as feces. This stage takes around 20 hours.

villus

blood vessel

gallbladder

liver

Liver

9 10 17

The liver produces a liquid called bile, which is stored in the gallbladder. Bile helps the digestion of fats. After a meal, the gallbladder squirts bile into the small intestine, where fats contained in food are broken down. The liver also removes and stores sugars from the blood. It releases them whenever the body needs energy.

Water

2 14

Our bodies are around two thirds water. This is used for many functions, such as digestion, as well as for blood and other fluids. If you feel thirsty, your body is telling you to drink more water.

Good food guide

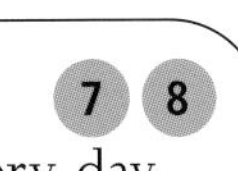

7 8

To stay healthy, eat different types of food every day. You need carbohydrates (sugars and starchy foods) and fats for energy; protein for bodybuilding; minerals for strong bones and teeth; and vitamins to prevent illnesses.

QUESTIONS: Inventors

Level 1

1. Is a telescope or a microscope used to see planets?
2. Are microscopes used by scientists or musicians to carry out experiments?
3. The Greek philosopher and scientist Aristotle studied plants and animals. True or false?
4. What is believed to have been the first writing instrument: a stylus made from reed or a pencil?

Level 2

5. The other planets in the solar system orbit Earth. True or false?
6. Rearrange MARINES US to name the ancient people who are believed to have invented the first writing system.
7. Which "O" is a building where astronomers study the sky?
8. When did Aristotle begin to study nature: around 3000 B.C., 350 B.C., or A.D. 1350?
9. Who built the first telescope: Galileo Galilei or Isaac Newton?
10. Rearrange REMOTE BAR to name a scientific instrument.
11. Which scientist figured out the movement of the planets: Aristotle, Galileo Galilei, or Isaac Newton?
12. Which scientist studied plants and animals: Aristotle, Galileo Galilei, or Isaac Newton?
13. Benjamin Franklin installed a lightning rod on his house. True or false?
14. Were the first writings made on clay, paper, or plant leaves?

Level 3

15. In which year did Alexander Graham Bell first successfully try his telephone?
16. Who discovered that electricity has positive and negative charges?
17. Who made the first star maps?
18. What shapes form the letters in cuneiform writing?

FIND THE ANSWER: Inventors

tradesman with stylus and clay tablet

The first observatories and calendars appeared in Egypt and Mesopotamia (modern-day Iraq) around 3000 B.C. Telescopes were invented in Europe in the 1600s, and they allowed scientists to observe planets that had not been seen before. Observations made by Galileo Galilei and Isaac Newton laid the foundations for modern science.

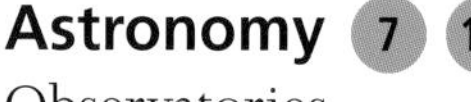

Astronomy 7 17

Observatories were built by ancient people to study the stars and planets. Chinese astronomers made the first maps of the stars. They recorded a solar eclipse in 2136 B.C.

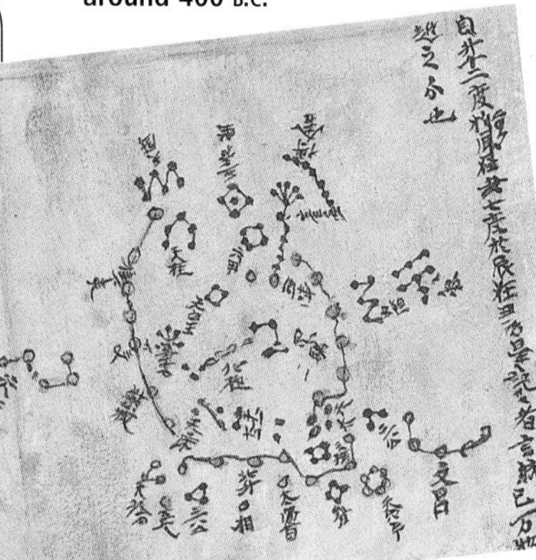

Chinese star map, around 400 B.C.

Sumerians and writing 4 6 14 18

The Sumerians in Mesopotamia are believed to have invented writing in around 3500 B.C. They used a stylus (a piece of reed) to press shapes into clay. They made lists of the goods that they traded, using triangles and lines to make images that stood for things such as fish, sheep, numbers, and days. This system is called cuneiform (wedge-shaped) writing.

The first scientist 3 8 12

Around 350 B.C. the Greek Aristotle (384–322 B.C.) became the first philosopher to observe nature and do experiments on plants and animals. He wrote descriptions of them and tried to figure out what their different parts—for example, brains, hearts, leaves, and stems—were for.

Aristotle

Galileo 1 5 9

Galileo Galilei (1564–1642) observed weights being dropped from the Leaning Tower of Pisa, in Italy. When the heaviest and lightest weights hit the ground at the same time, he realized that the speed of moving objects is not affected by weight. He built the first telescope and discovered that the planets orbit the Sun.

Newton's telescope (11)

Isaac Newton (1642–1727) designed a telescope that was more powerful than Galileo's. He figured out the laws behind the movement of the planets.

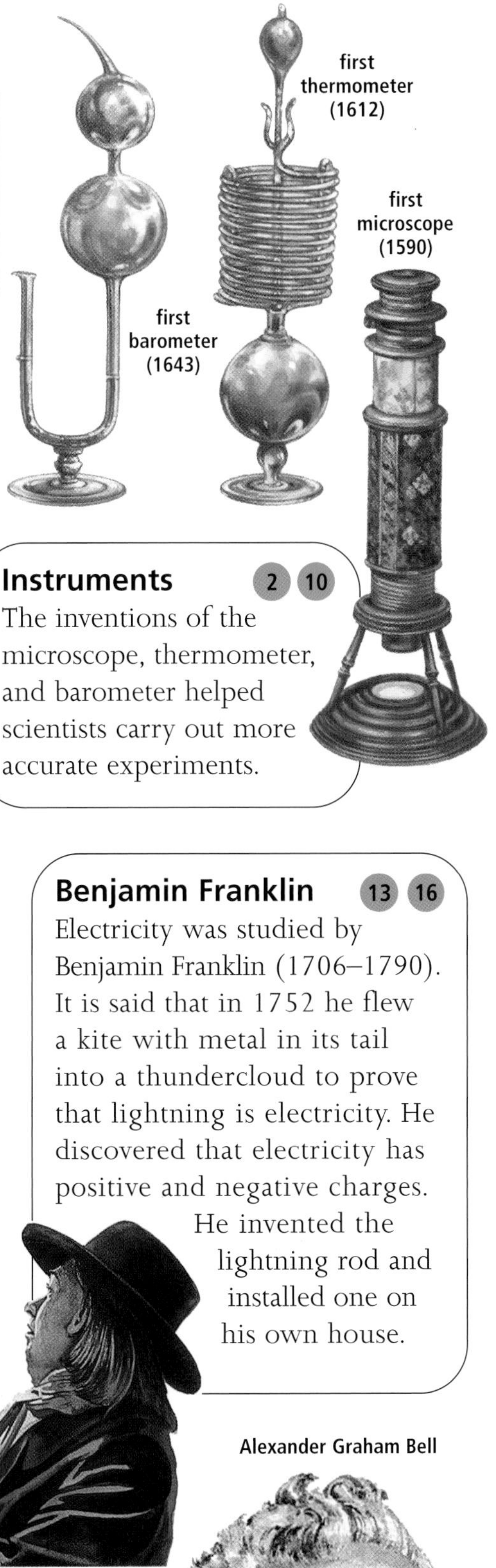

Instruments (2) (10)

The inventions of the microscope, thermometer, and barometer helped scientists carry out more accurate experiments.

Benjamin Franklin (13) (16)

Electricity was studied by Benjamin Franklin (1706–1790). It is said that in 1752 he flew a kite with metal in its tail into a thundercloud to prove that lightning is electricity. He discovered that electricity has positive and negative charges. He invented the lightning rod and installed one on his own house.

Alexander Graham Bell

Alexander Graham Bell (15)

Mass communication began when Alexander Graham Bell (1847–1922) had the idea of transmitting the human voice along waves of electricity. In March 1876 he spoke to his assistant on a telephone that he had invented. In 1877 he began the Bell Telephone Company.

QUESTIONS: Cars

Level 1

1. What "G" do most cars run on?
2. The Ford Model-T was the first affordable car. True or false?
3. The Mini was originally designed for driving where: in the city or in the countryside?
4. From where do solar-powered cars get their energy?

Level 2

5. How many wheels did Karl Benz's Motorwagen have: two, three, or four?
6. Rearrange ARE RELAX to name a part that is found in a car.
7. What nationality was Henry Ford: British, American, or Australian?
8. How many doors did the original Mini have?
9. Which type of car is better for the environment: a gasoline-powered car or a solar-powered car?
10. What "E" drives a car forward?
11. Was the Ford Model-T also known as "Thin Lizzie," "Tin Lizzie," or "Tin Dizzy"?
12. Which was the first vehicle to use a gasoline-powered engine?
13. In which decade was the Mini introduced: the 1950s, 1960s, or 1970s?
14. In 1914 a Ford Model-T could be assembled in 93 minutes. True or false?
15. Solar-powered cars can run all of the time. True or false?

Level 3

16. Is a propeller shaft a type of long rod, a series of gears, or a type of steering mechanism?
17. What "A" means the way that air flows over a moving car?
18. What "T" helps control the engine's speed?

Cars

The car is one of the most popular forms of transportation in the world today. Before motorized vehicles were invented, people traveled by horse-drawn carriages. People still refer to the "horsepower" of a car. Cars are one of the biggest causes of pollution in the world, so scientists are looking for ways to make them cleaner and safer for the environment.

Karl Benz (5) (12)

In 1885 the German inventor Karl Benz produced the three-wheeled Motorwagen—the first vehicle with a gasoline-powered engine. It could travel at around 9 mph (15km/h). The back wheels carried the engine and travelers. The front wheel was for steering.

Early cars (2) (7) (11) (14)

In 1908 the American inventor Henry Ford introduced the Ford Model-T (or "Tin Lizzie"). It was the first affordable car and was mass-produced on an assembly line. By 1914 a car could be assembled in just 93 minutes.

Mini revolution (3) (8) (13)

The Mini, introduced in the 1950s, is one of the most popular makes of car in the world. The original model only had two doors and was designed for driving around a city.

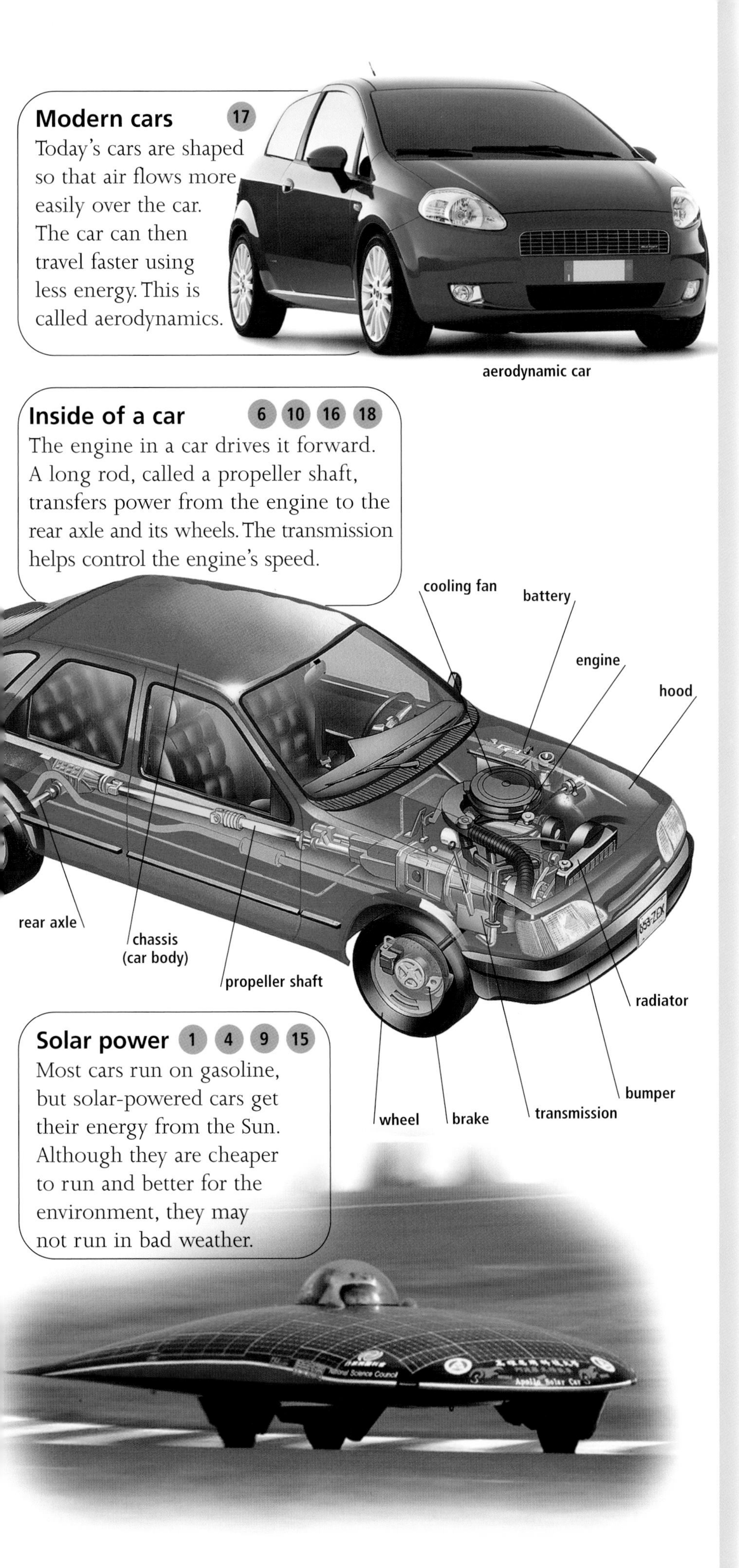

Modern cars (17)

Today's cars are shaped so that air flows more easily over the car. The car can then travel faster using less energy. This is called aerodynamics.

Inside of a car (6) (10) (16) (18)

The engine in a car drives it forward. A long rod, called a propeller shaft, transfers power from the engine to the rear axle and its wheels. The transmission helps control the engine's speed.

Solar power (1) (4) (9) (15)

Most cars run on gasoline, but solar-powered cars get their energy from the Sun. Although they are cheaper to run and better for the environment, they may not run in bad weather.

QUESTIONS: Motorcycles

Level 1

1. Is the Lambretta a scooter?
2. A "chopper" is a motorcycle that was changed by chopping off parts from its frame. True or false?
3. Rearrange EMPOD to name a very small type of motorcycle.
4. The first motorcycle was made in Germany. True or false?

Level 2

5. In racing do motorcycles have the same or different engine capacities?
6. Are the handlebars on choppers higher or lower than on other motorcycles?
7. What "S" is a bike that motocross racers use?
8. Was the Vespa introduced in 1946, 1956, or 1966?
9. What "S" is the name for a motorcycle carriage with only one wheel?
10. Did the Hildebrand brothers' 1889 trial motorcycle have a steam-driven or gasoline-driven engine?
11. Superbikes are not road bikes. True or false?
12. Scramblers race for how long: 10 to 40 minutes or one to two hours?
13. Is Harley Davidson known for scooters or choppers?

Level 3

14. Name two of the three engine classes for Grand Prix motorcycle circuit racing.
15. In what year did Eric Oliver first win the World Motorcycle Sidecar Championship?
16. What "P" is another word for a trial model?
17. What was the top speed of the motorcycle that was made by the Hildebrand brothers and Alois Wolfmuller?
18. What is the name of the largest sidecar maker?

FIND THE ANSWER: Motorcycles

The motorcycle was invented in 1885, when the German engineer Gottlieb Daimler attached a gasoline engine to a bicycle. Motorcycles are cheaper to buy and run than cars, which made them popular in the 1920s and 1930s and after World War II. World championship motorcycle racing began in 1949. Motorcycle sports, from road racing to speedway and hill-climb, are popular worldwide.

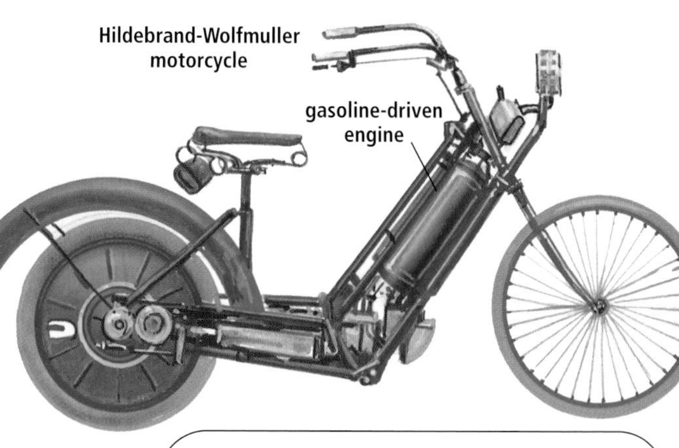

Early motorcycle 4 10 16 17

In 1889 the Hildebrand brothers from Munich, Germany, made a prototype (trial model) motorcycle with a steam engine. They made a gasoline-driven motorcycle with Alois Wolfmuller in 1894. Its top speed was 25 mph (40km/h).

Sidecars 9 15 18

One-wheeled motorcycle carriages are called sidecars. Watsonian-Squire, which began in the U.K. in 1912, is the largest sidecar maker. Eric Oliver won the first racing sidecar World Championship in 1949.

motorcycle and sidecar

Racing 5 11 14

In motorcycle racing bikes of the same engine capacity (size) race against each other. Grand Prix motorcycle circuit racing has three engine classes: 125cc, 250cc, and MotoGP (up to 800cc). Superbike racers use road bikes that are specially adapted for track racing.

Scooters

1 3 8

Mopeds have engines of up to 50cc, and scooters up to 250cc—smaller than most motorcycles. They have been popular since the Vespa was introduced in 1946 and the Lambretta in 1947.

chopper

The chopper

2 6 13

In the 1950s U.S. bikers lightened their motorcycles by chopping parts off the frame. They added raked (low-angled) front wheel forks and high handlebars. These motorcycles are called choppers. Harley Davidson now makes popular choppers.

Scrambling

7 12

Riding scrambler bikes with tough suspension, brakes, and tires, bikers race along a course for between 10 and 40 minutes. The course often involves jumps, as well as twisting uphill and downhill tracks. Motocross is one of the five types of off-road (dirt-track) racing for motorcyclists.

QUESTIONS: Airplanes

Level 1

1. Are the economy-class seats in an airplane usually in the back of the cabin or in the front?
2. Do aircraft taxi or train as they move along the ground?
3. Is cargo packed into containers before being loaded onto a plane?
4. Rearrange NICER SOUPS to name a really fast aircraft.

Level 2

5. At an airport passengers might be driven in a shuttle to aircraft that are parked on the runway. True or false?
6. Which "T" is the name of a building in an airport?
7. What "F" is the name of the part of an airplane where digital screens provide flight information?
8. Cargo decks can be found under the cabins. True or false?
9. What was the first wide-body jet plane: the Boeing 747 or the Airbus A380?
10. Do scissor trucks lift cargo containers into the cargo hold or lift passengers to the passenger cabins?
11. Did Concorde fly from London, Paris, New York City, or all of the above?
12. Which one is quieter: the Boeing 747 or the Airbus A380?
13. What "B" is the term used when a plane turns left or right in the air?
14. Where in an airport do passengers go when they want to board a plane?

Level 3

15. What do flaps on the wings do when they are open?
16. In which year did Concorde begin its passenger service?
17. What are the metal strips on the wings called that make the plane turn?
18. What is Mach 2.2 expressed as miles per hour?

FIND THE ANSWER:

Airplanes

The development of the airplane took a huge step forward in 1939 when the first jet aircraft was flown by a German pilot. Planes that have jet engines can carry more people greater distances than the first powered aircraft flown in 1903. Today's airplanes are designed to be quieter, use less fuel, and carry more people.

economy seating
cargo hold
first-class cabin
flight deck
jet engine

Inside an airplane (1) (7)

Digital screens in the flight deck provide flight information. There is also an instrument panel with more than 350 switches. The passengers sit in a first-class cabin behind the flight deck or in economy class farther back.

upper deck lounge
cargo containers

Airports (2) (6) (14)

At major airports airplanes taxi to and from docking bays outside of the terminal buildings. The departure lounge is where passengers go to board a plane. They enter and leave the aircraft through gangways.

Air freight (3) (8) (10)

Cargo is packed into huge containers. Some fit into the cargo decks under the cabins. Tow trucks haul the containers to the aircraft, and scissor trucks raise them to be level with the loading bay.

scissor truck

Jumbo jets 9 12

In 1970 the Boeing 747 was the first wide-body jet plane. It can carry up to 500 passengers. The Airbus A380 is now the largest jet plane. It is quieter and more fuel-efficient.

Supersonic jet 4 11 16 18

Concorde, the first supersonic passenger jet plane, was built by Great Britain and France. Its fastest speed was Mach 2.2 (1,364 mph, or 2,200km/h), more than twice the speed of any other passenger jet. It flew between London, Paris, and New York from 1976 until 2003.

Concorde

Wings and flaps 13 15 17

When flaps and slats along the wing open, they act like brakes. Ailerons are metal strips that move up and down to make the plane bank (turn).

Concorde

portable passenger gangway

Steps 5

If an aircraft parks on the runway away from the terminal, steps and gangways are brought to the aircraft. Passengers may be transported in an airport shuttle.

QUESTIONS: Where in the world?

Level 1

1. Did the U.S. use trains or tractors to haul goods up the Rocky Mountains in the 1940s?
2. Have astronauts ever visited the Moon?
3. Was the bullet train first used in Japan, the U.S., or Russia?

Level 2

4. What "H" was used to break the world record for water speed?
5. What "C" is a man-made waterway such as the 101-mi.-long (163km) one found in Egypt?
6. The Incas developed the wheel. True or false?
7. What was the fastest train in 1964?

Level 3

8. The Incas' road system covered how many miles?
9. Name the person who holds the world record for water speed.
10. In which year did *Sputnik 1* first orbit Earth?

FIND THE ANSWER: Where in the world?

Before the invention of the wheel around 5,000 years ago, people rarely traveled far from their homes. Since then inventors have developed cars, trains, and planes, as well as other types of transportation, that have changed how we travel. Many people now travel great distances that were not possible before.

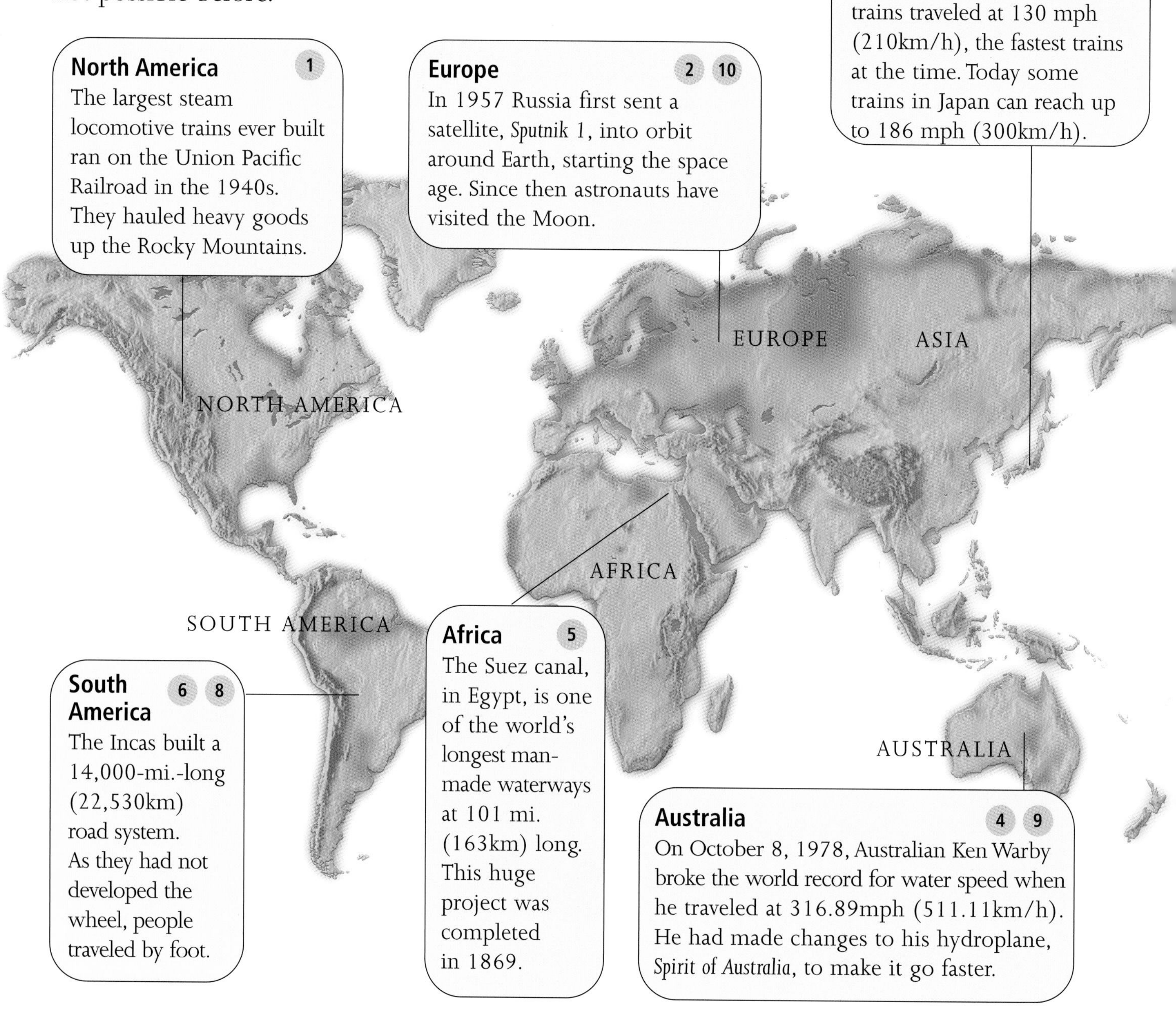

North America 1

The largest steam locomotive trains ever built ran on the Union Pacific Railroad in the 1940s. They hauled heavy goods up the Rocky Mountains.

Europe 2 10

In 1957 Russia first sent a satellite, *Sputnik 1*, into orbit around Earth, starting the space age. Since then astronauts have visited the Moon.

Asia 3 7

Japan began using high-speed bullet trains in 1964. These trains traveled at 130 mph (210km/h), the fastest trains at the time. Today some trains in Japan can reach up to 186 mph (300km/h).

South America 6 8

The Incas built a 14,000-mi.-long (22,530km) road system. As they had not developed the wheel, people traveled by foot.

Africa 5

The Suez canal, in Egypt, is one of the world's longest man-made waterways at 101 mi. (163km) long. This huge project was completed in 1869.

Australia 4 9

On October 8, 1978, Australian Ken Warby broke the world record for water speed when he traveled at 316.89mph (511.11km/h). He had made changes to his hydroplane, *Spirit of Australia*, to make it go faster.

Answers 1) Trains **2)** Yes **3)** Japan **4)** Hydroplane **5)** Canal **6)** False (they never used it) **7)** The bullet train **8)** 14,000 mph (22,530km) **9)** Ken Warby **10)** 1957

QUIZ FOUR

History

Ancient Egyptian daily life

Ancient Egyptian gods and goddesses

Ancient Greek warfare

Ancient Greek gods and goddesses

The Roman Empire

Roman warfare

The Aztecs

Aztec religion

QUESTIONS: Ancient Egyptian daily life

Level 1

1. What animals did the Egyptians hunt: hippopotamuses, horses, or hamsters?
2. Out of what material did Egyptians build boats: plastic, plywood, or papyrus?
3. Egyptians did not farm the land next to the Nile river. True or false?
4. Egyptians built houses out of mud bricks. True or false?

Level 2

5. Were Egyptian peasants ever beaten?
6. OH APRON can be rearranged to name what weapon that was used in hunting?
7. At what age did Egyptian children begin going to school: three, four, or five?
8. Egyptians drank beer. True or false?
9. When did the Nile river flood: in the spring, summer, or winter?
10. Who baked bread in ancient Egypt: the men or the women?
11. Only Egyptian boys went to school. True or false?
12. In what season did the Egyptian harvest take place?
13. What was a mertu: a type of person, type of food, or type of house?
14. What animals did the Egyptians use to help plow the land?
15. What "F" is used to make linen clothing?

Level 3

16. What did Egyptians call a team of five laborers?
17. What "S" was an Egyptian hairstyle that was worn by children?
18. What "B'"is a crop that was used by Egyptians to make a popular drink?

FIND THE ANSWER: Ancient Egyptian daily life

For most ancient Egyptian farmers life was tough. They worked hard for nine days out of ten on fields that were owned by wealthy noble people, and they were paid in beer, corn, or bread instead of money. How much they were paid depended on how successful the harvest was. Ordinary Egyptians also had to spend part of the year helping build enormous tombs for the pharaohs (rulers) of Egypt.

Peasants (5) (9) (13) (14)

Egyptian mertu (peasants) were the lowest members of society. Their working year began after the summer flooding of the Nile river. Some drove oxen to plow the land, while others scattered seeds. If the mertu did not work hard enough, their masters would beat them.

Hippos (1) (2) (6)

Egyptians hunted hippopotamuses because they trampled crops and ruined the harvest. Hunters traveled in boats made out of papyrus and carried harpoons (spears).

hunters using harpoons

Education (7) (11) (17)

The children of farmers began going to school at the age of four and left to start work when they were 12. At school boys and girls learned to read and write. They wore their hair in "side locks."

Harvest time

3 8 12 15 16 18

The ancient Egyptian harvest took place during the spring. The laborers worked in teams of five men, called "hands," collecting wheat to make bread, barley to make beer, and flax to make linen clothing. Oxen trod out the grains on the threshing floor. Egyptians only farmed the land next to the Nile river, which was kept fertile by flooding.

Housing

4 10

Laborers built small houses out of bricks of mud that had been dried out in the sun. Often they had no more than two or three rooms. Many families had a bread oven, which the women used for baking bread.

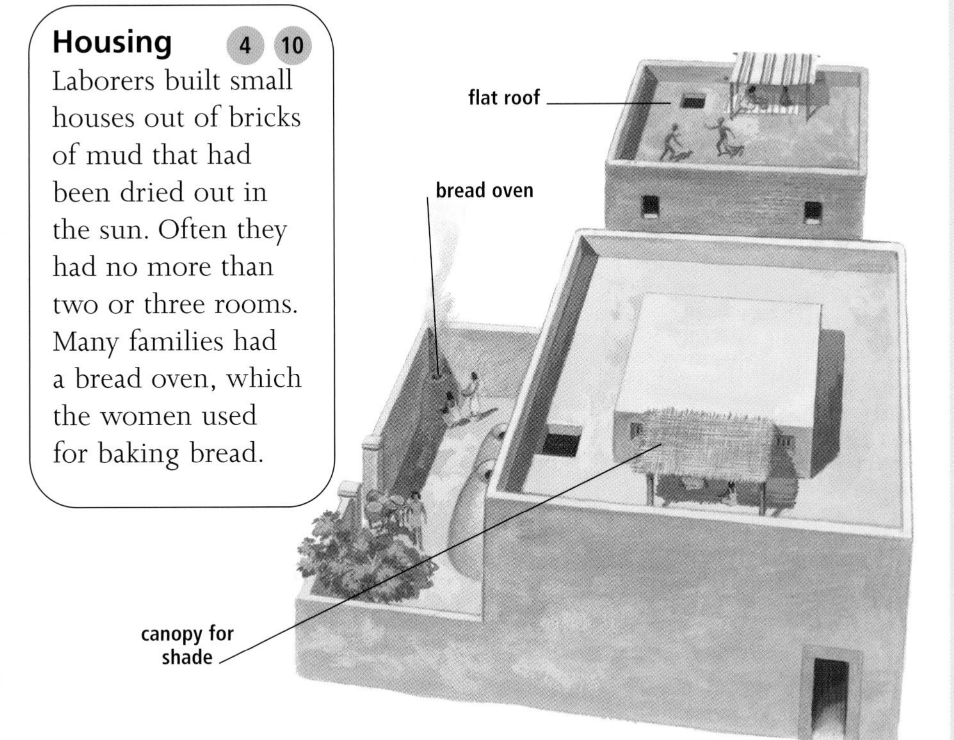

QUESTIONS: Ancient Egyptian gods and goddesses

Level 1

1. The ancient Egyptians believed in magic. True or false?
2. Who was a ruler of the gods: Ma, Ra, or Pa?
3. What name is given to evil magic: red, black, or blue?
4. Egyptians made statues of their gods. True or false?

Level 2

5. What was a "coming forth": a birth, death, or type of procession?
6. Only priests took part in daily rituals at the great temples. True or false?
7. ALE TUM can be rearranged to give the name of what item that was supposed to protect people against magic?
8. What type of animal bit the god Ra: a tiger, cobra, or spider?
9. Anubis had the head of which animal: a snake, jackal, or rhino?
10. Was Amun a god of fire or air?
11. On what item of jewelry would an Egyptian wear a model of a hand?
12. Which god was the guardian of the underworld?
13. Who was the husband of Isis?

Level 3

14. Who learned Ra's secret name?
15. What mask would priests wear when preparing a body for burial?
16. Which Egyptian god had a name that meant "The Hidden One"?
17. What "K" is the location of a great temple to Amun?
18. In which city was Amun originally worshiped?

FIND THE ANSWER:

Ancient Egyptian gods and goddesses

The ancient Egyptians worshiped many different gods and goddesses. Some looked like men and women; others took the forms of animals including the crocodile god, Sobek. The Egyptians built huge temples to their gods, which were taken care of by priests. Everyone participated in religious festivals and processions.

Anubis 9 12 15

Anubis was the guardian of the underworld. He protected the souls of dead people on their way to the afterlife. He had the body of a man and the head of a jackal. Priests often wore a jackal mask while preparing a body for burial.

Ra's secret name 2 8 13 14

Isis wanted her husband, Osiris, to rule Egypt, so she sent a cobra to bite Ra, the king of the gods. When Ra had been bitten, Isis promised to cure him if he told her his secret name, which was the key to his power. Ra gave in and surrendered his power to Osiris.

Amun 10 16 17 18
In Thebes the god Amun ("the Hidden One") was originally worshiped as a god of air, but eventually he was seen as the king of all gods. His great temple in Karnak took hundreds of years to build.

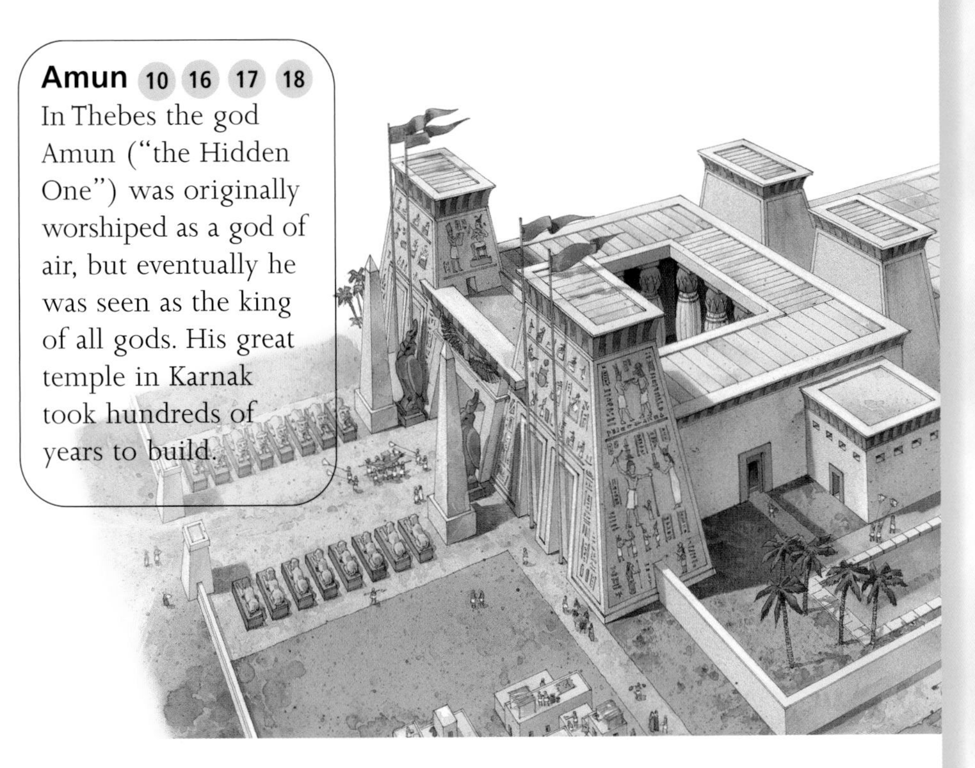

Magic 1 3 7 11
Egyptians believed that magic could help or harm them. Jewelry known as amulets protected the wearers from evil ("black") magic. Amulets of a hand were worn on bracelets and amulets of a foot were worn on anklets.

eye of Horus amulet   hand amulet   foot amulet

Inside of the temple 4 5 6
Only priests took part in daily rituals at the great temples. On some days there was a "coming forth" procession, during which a statue of the god was paraded outside of the temple.

mourning ritual in a temple of Amun

QUESTIONS:
Ancient Greek warfare

Level 1

1. What were Greek shields made out of: linen, paper, or wood?
2. REAPS can be rearranged to name what weapon that was used by the Greeks?
3. Where did the battle of Salamis take place: on land or at sea?
4. What did Greeks make helmets out of: bronze, copper, or aluminum?

Level 2

5. The main tactic of Greek warships was to ram the enemy. True or false?
6. What was a phalanx: a weapon, formation, or oar?
7. RIM TREE can be rearranged to name what Greek warship?
8. Spartans were Greeks. True or false?
9. At what age did boys start training in Sparta: seven, nine, or 11?
10. What color did Spartans paint on their shields: red or yellow?
11. Who won the battle of Salamis: the Greeks or the Persians?
12. Rearrange I PASS to name a Greek shield.
13. What "H" was the most common type of soldier in ancient Greece?
14. What part of the human body did a greave protect?
15. Who was Xerxes: a Persian king, Spartan general, or Theban god?

Level 3

16. What letter did Spartans paint on their shields?
17. What did Spartans call their country?
18. From what city were the Greeks who fought in Salamis?
19. What type of weapon was a xiphos?

FIND THE ANSWER:

Ancient Greek warfare

The ancient Greeks fought many wars, both among themselves and against foreign invaders such as the Persians. In the city of Athens every man had to fight in the army and provide his own weapons and armor. The Macedonians conquered all of Greece in the 300s B.C.

Sparta (8) (9)

Greeks from the city of Sparta began training for battle at the age of seven, enduring tough physical exercises. Sometimes they were whipped to see who could withstand the most pain. Sparta was said to have no walls so that its soldiers had to fight fiercely.

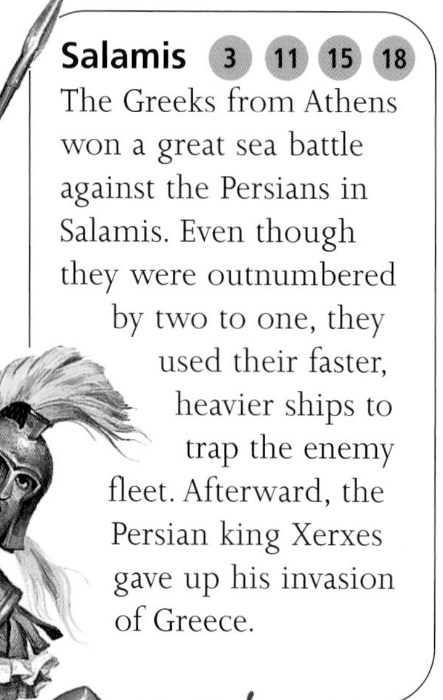

Salamis (3) (11) (15) (18)

The Greeks from Athens won a great sea battle against the Persians in Salamis. Even though they were outnumbered by two to one, they used their faster, heavier ships to trap the enemy fleet. Afterward, the Persian king Xerxes gave up his invasion of Greece.

Spartan shields (10) (16) (17)

Spartans painted large red "L"s on their shields—the first letter of "Lacedaemonia"—the name that they gave their country.

Ships (5) (7)

A Greek warship was known as a trireme. Their main tactic was to try to ram and sink enemy vessels.

Hoplite 4 13 14

Greek armies were mostly made up of foot soldiers called hoplites. They wore heavy bronze breastplates and helmets, as well as greaves to protect their shins. Some wore a horsehair crest on their helmet to scare opponents.

Arms 1 12 19

Hoplites carried a xiphos (a short double-edged sword) and a spear and had an aspis (a wooden shield) for protection.

Fighting 2 6

Hoplites fought in a tight formation known as a phalanx. The men created a wall of shields and used long spears to attack the enemy. If someone in the front row died or fell over, a hoplite from the second row would take his place.

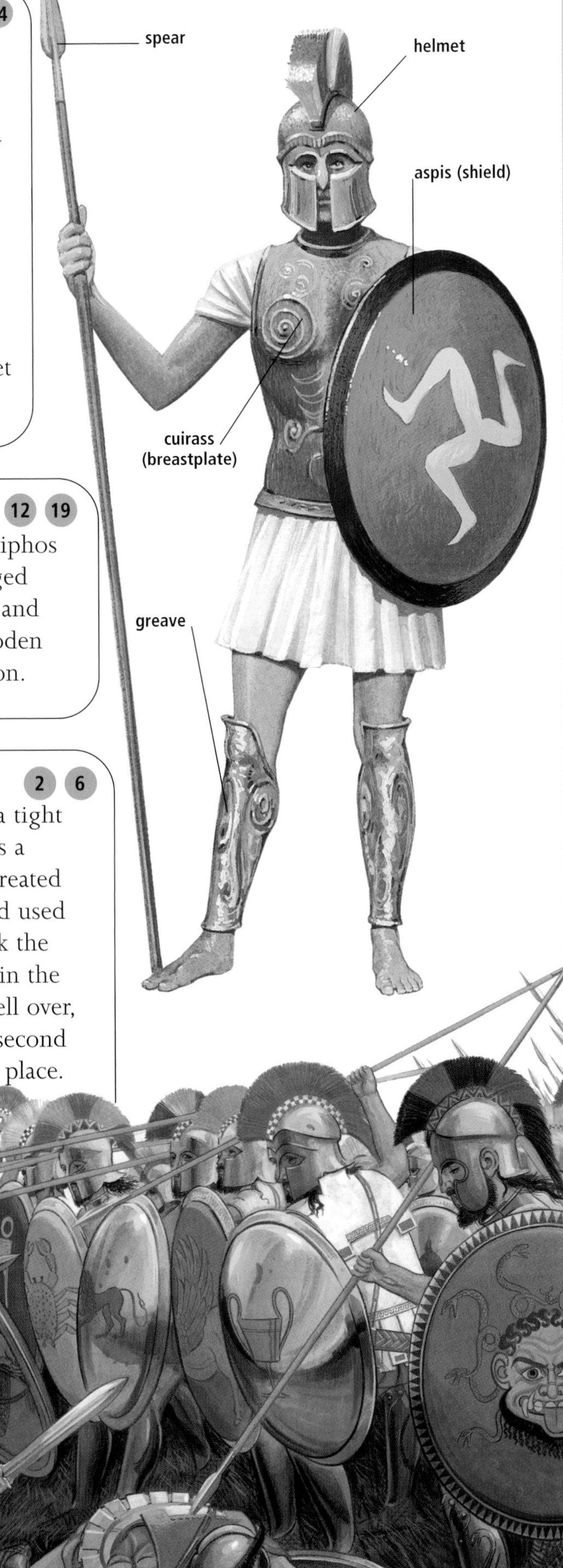

QUESTIONS: Ancient Greek gods and goddesses

Level 1

1. What "Z" was the king of the gods?
2. The Greeks sacrificed bulls to the gods. True or false?
3. Was Aphrodite the goddess of love and beauty or of hatred and ugliness?

Level 2

4. What "A" was the Greek god of war?
5. What was the symbol of Athene: the owl, eagle, or crow?
6. WORN RUDDLE can be rearranged to give the name of what place Greeks went to after death?
7. Was Asclepius the god of law or medicine?
8. Who was the Greek god of the Sun: Artemis, Poseidon, or Apollo?
9. Who went to the Elysian Fields: those who had led good lives or those who had led bad lives?
10. What "L" was a gift of wine poured onto an altar?
11. What "S" was the river that the Greeks crossed when they died?
12. Athene was the goddess of hunting. True or false?
13. Where was the Panathenaea held?
14. Rearrange STAR RUT to name a burning pit.
15. What animal appeared in the symbol of Asclepius: a snake, spider, or scorpion?
16. What "O" was a temple in which people could ask questions about the future?

Level 3

17. What gift did Athene give Athens?
18. Who was the husband of Aphrodite?
19. Which temple in Athens contained a huge gold and ivory statue of Athene?

FIND THE ANSWER: Ancient Greek gods and goddesses

The ancient Greeks believed that powerful gods and goddesses watched over the world and interfered in the affairs of people. These gods behaved just like humans, falling in love, having arguments, and trying to trick each other. The Greeks held festivals in honor of their gods and were always careful not to make them angry.

statue of Athene

Aphrodite

3 4 18

Although Aphrodite was the goddess of love and beauty, her husband was the ugly god Hephaestos, and she was in love with Ares, the god of war. She was often jealous of beautiful girls and punished them severely.

Aphrodite

Hades

Hades' wife Persephone

Asphodel Meadows

Elysian Fields

Athene

1 5 12 17 19

Zeus, the king of the gods, was the father of Athene, who was the goddess of wisdom and craft. Athene's symbol was the owl. Athene gave Athens its first olive tree. The tree provided food, wood, and olive oil, and so the grateful citizens chose Athene to be the patron of their city. They built a huge gold and ivory statue of the goddess, which stood in the Parthenon, a great temple in Athens.

Tartarus

The afterlife

6 9 11 14

The Greeks believed that after death they crossed the River Styx into the underworld. Hades, the king of the dead, judged how well they had lived their lives. Those who had led good lives went to the Elysian Fields. Those who had led bad lives went to the burning pit of Tartarus. People who had been neither good nor bad went to the Asphodel Meadows—a land of shadows.

Offerings

7 15

The Greeks left offerings at the statues of gods, hoping for their help. There (see right), sick people would ask to be healed by Asclepius, the god of medicine and healing. The god grasps his symbol in his left hand—a snake coiling around a rod.

Oracles

8 16

The sun god Apollo had an oracle (a temple where people asked questions about the future) in Delphi. Apollo replied through a priestess—the pythia.

Worship and sacrifice

2 10 13

The Greeks sacrificed animals to the gods. They considered a bull to be the best offering. They also gave the gods libations (gifts of wine poured onto an altar). There were large public festivals, such as the Panathenaea, held every four years in Athens, and almost every home had an altar for private worship.

QUESTIONS: The Roman Empire

Level 1

1. What could no one wear except for the emperor: polka dots, purple, or hats?
2. The Romans built winding roads. True or false?
3. SEA NET can be rearranged to give the name of what group of citizens?

Level 2

4. What were aqueducts used to transport: water, people, or food?
5. Was Rome founded by a pair of twins or a pair of lovers?
6. Which famous Roman was murdered: Hadrian, Augustus, or Julius Caesar?
7. What "V" looted Rome?
8. The name Augustulus meant "father of Augustus." True or false?
9. Augustus conquered the Dacians. True or false?
10. What was a toga: a crown, shoe, or robe?
11. How long is Zaghouan Aqueduct: more than 46 mi. (74km), more than 57 mi. (92km), or more than 68 mi. (109km)?
12. Was Odoacer a German or a Greek?
13. SOUL RUM can be rearranged to give the name of what founder of Rome?
14. Julius Caesar was the first emperor. True or false?
15. Augustus was the son of Julius Caesar. True or false?
16. Under which emperor was the empire at its largest: Nero, Trajan, or Vespasian?

Level 3

17. Who was the first Christian emperor?
18. Who said "I found Rome brick and left it marble"?
19. Who killed himself so that Trajan would not capture him?

FIND THE ANSWER:

The Roman Empire

The ancient Romans built up a huge empire that reached across Europe and into Asia and Africa. Its influence can still be seen today in languages, laws, and architecture. The Romans used their powerful armies to maintain control in their provinces (countries that they had conquered). They called foreigners "barbarians," and they believed that Romans had a duty to bring peace and civilization to the world.

Senate

1 3 10

The senate was a group of the most important citizens who helped govern Rome. They wore long, white robes called togas, which showed their status. Only the emperor could wear purple.

Empire

9 16 19

The empire reached its largest size under Emperor Trajan. An excellent general, Trajan conquered the Dacians in the southeast of Europe. The Dacian king Decebalus killed himself so that he would not be captured.

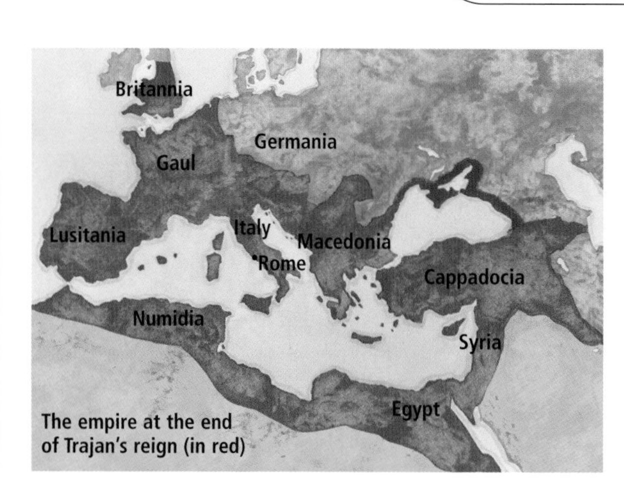

The empire at the end of Trajan's reign (in red)

The city

5 13 18

The Romans claimed that their city was founded by a pair of twins named Romulus and Remus. Over the years Rome grew into a huge metropolis. Emperor Augustus spent a lot of money making the city look beautiful. He boasted: "I found Rome brick and left it marble."

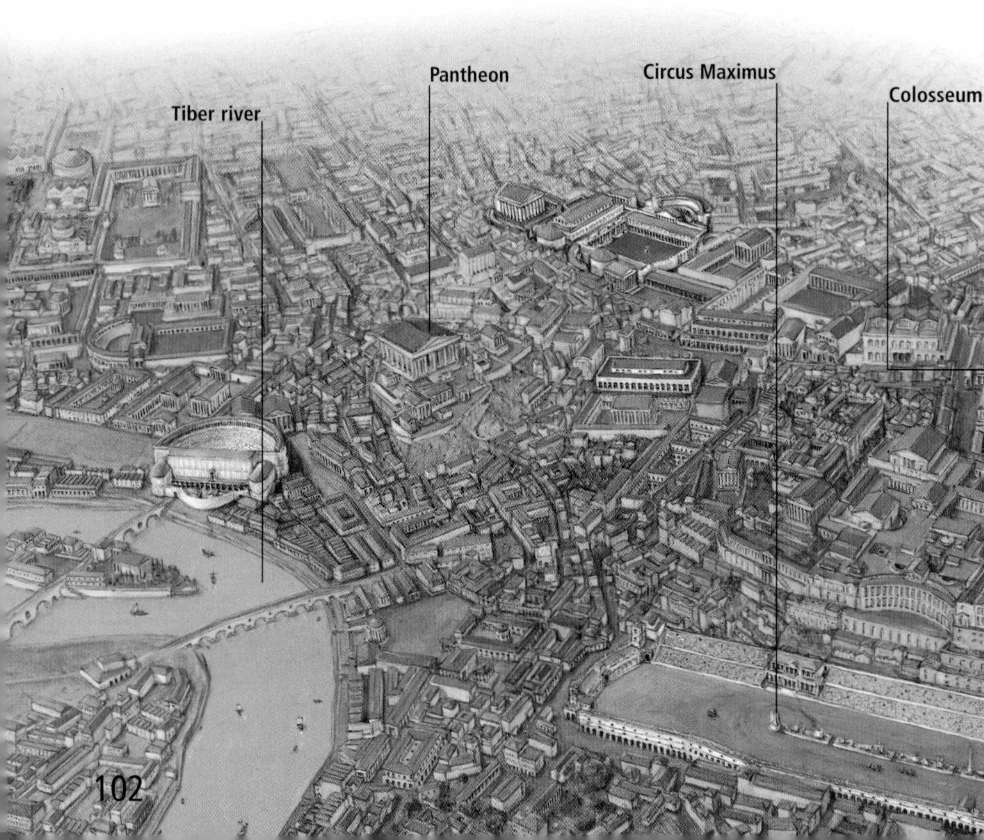

Julius Caesar

Augustus

Hadrian

Constantine

Rulers
6 14 15 17

Julius Caesar was murdered in 44 B.C. His grandnephew Augustus became the first emperor. Emperor Hadrian built huge walls around the empire. Constantine was the first Christian emperor.

Engineering
2 4 11

The Roman Empire brought new technologies and architecture to the lands that they conquered. They built long, straight roads and massive aqueducts to transport water. Some countries still use these today. Zaghouan Aqueduct, the longest that the Romans built, ran for more than 57 mi. (92km) through north Africa.

building an aqueduct

The end of Rome
7 8 12

In A.D. 455 an army of Vandals from Germany looted Rome. The last emperor, a 13-year-old boy named Augustulus ("little Augustus"), surrendered to the German chief Odoacer 20 years later. It was the end of the empire.

QUESTIONS: Roman warfare

Level 1

1. Roman soldiers fought together in formations. True or false?
2. What was the symbol of the Roman army: a mouse, eagle, or giraffe?
3. Would Roman soldiers be more likely to form a tiger, tortoise, or toad?

Level 2

4. What was an aquilifer: a general, doctor, or standard bearer?
5. What "L" was the name for a Roman foot soldier?
6. Was a ballista used to throw spears or rocks?
7. COIN TUNER can be rearranged to give the name of what army officer?
8. What was an onager: a war machine, soldier, or shield?
9. The Romans conquered the German tribes. True or false?
10. What "G" was a land conquered by Julius Caesar?
11. What name was given to soldiers from the provinces?
12. TOE STUD can be rearranged to give the name of what formation?
13. Roughly how many men were there in a legion: 50, 500, or 5,000?
14. What "P" was an empire to the east of Rome?
15. How many years did an auxiliary have to spend in the army before they were given citizenship?

Level 3

16. How many soldiers were there in a century?
17. Who fought Julius Caesar in a great civil war?
18. Which Roman general was killed in the battle of Carrhae?

Roman warfare

The Roman army was hardly ever defeated. As well as inventing many new battle tactics, the ancient Romans trained their soldiers to be disciplined and tough and never to run away. When they were not conquering new territories, the Roman army had to maintain the *pax romana* (Roman peace) throughout the empire, making sure that no one fought back against Roman rule.

Julius Caesar (10) (17)

Julius Caesar was an excellent general who conquered Gaul (France). He later defeated his rival Pompey in a great civil war and became the ruler of Rome.

centurion

legionary

Soldiers (5) (7) (13) (16)

Legionaries (foot soldiers) fought in legions of around 5,000 men. A centurion led a century consisting of 100 men.

The standard (2) (4)

The eagle was the symbol of the army, carried by a man called the aquilifer (standard bearer). Soldiers fought hard to protect the eagle, as it was seen as dishonorable to lose it in battle.

ballista

War machines (6) (8)

The Romans used powerful war machines when attacking towns or forts. The ballista could throw large spears like a giant bow and arrows. Catapults known as onagers were used to throw huge rocks.

Romans fighting German tribesmen

auxiliaries

Auxiliaries
11 15

Soldiers from the provinces—who often carried specialist weapons such as slings or bows—were called auxiliaries. After 25 years in the army they were allowed to retire and become Roman citizens.

Foes
9 14 18

The Romans never conquered the tribes of Germany or the Parthian Empire in the east. The Germans fought in forests and never risked open battles. The Parthians fought with bows and once won a great battle against the Romans in Carrhae, killing the Roman general Crassus.

Testudo
1 3 12

Legionaries fought in formations. The testudo (tortoise) formation protected them on all sides. Soldiers in the center held shields above their heads, and those at the sides held them in front.

QUESTIONS:
The Aztecs

Level 1

1. The Aztecs sometimes demanded prisoners for human sacrifices. True or false?
2. What did scribes do: write things down or fight in battles?
3. Most Aztec houses were made out of concrete. True or false?

Level 2

4. The Aztecs had a team of men who collected household garbage. True or false?
5. What does the name "tlatoani" mean: speaker or listener?
6. I BUTTER can be rearranged to name what type of payment that was made to the Aztecs?
7. Where was the Aztec capital built: on Lake Texcoco, Mount Texcoco, or the Texcoco river?
8. The Aztec capital had no streets. True or false?
9. Who conquered the Aztecs: the Spanish, French, or Portuguese?
10. The Aztec word "hueyi" means "small." True or false?
11. Aztec houses had no toilets. True or false?
12. A chinampa was a type of floating house. True or false?
13. What was a "snake woman": a warrior, doctor, or adviser?
14. What "G" did Aztecs use in writing?
15. How many days were there in the Aztec sacred calendar: 160, 260, or 360?

Level 3

16. How many types of calendars did the Aztecs have?
17. What was the Aztec capital city?

The Aztecs

The Aztecs settled in what is now Mexico in around A.D. 1325 and quickly became the leaders of a large empire. They developed a carefully ordered community with strict rules on how to behave—from the tlatoani, the ruler, right down to the slaves at the bottom of society. Their empire lasted until the 1500s, when Spanish conquistadors ("conquerors") invaded and destroyed their civilization.

Homes

3 4 11

Most Aztec homes were made out of wood, but some houses had stone walls and a central courtyard. The Aztecs were clean. Each house had a toilet, and a team of men collected household garbage.

Tenochtitlán

7 8 12 17

Around 200,000 people lived in the city of Tenochtitlán, the Aztec capital, which was built in the middle of Lake Texcoco. People traveled along canals instead of streets, while farmers grew crops on floating gardens called chinampas. Causeways were used to link the city with the mainland.

causeway

canal

The calendar

15 16

This Aztec calendar is shaped like the sun and has the face of the sun god carved in the center. The Aztecs had a solar calendar of 365 days and the tonalpohualli, a sacred calendar of 260 days, divided up between the Aztec gods. Priests used it to decide whether it would be lucky to do something on a certain day.

Tribute

1 6

The Aztecs demanded tribute (a yearly payment of goods) from the people who lived in their empire. Hundreds of foreign rulers came to the palace to deliver treasures of all types. The Aztecs punished those who did not pay with raids or demands for human prisoners to sacrifice.

Writing

2 9 14

Scribes kept track of the tribute that was paid to the Aztec rulers. They wrote lists using glyphs (small pictures) instead of words. When the Spanish conquered Tenochtitlán, they burned most of these papers.

Tlatoanis

5 10 13

Aztec nobles elected their ruler, whom they called the tlatoani ("the speaker"). The supreme ruler of all the Aztecs was called the hueyi tlatoani ("the great speaker"), and the people worshiped him as a god. The hueyi tlatoani had a head adviser, a man called the cihuacoatl ("snake woman"), who took care of most of the day-to-day running of Tenochtitlán.

QUESTIONS: Aztec religion

Level 1

1. The Aztecs only sacrificed animals. True or false?
2. What did Aztecs use to make the balls used in tlachtli: rubber, iron, or wood?
3. Was Huitzilopochtli the god of the Sun or the god of the night?

Level 2

4. Where did Aztecs perform sacrifices: on top of a temple, inside of a temple, or in front of a temple?
5. What was the Aztec color of sacrifice: red, yellow, or blue?
6. Aztec priests shaved off their hair. True or false?
7. What was cut out during a sacrifice: the tongue, liver, or heart?
8. Was Tlaloc the god of rain or the god of the Moon?
9. Where did Huitzilopochtli have a shrine: in all temples or at the Great Temple in the capital city?
10. Which Aztecs filed their teeth into points: warriors, priests, or rulers?
11. How often did the Aztecs make sacrifices to Huitzilopochtli: every hour, every day, or every five years?
12. What was the penalty for losing a game of tlachtli?
13. How long did the Aztecs claim it took to sacrifice 84,400 victims: four days, four months, or four years?

Level 3

14. BISON AID can be rearranged to name what volcanic rock, used by the Aztecs to make knives?
15. Players in tlachtli could only use their hands. True or false?
16. Which animal eating a snake was a sign to Aztecs to build a city?
17. What did Aztec priests use to paint their skin black?

FIND THE ANSWER:

Aztec religion

The Aztecs of Mexico and Central America believed that they had to sacrifice humans to the gods in order to keep the world in balance. Their priests killed around 10,000 people every year. Aztecs believed that there were five different eras (periods) of life on Earth and that they were living in the final era before the end of all time.

victim

priest

sacred stone

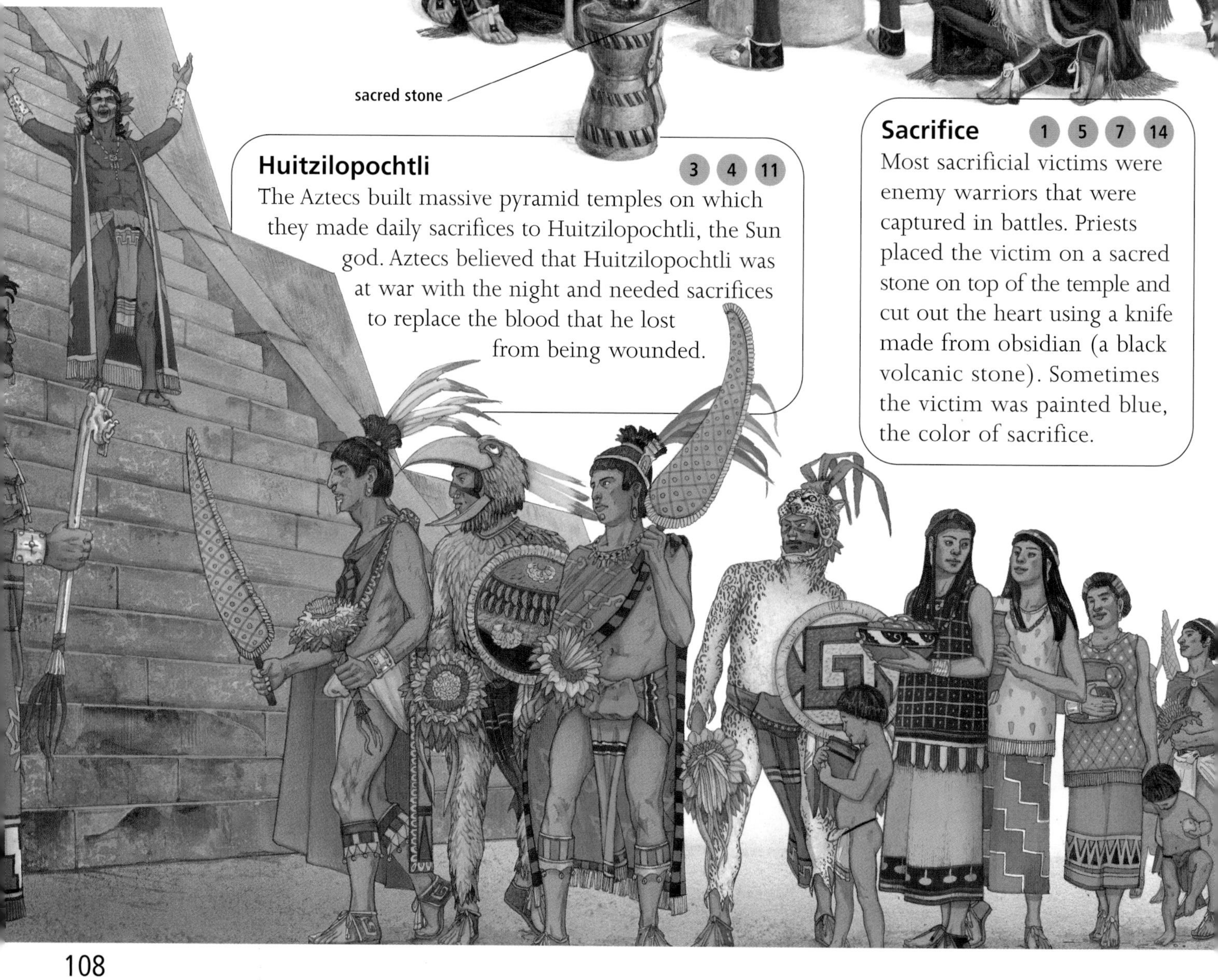

Huitzilopochtli

3 4 11

The Aztecs built massive pyramid temples on which they made daily sacrifices to Huitzilopochtli, the Sun god. Aztecs believed that Huitzilopochtli was at war with the night and needed sacrifices to replace the blood that he lost from being wounded.

Sacrifice

1 5 7 14

Most sacrificial victims were enemy warriors that were captured in battles. Priests placed the victim on a sacred stone on top of the temple and cut out the heart using a knife made from obsidian (a black volcanic stone). Sometimes the victim was painted blue, the color of sacrifice.

Tlachtli

2 12 15

In the sacred game of tlachtli players won by passing a small rubber ball through a stone hoop, without using their hands. The game represented the battle between night and day. Afterward the players on the losing team were offered as a sacrifice to the gods.

priest holding sacrificial mask

Priests

6 10 17

Aztec priests held a high rank in society. They painted their skin with black soot and grew their hair long. Some filed their teeth into sharp points.

Signs

16

The eagle, sitting on a prickly pear and eating a snake, was a sign from the gods to the early Aztecs to build their city on that spot.

Temples

8 9 13

The Great Temple pyramid in the Aztec capital city of Tenochtitlán had two shrines at its summit—one to the rain god Tlaloc and one to Huitzilopochtli. The Aztecs claimed to have sacrificed 84,400 victims in four days at this temple.

QUESTIONS:

Where in the world?

Level 1

1. Where did the ancient Greek civilization begin: in Rome or in Athens?
2. The Olmec was the first Mexican civilization, before the Aztecs. True or false?
3. Did people first travel to islands in the Pacific Ocean by swimming, in boats, or in planes?

Level 2

4. What kind of political organization did the ancient Greeks pioneer: dictatorship or democracy?
5. China's Terra-Cotta Army has statues of soldiers and which "H" animal?
6. Which "I" people were excellent engineers but could not write?
7. Which ancient civilization built temples, cities, and pyramids around 3000 B.C.?
8. Which ancient Mexican civilization carved gigantic heads out of stone: the Incas or the Olmecs?

Level 3

9. Who was the first Chinese emperor?
10. When did Greek civilization begin?

FIND THE ANSWER:

Where in the world?

Civilizations emerged in different regions at different times. The first great civilization began around 5,000 years ago in Mesopotamia (modern-day Iraq). There, the Sumerians built temples, invented wheeled transportation, made pottery, and invented writing. The Roman civilization began 3,000 years ago and spread north from Greece and Mesopotamia to Britain.

North America 2 8
The first civilization in Mexico, before the Aztec, was the Olmec, which arose around 1150 B.C. They carved gigantic human heads out of stone.

Europe 1 4 10
The ancient Greek civilization began in Athens before 1000 B.C. Greek philosophy, democracy, and science have influenced Europe for almost 2,000 years.

Asia 5 9
Qin Shi Huangdi, the first Chinese emperor, ruled from 221–210 B.C. He built the Great Wall of China and was buried with the Terra-Cotta Army—huge statues of soldiers and horses.

South America 6
The Incas ruled a huge area from Ecuador to Chile c. A.D. 1438–1532. They were expert engineers but did not write or use the wheel.

Africa 7
The ancient Egyptians established one of the earliest civilizations in north Africa around 3000 B.C. They built huge temples, cities, and pyramids.

Polynesia 3
In c. 2500 B.C. voyagers from southeast Asia began using boats to reach islands in Polynesia, a group of islands in the Pacific Ocean. It is thought that they used the stars and migrating birds to guide them.

NORTH AMERICA
EUROPE
ASIA
SOUTH AMERICA
AFRICA
AUSTRALIA

Answers 1) Athens **2)** True **3)** In boats **4)** Democracy **5)** Horses **6)** Incas **7)** The ancient Egyptians **8)** The Olmecs **9)** Qin Shi Huangdi (he ruled 221–210 B.C.) **10)** Before 1000 B.C.

QUIZ FIVE

Sports and art

Fairy tales

Theater

William Shakespeare

Famous ballets

Basketball

Horse and pony care

Martial arts

Motorsports

QUESTIONS:
Fairy tales

Level 1

1. Cinderella marries a prince. True or false?
2. Are Hansel and Gretel abandoned in the woods or in a town?
3. Is Gretel, Cinderella, or Sleeping Beauty woken up by a kiss from a prince?
4. Does the Pied Piper lure children away from town or get them to return to town?

Level 2

5. For how long does Sleeping Beauty sleep: ten years, 50 years, or 100 years?
6. In *Rumpelstiltskin* is straw, palm leaves, or sheep's wool spun into gold?
7. What "G" is the witch's house made of in later versions of *Hansel & Gretel?*
8. What "F" does the Pied Piper play to lure away the children?
9. Are there more than 30, 340, or 560 versions of *Cinderella?*
10. What are mermaids: half men and half goat, half men and half fish, or half women and half fish?
11. Is Hamelin a German, French, or Austrian town?
12. Are Hansel and Gretel the children of a miller, prince, or woodcutter?
13. Who told the king that it was possible to spin gold: Rumpelstiltskin, the miller, or his daughter?

Level 3

14. In the Chinese version of *Cinderella* which "W" finds the slipper?
15. Who wrote *The Little Mermaid?*
16. In which story does a fairy cast a spell?
17. In what year did the children really leave Hamelin?
18. When was the earliest version of *Cinderella* written?

FIND THE ANSWER: Fairy tales

Storytelling has been popular for hundreds of years. Instead of being written down, stories were originally passed down by mothers and grandmothers. The characters in fairy tales are based on ordinary people, but something about their character has been exaggerated such as a wise old woman or an evil old man. These are ordinary people, but unusual or even magical things happen to them.

Pied Piper

4 8 11 17

The tale of a piper playing a flute to lure away first the rats and then the children from a German town is based on children really leaving Hamelin in 1284. No one is sure why they left, but it may have been to go on a crusade.

Cinderella

There are more than 340 versions of *Cinderella*—a story about a poor girl who goes to a ball and loses a glass slipper. The prince finds the slipper and marries Cinderella. The earliest version, from China, was written around A.D. 850. Instead of a ball and a prince, there is a festival and a warlord.

Rumpelstiltskin (6) (13)

The story of spinning straw into gold can be seen as a tale to warn against bragging. A miller bragged to the king that his daughter could spin gold, but his daughter was punished for his lies.

Mermaids (10) (15)

Stories about mermaids, creatures that are half women and half fish, are told in many countries. In Hans Christian Andersen's well-known tale *The Little Mermaid* a mermaid falls in love with a human prince.

Sleeping Beauty (3) (5) (16)

There are different versions of the tale of fairies offering gifts to a princess. One fairy casts an evil spell on her, which involves a spindle used for spinning. In the best-known version the princess pricks her finger on a spindle and sleeps for 100 years, until she is kissed by a prince.

Hansel & Gretel (2) (7) (12)

The story of a woodcutter abandoning his children in the woods often happened for real in the Middle Ages, when food was often scarce. In the original story the children find a witch's house, which was made of bread to attract children. In later versions the house is made of gingerbread.

QUESTIONS: Theater

Level 1

1. Stage carpenters work with wood. True or false?
2. Stagehands are normally in charge of the actors' costumes. True or false?
3. Does a costume designer or a set designer plan the layout of the stage?
4. Set builders build theater scenery. True or false?
5. Is stage smoke a type of special effect?

Level 2

6. What "C" is the name for the clothing that performers wear?
7. Does a costume designer work with a set designer?
8. Which "D" cleans and fixes the costumes?
9. Does New York's Metropolitan Opera House require 200, 500, or 1,000 staff to put on a performance?
10. Is the place where the audience sits called the wings, backstage, or the auditorium?
11. On stage what would a suitcase be considered: a set, costume, or prop?
12. Are the sides of the stage that are out of the audience's view called the wings, upstage, or front of house?
13. New York's Metropolitan Opera House is also known as what: the Op House, the Met, or the Big Stage?
14. Rearrange AT BELL to name a type of performance that may need a dresser.

Level 3

15. Where are sets often assembled?
16. What is the largest number of people that can watch a single performance in New York's Metropolitan Opera House?
17. Which theater staff sometimes help actors make quick costume changes?
18. Who uses scale models of the stage in their work?

FIND THE ANSWER: Theater

A theater is where plays and other forms of entertainment, such as ballet or opera, are staged. A theater can be as simple as a piece of ground outdoors or a huge and complex theater building that has been designed specifically for staging plays. A major production requires a number of different staff, from the director and producer to the stagehands.

A large theater 9 10 13 16

New York's Metropolitan Opera House, known as the Met, is a big theater. The auditorium—the place where the audience sits—can hold up to 3,800 people. The theater employs around 1,000 people for each performance.

rehearsal space

Costumes 6 7

The clothes that the performers wear are called costumes. They are carefully designed, because fabric looks different on stage and under lights than it does in daylight. The costume designer works with the lighting designer and set designer.

Set designers 3 18

The person who designs the layout of the stage and the scenery is called the set designer. A set designer often makes a scale model so that others can see the design.

Set builders 1 4 15

The people who produce the scenery are known as set builders. Some may be stage carpenters working with wood. Others may be skilled scenery painters, plasterers, or steel welders. A set is often built in a workshop and then assembled on the stage.

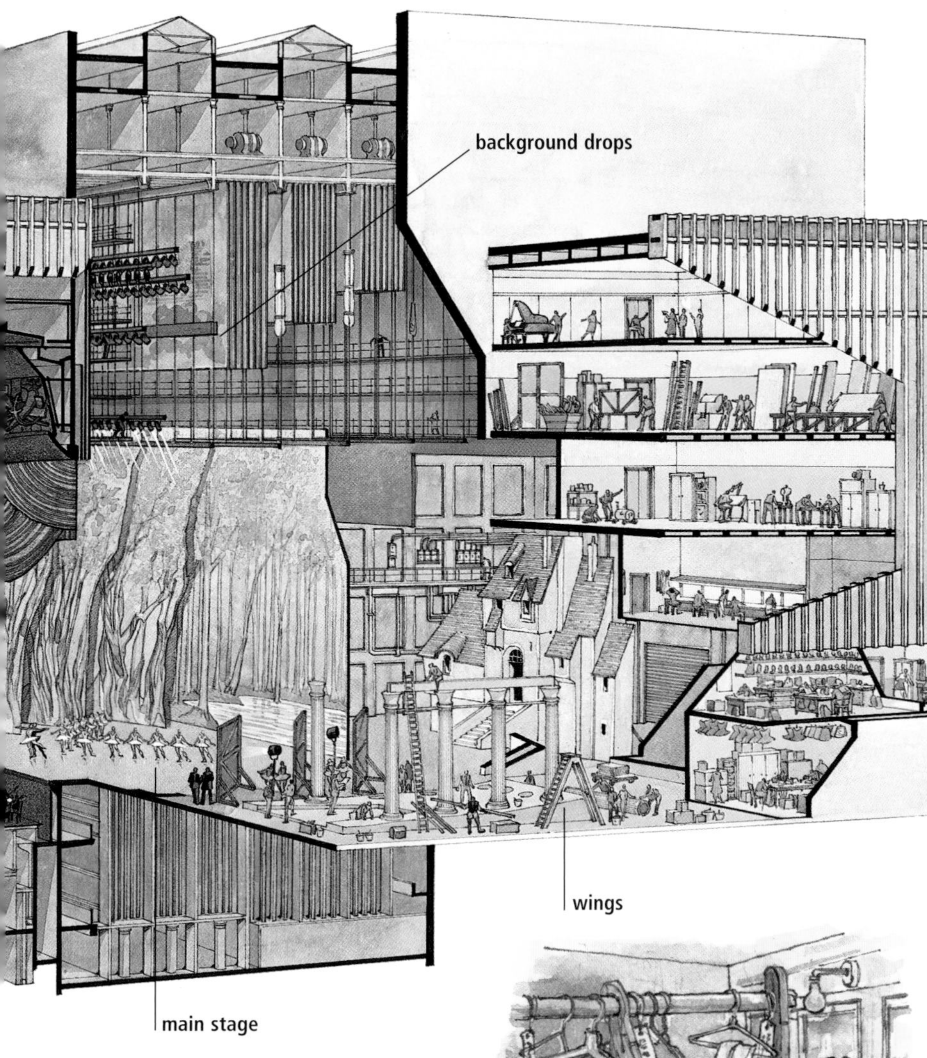

Stagehands

2 5 11

The people who run the sound, lighting, scenery, and special effects, such as stage smoke, are called stagehands. They are also responsible for props. These are objects that are used in the play such as a suitcase or tray.

Dressers

8 12 14 17

The people who take care of the costumes for a play or a ballet are called dressers. They keep the clothes clean and fix them if they get torn or damaged. Dressers also help the performers get dressed. They may need to help them make a quick change, sometimes in the wings (the sides of the stage, out of sight of the audience).

QUESTIONS: William Shakespeare

Level 1

1. *Macbeth* is a play about a figure from Scottish history. True or false?
2. Was Shakespeare's theater called the Swan or the Globe?
3. *Hamlet* is a comedy. True or false?
4. Did Shakespeare write a play called *Romeo and Juliet* or *Verona and Juliet*?

Level 2

5. Were people who watched a play from the pit called pitlings, groundlings, or watchlings?
6. Was Shakespeare born in London, Stratford-upon-Avon, or Paris?
7. What was the name of the uncovered part of the theater where people stood to watch plays?
8. Richer people watched plays in the Globe in a covered area. True or false?
9. Could the Globe hold 500, 1,500, or 3,000 people?
10. Which "M" is Shakespeare's bloodiest tragedy?
11. Is the line "To be, or not to be" from *Macbeth*, *Hamlet*, or *Romeo and Juliet*?
12. Is *Romeo and Juliet* based on real lovers or a made-up tale?
13. The Globe was built close to which river in London?
14. Was *Hamlet* first performed around 1550, 1600, or 1625?

Level 3

15. Where was the home of the real couple on whose story Shakespeare based *Romeo and Juliet*?
16. Which British king had a friendship with Shakespeare?
17. In what year was the Globe rebuilt after it had burned down?
18. By which year was Shakespeare recognized as a playwright?

FIND THE ANSWER: William Shakespeare

The English writer William Shakespeare wrote plays, long poems, and shorter poems known as sonnets. During his life, he wrote dozens of famous comedies, tragedies, and history plays, which are still popular today. They are performed in theaters around the world. Shakespeare is thought of as the greatest English playwright, and many of his plays have now been turned into movies.

The writer 6 18
William Shakespeare (1564–1616) was born in Stratford-upon-Avon, England. He moved to London, and by 1592 he became known as a playwright.

William Shakespeare

Macbeth 1 10 16
Shakespeare's shortest, but bloodiest, tragedy is *Macbeth*. It is based on a figure from Scottish history. The play reflects the author's friendship with King James I, who claimed Scottish lineage.

Hamlet 3 11 14
"To be, or not to be" is the most famous line from this tragedy, first performed in around 1600. It was a great success at the time and is still one of Shakespeare's most performed plays.

Romeo and Juliet 4 12 15
The tragedy of two lovers who died for each other is based on two real lovers in Verona, Italy, who died in 1303. Shakespeare turned the story into a play early on in his career, around 1594–1595.

The pit (7) (8)

The area in front of the theater stage was called the pit. It was uncovered, and people had to stand there to watch the play. Richer people watched from seats that were covered by the roof.

The Globe (2) (9) (13) (17)

Shakespeare's original Globe Theatre opened in 1599 on the south bank of the Thames river in London, England, and held an audience of 3,000 people. Many of his best-known plays were performed there. It burned down in 1613 but was rebuilt the next year. In 1997 a replica of the Globe Theatre opened close to the original site. People go there to watch Shakespeare's plays.

the Globe Theatre

Groundlings (5)

People who paid to watch plays in the pit were called groundlings. They paid an admission fee of one penny to watch a play in the pit.

QUESTIONS: Famous ballets

Level 1

1. *The Nutcracker* features a nutcracker turned into a prince. True or false?
2. Is *Swan Lake* a difficult ballet to perform?
3. Was *Giselle* first performed in London, England, or Paris, France?
4. Junior ballet dancers sometimes do solo performances. True or false?

Level 2

5. Is *The Firebird* based on a Shakespeare play or on Russian folk tales?
6. Who composed the music for the ballet *The Sleeping Beauty*: Tchaikovsky or Petipa?
7. Is *Giselle* still performed the same way it was in the first production?
8. In *The Firebird* the dancer performing the part of the firebird often wears a plain costume. True or false?
9. Odile in *Swan Lake* is what type of creature?
10. Which "P" roles are unsuitable for junior soloists?
11. Was the composer for *The Sleeping Beauty* Russian, French, or American?
12. *The Nutcracker* is a popular production at what time of year?
13. Aside from Odile, what is one of the other characters that is seen in *Swan Lake*?

Level 3

14. What is the first name of the composer of the music for *The Firebird*?
15. In which year was the first production of *The Nutcracker*?
16. Puss in Boots makes an appearance in which ballet?
17. In which year was *Giselle* first performed?
18. Who choreographed the ballet *The Sleeping Beauty*?

FIND THE ANSWER:

Famous ballets

Ballets are set to music that has been written by a composer, with the dance movements arranged by a choreographer. Many early ballets were produced in Russia. The Ballets Russes was a ballet company that toured Europe and the U.S. in the early 1900s, sparking great interest in ballet.

Sleeping Beauty

6 11 18

The Russian composer Peter Tchaikovsky wrote the music for *The Sleeping Beauty*. It was his first successful ballet. His success was largely due to his working with the choreographer Marius Petipa.

Nutcracker

1 12 15

After working on *The Sleeping Beauty*, Tchaikovsky and Petipa created *The Nutcracker* in 1892, a ballet about a girl who dreams of a toy nutcracker turned into a prince. Today it is often performed at Christmastime.

Puss in Boots

4 10 16

The main character from the fairy tale Puss in Boots—the cat who helps his master—makes an appearance in *The Sleeping Beauty* ballet. This lighthearted character and the White Cat are often danced by junior soloists who are not ready for principal, or main, roles.

Swan Lake

2 9 13

Swan Lake is one of the most difficult ballets to perform. It includes the black swan maiden Odile, a prince, and an evil sorcerer.

Giselle 3 7 17

First performed in Paris, France, in 1841, *Giselle* is one of the oldest ballets to still be performed—although changes have been made since the first production.

The Firebird 

In 1910 the Russian composer Igor Stravinsky wrote the music for *The Firebird*, based on Russian folk tales about a magical bird. It was the first time that the Ballets Russes had music specially composed for them, and it is one of Stravinsky's best works. The ballet features an energetic dance by the firebird wearing an elaborate costume.

QUESTIONS: Basketball

Level 1

1. Children can play basketball. True or false?
2. Is Michael Jordan British or American?
3. A regular shot in basketball scores two points. True or false?
4. Are competition basketballs orange, yellow, or green?

Level 2

5. How many feet off the ground is the basket: 7 ft. (2m), 10 ft. (3m), or 16 ft. (5m)?
6. In which year was basketball invented: 1891, 1911, or 1931?
7. Does a basketball weigh 21–23 oz. (600–650g), 24–26 oz. (700–750g), or 28–30 oz. (800–850g)?
8. What "H" is the line across the middle of a basketball court?
9. Rearrange CHAIN to spell the country that basketball player Yao Ming is from.
10. In which part of the basketball court can players only stay with the ball for three seconds: the key, the center of the court, or in the corners of the court?
11. How many panels make up a basketball: three, six, or eight?
12. Are the balls that are used by children smaller, bigger, or the same size as the balls that are used by adults?
13. What type of basket was first used to play basketball: a basket for peaches, blueberries, or tomatoes?

Level 3

14. How many feet wide is a basketball court?
15. How many inches taller is Yao Ming than Michael Jordan?
16. Who invented basketball?
17. In basketball what is the highest number of points that a single shot can score?
18. How much is a foul shot worth?

FIND THE ANSWER: Basketball

Basketball is a fast-paced team sport that is popular around the world. The ball is passed between teammates or dribbled by bouncing it along the floor. The goal of the game is to score points by shooting the ball through a basket, scoring one, two, or three points. The team with the most points at the end of the game wins.

The first game (6) (13) (16)

Since its invention by James Naismith in 1891, basketball has blossomed as a sport. At first players aimed a ball into a peach basket. Open nets were first used in 1903. Before then, players retrieved the balls from the baskets.

The ball (4) (7) (11)

A soccerball was the first ball used to play basketball. The basketball that is used in competitions today is orange and has eight panels. It weighs 21–23 oz. (600 to 650g).

basket

key

halfway line

Court (5) (8) (10) (14)

A basketball court is 92 ft. (28m) long and 50 ft. (15m) wide, and the basket is 10 ft. (3m) off the ground. The court is divided by a halfway line. Under each basket is the key, where players can only stay with the ball for three seconds.

A child's game (1) (12)

Smaller and lighter balls are made for children. Basketball is a good game for helping children improve their physical fitness and coordination.

Scoring (3) (17) (18)

Two points are scored by making a successful regular shot. A long-distance shot is worth three points. Each foul shot is worth one point.

competing for the ball

Great heights (2) (9) (15)

Most professional basketball players are very tall, which gives them an advantage. American player Michael Jordan is 6 ft. 5 in. (1.98m) tall. China's Yao Ming is 7 ft. 6 in. (2.29m) tall. You don't need to be tall to join in this sport, though.

QUESTIONS: Horse and pony care

Level 1

1. Horses and ponies do not like being groomed. True or false?
2. Are horses and ponies sometimes massaged?
3. Is the seat that a rider sits on called a bridle or a saddle?
4. Horses and ponies mostly eat hay and grass. True or false?
5. Horses and ponies are kept in buildings called what: stables or pastures?

Level 2

6. What is the cloth that is used after grooming called: a rubber glove, stable glove, or stable cloth?
7. Is braiding done before or after clipping and grooming?
8. What type of "C" comb can remove dried mud from a horse's or pony's body?
9. What "M" name is the hair on a horse's or pony's neck?
10. Rearrange DIG BEND to give the name of something that is replaced in the stable every day.
11. How many times a day must a horse or pony be fed: once, twice, or three times?
12. Name one of two "B" grains that are used in concentrated feeds for horses and ponies.
13. Is a sponge, tack, or saddle soap used to clean around a horse's or pony's eyes?
14. Can horses and ponies only eat small amounts of grains or large amounts?

Level 3

15. How much manure can an adult horse produce in a week?
16. What is the term that is used for putting a saddle and bridle on a horse or pony?
17. What object containing horse and pony food is hung up in the stall?
18. How many pounds of hay can an adult horse eat in a day?

Horse and pony care

Owning a horse or pony is a lot of hard work. The owner must take care of the horse or pony, keeping it clean and well fed and exercising it regularly. Most horses and ponies live outside in a fenced-off area of a field that is called a pasture. When it is cold or wet, or when a horse is sick, it may stay inside in a stable. Some competition horses spend every night in a stable. Warm winter blankets are put on horses and ponies during cold weather.

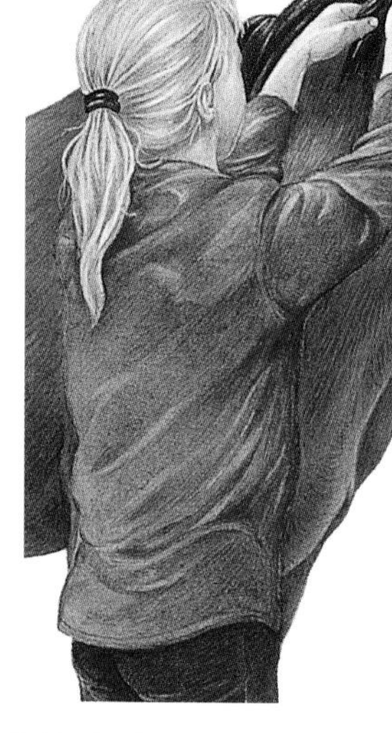

braiding the mane

bridle

Braiding (7) (9)

After clipping and grooming, the mane—the hair on the horse's or pony's neck—can be braided, especially if it is going to a show. This makes it neat and tidy. The tail can be braided too.

The stable (5) (11) (18)

Horses and ponies that are kept in a stable—a building made to house them—have to be fed at least twice a day. Daily tasks include grooming, exercising, mucking out, and filling haynets and water buckets. An adult horse can eat 22 lbs. (10kg) of hay a day.

Mucking out (10) (15)

Keeping a horse's stable clean is called mucking out. An adult horse can produce 44 lbs. (20kg) of manure a day. Old bedding is removed with a pitchfork and replaced with fresh bedding daily.

saddle

straw bedding

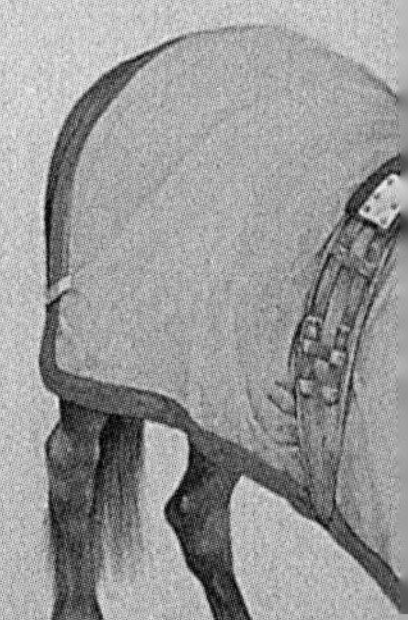

Tacking up (3) (16)

The saddle is the rider's seat, and the bridle is the horse's headgear. Together these items are called tack. Putting them on a horse is called tacking up.

Grooming (1) (8) (13)

Many tools are used to keep horses' and ponies' skin and coats clean and healthy. Most horses and ponies enjoy grooming. A rubber or plastic curry comb removes dried mud. A damp sponge cleans around a horse's or pony's eyes.

Feeds (4) (12) (14) (17)

Hay and grass are called bulk feed and make up most of horses' and ponies' diets. Hay is hung in a haynet so that the horse or pony can eat when it wants. Horses and ponies can only eat a small amount of grains such as bran, oats, and barley. These are concentrated feeds.

Stable cloth (2) (6)

A stable cloth, or towel, is used after grooming to remove any dust. It is also used to massage horses' and ponies' muscles.

QUESTIONS:
Martial arts

Level 1

1. Are martial artists often trained to use their skills to defend or to fight?
2. Tai chi movements are sharp and sudden. True or false?
3. Is karate a type of striking martial art?
4. Are throwing techniques and armlocks part of judo or kung fu?

Level 2

5. Does kickboxing, tai chi, or karate combine boxing with kicking moves?
6. Does a kickboxer score points by striking with their hands, feet, or both?
7. Training for karate is divided into three parts: basics, forms, and sparring. True or false?
8. Which "J" country does kendo come from?
9. Which color is usually the highest in the colored belt system that is used in many martial arts: brown, black, or purple?
10. Which qualities are required for success in martial arts: discipline and self-control or taking your own lead and being quick to respond?
11. Which "K" is a form of martial art that is known for its kicks and open-hand techniques?
12. Which martial art is based on animal poses: tai chi, karate, or kendo?
13. Which European country does the form of kickboxing called "savate" come from: Italy, Spain, or France?

Level 3

14. Why does the color of a belt worn by a judo or karate student change?
15. What is the name of the sword that is used in kendo?
16. The teachings of which Buddhist led to the beginning of many martial arts?
17. Which martial art is based on jujitsu?

FIND THE ANSWER: Martial arts

Martial arts are a collection of combat sports and skills. Many of these developed in different countries in Asia over hundreds of years. Millions of people all over the world now enjoy martial arts as a form of exercise. Others practice a martial art as a competitive sport or to learn self-defense.

Origin (16)

Many martial arts are based on teachings by Bodhidharma—a 5th-century Buddhist who visited the Shaolin Temple in China.

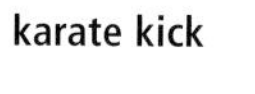

Judo (4) (17)

Based on the ancient art of jujitsu, the sport of judo uses throwing techniques. During a bout, people grapple on the ground using armlocks, control holds, and special choking techniques.

Karate (3) (7) (11)

A type of striking martial art, karate features kicks, punching, knee and elbow strikes, and open-hand techniques. Training is divided into the basics: forms—patterns using movements—and sparring with another person.

Training (1) (10)

Success in martial arts requires discipline. People practice for many hours. Martial artists are often trained to keep self-control all the time, using their skills to defend, not to fight.

blue belt

black belt

Belt colors (9) (14)

In many martial arts the color of a belt indicates a student's progress. A black belt is usually the highest color. The colors and their order varies among schools.

Kendo

8 15

The Japanese sport of sword fighting is called kendo. Swords, called "shinai," are made out of four sections of bamboo that are bound together. Competitors wear body protection called "do" and a helmet with a grille called a "men."

5 6 13

Kickboxing

In this mixture of boxing and martial arts the kickboxer uses their hands and feet to strike and score points. In French kickboxing, called savate, the fighters usually wear shoes.

Tai chi

2 12

Based on animal poses, tai chi is a gentle form of exercise. The movements are linked in a graceful, flowing sequence.

QUESTIONS: Motorsports

Level 1

1. A driver's helmet protects them against what: ice, wind, or fire?
2. Rearrange GEE INN to spell the name of a part of a car.
3. Formula One cars are low and streamlined. True or false?
4. Does the team decide on a plan in order to win the race?

Level 2

5. Which "M" is the name of the stewards who are in charge of fire safety?
6. How fast can an F1 pit crew change four wheels: seven, 17, or 37 seconds?
7. Many F1 drivers consider Silverstone to be one of the fastest F1 racetracks. True or false?
8. How many gallons of gasoline does an F1 car normally use to drive 60 mi. (100km): seven, 13, or 20?
9. What was the world land speed record for an F1 car set in 2006: 22 mph (35km/h), 220 mph (355km/h), or 960 mph (1,550km/h)?
10. What are the top three NASCAR championships?
11. What is the important difference between ordinary tracksuits and the race suits that are worn by racecar drivers?
12. What is the strong frame that makes up a NASCAR's structure made out of?
13. The average speed over the entire racetrack of the Talladega Superspeedway is what: 100 mph (160km/h), 188 mph (303km/h), or 220 mph (354km/h)?

Level 3

14. What must a driver do at a pit stop?
15. What are g-forces?
16. What does the pit crew do to a race car during a pit stop?
17. What is the advantage of starting a Formula One race with tanks that are half full?

FIND THE ANSWER:

Motorsports

Motorsports are very popular and take place around the world. Two of the most popular types are Formula One (F1, or first-class racing) and NASCAR. F1 began in 1950, and in 2006, 19 races were held on circuits (racetracks) worldwide. NASCAR, the National Association for Stock Car Auto Racing, was set up in 1948.

Formula One car

open wheel

monocoque body (made in one piece)

engine

rear wing

front wing

The car 2 3 8 12

Race cars are low and streamlined. Powerful F1 engines consume around 20 gallons of gasoline per 60 mi. (100km). Each NASCAR vehicle is custom-built around a strong steel frame.

helmet

underwear

outer suit

glove

shoe

Race suits 1 5 11

Drivers' race suits, shoes, gloves, and underwear are fireproof—if the car catches on fire, they protect the driver until track marshals use fire extinguishers. The strong, flexible helmets are also fireproof.

NASCAR 10 13

NASCAR is now the U.S.'s favorite motorsport, with more than 75 million fans. Races feature top speeds of more than 198 mph (320km/h) and close finishes. The big three competitions are the Busch Series, the Craftsman Truck Series, and the Nextel Cup.

Strategy 4 17

In order to win, the team needs to have a plan. For example, tanks that are half full will make the car lighter and faster, but full tanks will need fewer pit stops to refuel. The team decides which strategy is best.

refueling

lollypop

fire safety

changing wheels

Pit stops 6 14 16

F1 mechanics can change four wheels (which is faster than replacing worn tires) and refuel in seven seconds. They also make repairs. The driver has to stop the car in an exact spot and wait for a signal before starting again.

Speed 7 9 15

In 2006 Honda set a world land speed record of 220 mph (355km/h) for an F1 car. When racing, faster cars, such as Ferraris, exceed 186 mph (300km/h). One of the fastest circuits is Silverstone, in the U.K. During fast turns, drivers can suffer neck injuries from high g-forces (acceleration due to gravity).

ANSWERS

Did you get it right? Now that you have finished *Quiz Quest 2*, you can turn over the pages to find the answers. Remember, with the help of a friend, you can also use the answer section for a quick quiz. Why not take turns and see who gets the most right?

ANSWERS: Desert creatures

Level 1

1. What is a coyote: a wild dog or a wild cat?
   Answer: A wild dog
2. What are the thorny devil and the Gila monster: reptiles, birds, or insects?
   Answer: Reptiles
3. Desert foxes have large ears to help keep them cool. True or false?
   Answer: True

Level 2

4. Some desert birds build their nests in cacti. True or false?
   Answer: True
5. Desert birds of prey eat prickly plants. True or false?
   Answer: False (they eat rodents, rabbits, and snakes)
6. Which desert lizard is poisonous: the Gila monster or the chameleon?
   Answer: The Gila monster
7. Which bird is not a desert bird of prey: the turkey vulture, lappet-faced vulture, or kestrel?
   Answer: The kestrel (it doesn't live in the desert)
8. What kind of fox lives in the desert: the red fox, arctic fox, or fennec fox?
   Answer: The fennec fox
9. Does the thorny devil collect dew on its body or from plants?
   Answer: On its body
10. Which characteristics help desert hunters: swift movement, good eyesight, claws, or all of the above?
    Answer: All of the above
11. Does the Peruvian fox live in the Atacama Desert in South America or the Sahara in north Africa?
    Answer: The Atacama Desert in South America
12. Which animal does the bobcat eat: rodents or coyotes?
    Answer: Rodents

Level 3

13. Which type of lizard lives its entire life in a decaying cactus?
    Answer: The yucca night lizard
14. Does the desert coyote weigh more or less than a coyote that lives in the mountains?
    Answer: Less
15. Which feature of a bobcat helps its hearing?
    Answer: The hairs on its ears
16. Which "B" is a flying creature that eats the nectar found in cactus flowers?
    Answer: Bat
17. What is another name for the Peruvian fox?
    Answer: The Sechuran fox
18. Which "G" lizard can live for months without food?
    Answer: Gila monster

ANSWERS: Spiders

Level 1

1. Is the spider's body made up of two, three, or eight parts?
   Answer: Two parts
2. How many wings do spiders have: one pair, two pairs, or none?
   Answer: None
3. Spiders spin silk to make spider webs. True or false?
   Answer: True
4. Most spiders have no eyes. True or false?
   Answer: False (most spiders have six or eight eyes)

Level 2

5. The trapdoor spider catches its prey in a web. True or false?
   Answer: False (it catches its prey with a trap)
6. What shape does an orb weaver spin after it makes a frame: "X," "Y," or "Z"?
   Answer: "Y"
7. A spider's silk-making organs are in its abdomen. True or false?
   Answer: True
8. Are a spider's legs attached to the front part of its body or its abdomen?
   Answer: The front part of its body
9. Can some spiders only see shadows and light?
   Answer: Yes
10. How does a spider eat its prey: by chewing it, by turning its insides into liquid and sucking them out, or by eating it whole?
    Answer: By turning its insides into liquid and sucking them out
11. In what "A" part of the body are the organs that a spider uses for digesting food?
    Answer: Abdomen
12. Which spider is the largest in the world?
    Answer: The Goliath bird-eating spider
13. The Goliath bird-eating spider only eats birds. True or false?
    Answer: False (it usually eats insects, mice, or lizards)

Level 3

14. A dry silk thread stays on the web when a spider finishes spinning. True or false?
    Answer: False (it is removed)
15. What type of spiders are the wolf spider and tarantula?
    Answer: Hunting spiders
16. What do a spider's hollow fangs hold?
    Answer: Poison from venom glands
17. Is it believed that jumping spiders have good or bad eyesight?
    Answer: Good eyesight
18. How does a bird-eating spider detect movement?
    Answer: With the hairs on its body
19. How does a spider turn its prey's insides into liquid?
    Answer: By injecting the prey with special juices

ANSWERS: Bees

Level 1

1. Honey comes from which creatures: bats, bees, or bears?
   Answer: Bees
2. What "D" are male honeybees called?
   Answer: Drones
3. Wild honeybees build their own nest, called a hive. True or false?
   Answer: True
4. Bees do not have an abdomen. True or false?
   Answer: False

Level 2

5. Are a bee's wings attached to its thorax (the middle section of its body) or to its head?
   Answer: To its thorax
6. Worker bees collect pollen and nectar. True or false?
   Answer: True
7. What "N" is honey made from?
   Answer: Nectar
8. What "H" shape is a cell in a beehive?
   Answer: Hexagonal
9. Does a honeybee have two or three types of wings?
   Answer: Two (forewings and hind wings)
10. Do bees' eggs hatch in three days, one week, or one month?
    Answer: Three days
11. Bees have special glands that produce what: wax, oil, or fat?
    Answer: Wax
12. Some bees have a special "honey stomach" for storing nectar. True or false?
    Answer: True
13. What is the average number of flowers that a bee will visit in a single trip: 5–10, 50–100, or 500–1,000?
    Answer: 50–100

Level 3

14. Where do honeybees store pollen when they are collecting it?
    Answer: In a pollen "basket" on their hind legs
15. Name the special tube that bees use to suck out nectar.
    Answer: Proboscis
16. On average, how many eggs might a queen bee lay in one month?
    Answer: 16,666
17. How is honey removed from a honeybee?
    Answer: It is sucked out by a worker bee
18. Name a substance made by worker bees that is fed to future queen bees.
    Answer: Royal jelly
19. What does a honeybee do when it finds a new supply of food?
    Answer: It does a special "dance"

ANSWERS: Deadly creatures

Level 1

1. Some snakes are poisonous. True or false?
   Answer: True
2. What do great white sharks hunt: seals, porpoise, or both?
   Answer: Both
3. Female black widow spiders are dangerous to people. True or false?
   Answer: True
4. Which creature wraps its body around its victim to kill it: the boa constrictor or the jellyfish?
   Answer: The boa constrictor

Level 2

5. What "T" do jellyfish have?
   Answer: Tentacles
6. How does a crocodile kill its prey: by tossing it into the air or by drowning it?
   Answer: By drowning it
7. The cobra kills its prey by wrapping its body around it. True or false?
   Answer: False (it uses a poisonous bite)
8. How do sharks find prey: by smell, by using special cells that sense movement, or both?
   Answer: Both
9. What does a jellyfish eat: small fish, worms, or both?
   Answer: Small fish
10. How heavy is a great white shark: 440 lbs. (200kg), 2,200 lbs. (1,000kg), or 4,400 lbs. (2,000kg)?
    Answer: 4,400 lbs. (2,000kg)
11. Is the tiger shark considered to be safe or dangerous to people?
    Answer: Dangerous (it is a fierce predator)
12. Does the crocodile hide from its prey?
    Answer: Yes (it hides underwater)

Level 3

13. What is another name for a box jellyfish?
    Answer: Sea wasp
14. How many clusters of tentacles does a box jellyfish have?
    Answer: Four
15. Which piranha is the most dangerous?
    Answer: The red-bellied piranha
16. Which spider is the most dangerous?
    Answer: The Brazilian wandering spider
17. The crocodile has what type of special feature to stay underwater?
    Answer: Waterproof flaps to seal its eyes, ears, nostrils, and throat
18. What "B" does a piranha detect with a special sensory system?
    Answer: Blood

ANSWERS: Frogs

Level 1

1. A baby frog is called a tadpole. True or false?
   Answer: True
2. Do flying frogs have feathers, like birds, or flaps of skin?
   Answer: Flaps of skin
3. Adult frogs have tails. True or false?
   Answer: False
4. Do frogs lay their eggs in water or in nests made in trees?
   Answer: In water

Level 2

5. Tadpoles have tails, gills, and legs. True or false?
   Answer: False (they do not have legs)
6. How often do most frogs shed their skin: once a week, once a year, or never?
   Answer: Once a week
7. How far can a flying frog glide: 6 ft. (2m), 40 ft. (12m), or 70 ft. (22m)?
   Answer: 40 ft. (12m)
8. All frogs catch food with their tongues. True or false?
   Answer: False (some frogs use their feet)
9. How many days does it take for a frog's eggs to hatch: 3–5 days, 3–25 days, or 25–35 days?
   Answer: 3–25 days
10. FRET LOG can be rearranged to give the name of what stage of a frog before it becomes an adult?
    Answer: Froglet
11. Are frogs' ears specially tuned in to hear the calls of predators or to hear the calls of their own species?
    Answer: To hear the calls of their own species
12. Would a frog puff out its throat to call another frog, to scare a predator, or both?
    Answer: Both
13. What "A" do tadpoles eat?
    Answer: Algae

Level 3

14. Where do poison dart frogs live?
    Answer: Tropical rain forests in Central and South America
15. Can a cricket frog jump twice its body length, ten times its body length, or more than 30 times its body length?
    Answer: More than 30 times
16. What "M" is the term that is used to describe the changes that a tadpole undergoes?
    Answer: Metamorphosis
17. Name a species of frog that guards its eggs from predators.
    Answer: Darwin's frog or poison dart frog (plus many other types of frogs)
18. The poison from the poison dart frog is used by some tribespeople to do what?
    Answer: Hunt
19. Give a reason why frogs need to keep their skin wet.
    Answer: To get oxygen

ANSWERS: Coral reef creatures

Level 1

1. Do most corals like warm, shallow water?
   Answer: Yes
2. Is the anemone fish one of the many species of fish that live in the coral reef?
   Answer: Yes
3. Starfish are not really fish. True or false?
   Answer: True
4. Do jellyfish have brains?
   Answer: No (they have a "nerve net")

Level 2

5. Some fish are colorful or patterned so that they can recognize each other. True or false?
   Answer: True
6. CLEAT NETS can be rearranged to give the name of what part of a jellyfish?
   Answer: Tentacles
7. What does a jellyfish's nerve net detect: touch or light?
   Answer: Touch
8. How many species of fish inhabit the coral reef: more than 3,000, more than 4,000, or more than 5,000?
   Answer: More than 4,000
9. Which coral reef creature looks as harmless as a rock?
   Answer: The stonefish
10. Are brain coral and elkhorn types of hard corals or soft corals?
    Answer: Hard corals
11. What do corals use their tentacles for: to walk along the seabed, to feed themselves, or to swim?
    Answer: To feed themselves
12. Do sea anemones protect anemone fish or eat them?
    Answer: They protect them

Level 3

13. What "P" do corals eat?
    Answer: Plankton
14. What "S" means "life together"?
    Answer: Symbiosis
15. What is the name for a large group of jellyfish?
    Answer: A bloom
16. How many tentacles do soft corals have?
    Answer: Eight
17. What part of their body do most fish move in order to swim?
    Answer: Their tail
18. Which "S" creature is an echinoderm?
    Answer: Starfish

ANSWERS: Dolphins and porpoise

Level 1

1. Is the bottle-nosed a type of dolphin, crab, or lobster?
   Answer: Dolphin
2. Most porpoise are smaller than dolphins. True or false?
   Answer: True
3. What game do dolphins like to play: soccer, tennis, or bow riding?
   Answer: Bow riding
4. Which type of animal is a dolphin: a mammal or a reptile?
   Answer: A mammal

Level 2

5. Dolphins have a "melon" in their head to help them find fish. True or false?
   Answer: True (they use it for echolocation)
6. Do dolphins make clicks, whistles, or both to communicate with each other?
   Answer: Both
7. Why do porpoise swim upside down: to attract a mate or to eat their food?
   Answer: To attract a mate
8. How fast does a Dall's porpoise swim?
   Answer: 34 mph (55km/h)
9. What "S" do dolphins like to play with?
   Answer: Seaweed
10. Does a porpoise or a dolphin have a triangular dorsal fin?
    Answer: A porpoise
11. Where do female dolphins give birth to their babies: close to the seabed or just below the surface of the water?
    Answer: Just below the surface of the water
12. How many games are dolphins believed to play: more than three, more than 30, or more than 300?
    Answer: More than 300
13. What is the function of a "babysitter" dolphin?
    Answer: To help the mother teach her young
14. Do female dolphins give birth to calves, kittens, or pups?
    Answer: Calves

Level 3

15. How many species of porpoise are there?
    Answer: Six
16. Which species is the smallest porpoise?
    Answer: The Vaquita
17. What is a dolphin's beak called?
    Answer: A rostrum
18. What is bow riding?
    Answer: Surfing on the waves that are created by boats
19. What "C" sound do dolphins use to learn about their surroundings and find fish?
    Answer: Clicking sound

ANSWERS: Killer whales

Level 1

1. Do killer whales live in a family group called a pod?
   Answer: Yes
2. Another name for the killer whale is the orca. True or false?
   Answer: True
3. Do adult killer whales take care of their young, or do they let their young take care of themselves?
   Answer: Adults take care of their young
4. What is a whale jump called: a breach, hop, or bungee?
   Answer: A breach

Level 2

5. Is a killer whale also called a shark of the ocean or a wolf of the sea?
   Answer: A wolf of the sea
6. How long is a male killer whale: up to 12 ft. (4m), 20 ft. (6m), or 32 ft. (10m)?
   Answer: Up to 32 ft. (10m)
7. Killer whales sometimes hunt young blue whales. True or false?
   Answer: True
8. Why would a whale breach: to scare prey, warn of danger, attract a mate, or all of the above?
   Answer: All of the above
9. What "C" and "W" noises will a whale use to send messages to another whale?
   Answer: Clicks and whistles
10. A clan is made up of several pods. True or false?
    Answer: True
11. Does a killer whale poke its tail or its head out of the water when it is spyhopping?
    Answer: Its head
12. Are killer whales mammals or large fish?
    Answer: Mammals
13. Do killer whales protect injured and sick members of their pod, attack them, or chase them away?
    Answer: Protect them

Level 3

14. What is a killer whale's cruising speed?
    Answer: 6 mph (10km/h)
15. What is a lobtail?
    Answer: A smack on the water with the tail
16. How much faster does a killer whale swim when it's hunting and not cruising?
    Answer: 24 mph (38km/h) faster
17. LEAD CIT can be rearranged to give what name for the common calls that are shared by a whale pod?
    Answer: Dialect
18. For how long can a whale hold itself up while it is spyhopping?
    Answer: Up to 30 seconds

ANSWERS: Baleen whales

Level 1

1. Is the blue whale the largest mammal on Earth?
   Answer: Yes
2. What do baleen whales eat: birds or shrimplike krill?
   Answer: Shrimplike krill
3. Whales never migrate with their young. True or false?
   Answer: False
4. The blue whale is the loudest animal, much louder than humans. True or false?
   Answer: True

Level 2

5. Only the blue whale has two blowholes. True or false?
   Answer: False (all baleen whales have two blowholes)
6. The bowhead likes the warm waters of the Mediterranean Sea. True or false?
   Answer: False (it lives in Arctic waters)
7. The gray whale migrates along which coast of the U.S.: the eastern or the western coast?
   Answer: The western coast
8. What are baleen plates used for: tossing fish, trapping krill, or swimming?
   Answer: Trapping krill
9. Do humpback whales use bubbles to trap krill?
   Answer: Yes (they form a bubble netting)
10. Name one of two reasons why baleen whales migrate.
    Answer: To breed or to feed
11. Why does the bowhead have a thick layer of blubber?
    Answer: To keep it warm
12. How far can the gray whale migrate: 600 mi. (1,000km), 3,000 mi. (5,000km), or 6,000 mi. (10,000km)?
    Answer: 6,000 mi. (10,000km)
13. Rearrange FREET FIELDS to describe how a baleen whale eats.
    Answer: Filter feeds

Level 3

14. How loud is a blue whale's call?
    Answer: Up to 188 decibels
15. Do humpback whales eat the food that they catch by bubble netting on the seabed or at the surface?
    Answer: At the surface
16. What percentage of its total length is the head of the bowhead?
    Answer: 40 percent
17. How many krill can a blue whale eat in a single day?
    Answer: Four million

ANSWERS: Birds of prey

Level 1

1. Which bird is the national bird of the U.S.: the golden eagle, harpy eagle, or bald eagle?
   Answer: The bald eagle
2. Does the osprey live close to water or in the mountains?
   Answer: Close to water
3. The peregrine falcon is faster than any other creature in the world. True or false?
   Answer: True
4. What are talons: claws, wings, or legs?
   Answer: Claws

Level 2

5. How many species of falcons are there: around five, 35, or 75?
   Answer: Around 35
6. What type of eagle is the South American harpy: a snake eagle, buzzardlike eagle, or sea eagle?
   Answer: Buzzardlike eagle
7. How fast can a peregrine falcon dive: 14 mph (23km/h), 140 mph (230km/h), or 200 mph (320km/h)?
   Answer: 200 mph (320km/h)
8. Which birds of prey have longer talons: those that catch rabbits or those that catch fish?
   Answer: Those that catch fish
9. How many species of eagles are there: around 20, 40, or 60?
   Answer: Around 60
10. Which bird of prey has the largest wingspan?
    Answer: The Andean condor
11. What is the world's largest eagle?
    Answer: The South American harpy
12. What does the bald eagle eat: small animals, fish, or both?
    Answer: Both
13. What type of wings enable eagles and buzzards to soar for long periods: broad wings or long, tapered wings?
    Answer: Broad wings
14. Is the kestrel a type of falcon or eagle?
    Answer: Falcon

Level 3

15. Which wing shape allows birds to maneuver easily?
    Answer: Short and round
16. The golden eagle is which type of eagle?
    Answer: A booted eagle
17. What is unusual about the bottom of an osprey's feet?
    Answer: They are covered with spiny scales for gripping prey
18. What happens to a bald eagle at three or four years of age?
    Answer: It develops its white head and yellow beak

ANSWERS: Rats and mice

Level 1

1. To what animal group do rats and mice belong: rodents, insects, or reptiles?
   Answer: Rodents
2. Is the Swiss albino mouse the most common pet mouse?
   Answer: Yes
3. The Norway rat is the most common rat in the world. True or false?
   Answer: True
4. What disease were rats blamed for spreading: the Plague, flu, or colds?
   Answer: The Plague

Level 2

5. A mouse has a lot of fur when it is born. True or false?
   Answer: False (it has no fur)
6. The Norway rat killed off many black rats when it arrived in Europe. True or false?
   Answer: True
7. Do some rats live in houses and other buildings?
   Answer: Yes
8. Do dormice build nests or live in caves?
   Answer: They build nests
9. Where did the Norway rat originate: Europe, Asia, or Africa?
   Answer: Asia
10. What "I" are teeth that both rats and mice have?
    Answer: Incisors
11. How many species of mice are there: less than ten, between ten and 100, or more than 100?
    Answer: More than 100
12. What is another name for the Norway rat?
    Answer: The brown rat
13. What "H" do dormice do during the winter?
    Answer: Hibernate

Level 3

14. What "H" is one of the smallest types of mice?
    Answer: Harvest mouse
15. In which areas is the black rat more common than the brown rat?
    Answer: Tropical areas
16. What does the Latin word *rodere* mean?
    Answer: "To gnaw"
17. How did the Norway rat arrive in North America?
    Answer: On the ships of the new settlers
18. How fast can a mouse run?
    Answer: Up to 8 mph (13km/h)
19. How many baby mice might a female mouse give birth to in a year?
    Answer: Around 40

ANSWERS: Bats

Level 1

1. Bats are flying mammals. True or false?
   Answer: True
2. Vampire bats drink the blood of which animals: cattle, lizards, or snails?
   Answer: Cattle
3. Are a bat's bones light in weight to make flying easier?
   Answer: Yes

Level 2

4. What are fruit bats sometimes called: flying cats, flying foxes, or flying monkeys?
   Answer: Flying foxes
5. All bats use echolocation to help them find food. True or false?
   Answer: False (some use their sense of smell)
6. Some baby bats can fly when they are only two weeks old. True or false?
   Answer: True
7. What do bats use the clawed fingers on their wings for: climbing or hanging upside down?
   Answer: Climbing
8. How many squeaks per second might a bat use during echolocation: two, 200, or two million?
   Answer: 200
9. Which part of its body does a vampire bat use to detect heat?
   Answer: Heat sensor
10. TURF BAITS can be rearranged to name which bats found in Asia, Africa, and Oceania?
    Answer: Fruit bats
11. Do bats have strong legs or weak legs?
    Answer: Weak legs
12. What is the wingspan of the largest bat: 5 ft. (1.5m), 7 ft. (1.8m), or 8 ft. (2.5m)?
    Answer: 7 ft. (1.8m)

Level 3

13. Why does the vampire bat have less teeth than other bats?
    Answer: It does not need to chew its food
14. What is another name for the bumblebee bat?
    Answer: Kitti's hog-nosed bat
15. How do the fingers of fruit bats differ from other bats?
    Answer: They also have a claw on the second fingers
16. What is the difference in wingspan between the smallest bat and the largest bat?
    Answer: More than 5 ft. (165cm)
17. How do some bats find fruits and nectar?
    Answer: By using their sense of smell
18. Where can a flap of skin be found on a bat?
    Answer: Between its legs and its tail

ANSWERS: Big cats

Level 1

1. Lions hunt their prey in a group. True or false?
   Answer: True
2. What is a group of lions called: a pride or a school?
   Answer: A pride
3. Do lions and tigers both roar?
   Answer: Yes
4. All big cats are mammals. True or false?
   Answer: True
5. What does a lion eat: zebras, penguins, or lobsters?
   Answer: Zebras

Level 2

6. The tiger, leopard, jaguar, and lynx are all big cats. True or false?
   Answer: False (the lynx is not a big cat)
7. How much can a tiger eat in one meal: 22 lbs. (10kg), 88 lbs. (40kg), or 176 lbs. (80kg) of meat?
   Answer: 88 lbs. (40kg) of meat
8. Which animal is the fastest on land: the jaguar, lion, or cheetah?
   Answer: The cheetah
9. Which cat is the largest: the lion, tiger, or cheetah?
   Answer: The tiger
10. Rearrange ROD LEAP to name a big cat that feeds on impalas, hares, and birds.
    Answer: Leopard
11. Each tiger has the same pattern of stripes on both sides of its body. True or false?
    Answer: False (there is a different pattern on each side)
12. Which cat will hide its kill in a tree: a lion, tiger, or leopard?
    Answer: A leopard
13. Which is the only big cat that lives in the Americas: the cheetah, jaguar, or ocelot?
    Answer: The jaguar
14. Which "S" describes the way that lions and tigers hunt?
    Answer: Stalking

Level 3

15. Which small tiger is native to Asia?
    Answer: The Sumatran tiger
16. Which mammal group includes lions, tigers, leopards, and jaguars?
    Answer: Panthera
17. What two things help hide a big cat when it is hunting?
    Answer: Tall grass and the coloring of its fur
18. How far can a cheetah travel in just three strides?
    Answer: 60 ft. (18m)
19. Which is the only big cat that cannot fully retract its claws?
    Answer: The cheetah

ANSWERS: Great apes

Level 1

1. Chimps live together in groups. True or false?
   Answer: True
2. What is an adult male gorilla called: a silverback, grayfront, or bluetop?
   Answer: Silverback
3. Chimps have calls to communicate with each other. True or false?
   Answer: True
4. Because rain forests are being destroyed, are all of the great apes in danger of becoming extinct?
   Answer: Yes

Level 2

5. Gorillas and chimps live in both Africa and Asia. True or false?
   Answer: False (they only live only in Africa; orangutans live in Asia)
6. At what age do gorillas learn to "knuckle walk": three weeks, nine months, or nine years?
   Answer: Nine months
7. The orangutan is a sociable creature. True or false?
   Answer: False (it lives alone after leaving its mother)
8. Is blackback another name for a young male gorilla, a young male orangutan, or a young male chimpanzee?
   Answer: A young male gorilla
9. Which is an enemy of the gorilla: the leopard, tiger, or jaguar?
   Answer: The leopard
10. How long will a juvenile male gorilla stay with his family: until he is three years old, eight years old, or 11 years old?
    Answer: Until he is 11 years old
11. How many gorillas do the largest wild groups contain: ten, 30, or 200?
    Answer: 30
12. What feature identifies an adult male gorilla: a silver, black, or brown patch of fur along its back?
    Answer: A silver patch of fur
13. What is a gorilla group called: a clan, troop, or family?
    Answer: A troop
14. Where do orangutans live: in trees, caves, or tall grass?
    Answer: In trees

Level 3

15. Bonobo is another name for what type of chimp?
    Answer: Pygmy chimp
16. How many nests can an orangutan make in seven days?
    Answer: 14
17. What do opposable thumbs allow a great ape to do?
    Answer: Use tools
18. Which member of a gorilla group decides when it is time to move on?
    Answer: The silverback
19. What do gorillas eat?
    Answer: Mostly plants, but they will also eat insects

ANSWERS: Bears

Level 1

1. Bears hibernate by going into a long sleep. True or false?
   Answer: True
2. Where do polar bears live: the Arctic, the Antarctic, or South America?
   Answer: The Arctic
3. Are baby bears called kittens, pups, or cubs?
   Answer: Cubs
4. Where do mother bears give birth: underwater, by a lake, or in a den?
   Answer: In a den
5. Bears are sometimes scavengers. True or false?
   Answer: True

Level 2

6. The grizzly bear is a type of brown bear. True or false?
   Answer: True
7. For how long can a black bear hibernate: 50, 100, or 200 days?
   Answer: 100 days
8. Is the sun bear, Kodiak bear, or spectacled bear the smallest bear?
   Answer: The sun bear
9. Does a polar bear have a 1 in. (2.5cm), 4 in. (10cm), or 20 in. (50cm) layer of fat around its body?
   Answer: A 4 in. (10cm) layer
10. At what age does a bear cub leave its mother: one year old, two years old, or three years old?
    Answer: Three years old
11. What "S" do Alaskan brown bears love to eat?
    Answer: Salmon
12. Where does the spectacled bear live: in mountains, deserts, or tundra?
    Answer: In mountains

Level 3

13. If a black bear weighs 400 lbs. (180kg) in the spring, how much would it weigh at hibernation?
    Answer: 800 lbs. (360kg)
14. What "S" is a marine animal that is eaten by polar bears?
    Answer: Seals
15. Name one of two main things that cubs learn from their mothers.
    Answer: How to hunt or make shelters
16. What is an omnivore?
    Answer: An animal that eats both plants and meat
17. Which is the largest bear?
    Answer: The polar bear
18. Which bear eats bromeliad plants?
    Answer: The spectacled bear
19. In the fall how many hours a week, on average, does a bear spend eating?
    Answer: 140

ANSWERS: Pets

Level 1

1. Pet fish are kept in a tank called an aquarium. True or false?
   Answer: True
2. Cats use their whiskers to find their way around at night. True or false?
   Answer: True
3. Are rabbits fast runners or slow animals?
   Answer: Fast runners
4. Is a cat happy or unhappy if it holds its tail high?
   Answer: Happy

Level 2

5. Cavies are also called guinea pigs. True or false?
   Answer: True
6. Do domestic cats have short hair, long hair, or either type?
   Answer: Either type
7. Are dogs most closely related to rabbits, foxes, or wolves?
   Answer: Wolves
8. Can a rabbit see almost 90 degrees, 180 degrees, or 360 degrees?
   Answer: Almost 360 degrees
9. Which is not a type of parrot: macaw, parakeet, or quetzal?
   Answer: Quetzal
10. What "H" means an animal that eats plants?
    Answer: Herbivore
11. The Abyssinian guinea pig has smooth, short hair. True or false?
    Answer: False (it has a rough coat of swirled hair)
12. Which animal is also known as a desert rat: the guinea pig, gerbil, or rabbit?
    Answer: The gerbil
13. Rearrange DEER BURP to spell a word used to describe cats of a particular type.
    Answer: Purebred

Level 3

14. What must a hamster do because its teeth grow all the time?
    Answer: Gnaw on anything available
15. What ability is the African gray parrot known for?
    Answer: Being one of the best mimics
16. What "S" is another name for the golden hamster?
    Answer: Syrian hamster
17. Pet fish owners need to make sure that what "T" in an aquarium is properly controlled to suit the type of fish?
    Answer: Temperature
18. How many breeds of dogs are there?
    Answer: More than 400 breeds
19. Rabbits are most active during which times of the day?
    Answer: At dawn and dusk
20. In which states is it illegal to keep gerbils?
    Answer: California and Hawaii

ANSWERS: Africa

Level 1

1. Is Mount Kilimanjaro Africa's highest point?
   Answer: Yes
2. The Sahara is the largest desert in the world. True or false?
   Answer: True
3. Which "N" in Africa is the longest river in the world?
   Answer: Nile river
4. Who built the pyramids: the ancient Europeans, ancient Egyptians, or ancient Americans?
   Answer: The ancient Egyptians

Level 2

5. The Serengeti is a sandy desert. True or false?
   Answer: False (it is a grassland)
6. Lake Tanganyika is the longest lake in the world. Is it also the deepest in Africa?
   Answer: Yes
7. Where does the Nile river flow to: the Mediterranean Sea, Red Sea, or Atlantic Ocean?
   Answer: The Mediterranean Sea
8. Is the Serengeti in Tanzania and Kenya, or Botswana and South Africa?
   Answer: Tanzania and Kenya
9. What happens every year along the Nile river: does the river dry up, stay the same, or flood its banks?
   Answer: It floods its banks
10. How many blocks of stone make up the Great Pyramid: 23,000, 230,000, or 2,300,000?
    Answer: 2,300,000
11. What "N" are people who live in the Sahara?
    Answer: Nomads
12. How many animals migrate in the Serengeti each year: almost 200,000, two million, or five million?
    Answer: Two million
13. Rearrange MAIN GOLF to name a bird that migrates to Lake Tanganyika.
    Answer: Flamingo

Level 3

14. How long is Lake Tanganyika?
    Answer: 415 mi. (670km) long
15. Name the highest point on Mount Kilimanjaro.
    Answer: Kibo
16. For which "C" pharaoh was the Great Pyramid built?
    Answer: Cheops
17. What is a stratovolcano?
    Answer: A volcano that is made of hardened lava and volcanic ash
18. How large is the Sahara?
    Answer: 3,500,000 sq. mi. (9,000,000km^2)

ANSWERS: The Middle East

Level 1

1. The Blue Mosque is in Istanbul. True or false?
   Answer: True
2. Do Muslims make pilgrimages to Mecca?
   Answer: Yes
3. Is the tallest hotel in the world in Dubai or in Antarctica?
   Answer: Dubai
4. Minarets are tiny Islamic dancers. True or false?
   Answer: False (minarets are spiral towers)

Level 2

5. Diriyah was the capital of which country: Saudi Arabia, Greece, or Spain?
   Answer: Saudi Arabia
6. How many blue tiles are inside of the Blue Mosque: more than 200, more than 2,000, or more than 20,000?
   Answer: More than 20,000
7. Was the Blue Mosque completed in 3600 B.C. or A.D. 1616?
   Answer: A.D. 1616
8. Was Diriyah destroyed by a flood or an Egyptain-led army?
   Answer: An Egyptian-led army
9. Which is a servant in an Islamic mosque: the muezzin or the serf?
   Answer: The muezzin
10. In which "S" country was the Krak des Chevaliers built?
    Answer: Syria
11. The Blue Mosque is also known as the Sultan Ahmed Mosque. True or false?
    Answer: True
12. What is a caliph: an Islamic leader or a Jewish leader?
    Answer: An Islamic leader
13. What "G" once covered the Dome of the Rock?
    Answer: Gold

Level 3

14. Who ordered the building of the Dome of the Rock?
    Answer: Abd al-Malik
15. Mecca is in which country?
    Answer: Saudi Arabia
16. What does Krak des Chevaliers mean?
    Answer: Fortress of the Knights
17. Around how much higher than the Burj al-Arab will the Burj Dubai be?
    Answer: 1,604 ft. (489m) higher
18. When were the Crusades?
    Answer: Between the 1000s and 1200s

ANSWERS:
Asia

Level 1

1. Mount Everest is the tallest mountain in the world. True or false?
   Answer: True
2. Is the Taj Mahal in India, Croatia, or Spain?
   Answer: India
3. In building the Taj Mahal, more than 1,000 elephants were used to haul marble. True or false?
   Answer: True
4. Mount Fuji in Japan is a dormant volcano. True or false?
   Answer: True

Level 2

5. Shah Jahan built the Taj Mahal for his favorite daughter. True or false?
   Answer: False (Shah Jahan built it in memory of his wife)
6. What "T" does "wat" mean?
   Answer: Temple
7. Where is the Potala Palace: in Japan, Malaysia, or Tibet?
   Answer: In Tibet
8. Which building was built in Kuala Lumpur, the capital of Malaysia: Angkor Wat, the Great Wall, or Petronas Twin Towers?
   Answer: Petronas Twin Towers
9. How many people climb Mount Fuji's summit to pray each year: 5,000, 50,000, or 500,000?
   Answer: 500,000
10. When was Angkor Wat built: in the 1000s, 1100s, or 1200s?
    Answer: In the 1100s
11. The Sarawak Chamber is the world's largest cave chamber. True or false?
    Answer: True
12. Name one of the first two people to reach the summit of Mount Everest.
    Answer: Edmund Hillary or Tenzing Norgay
13. During which dynasty did the building of the Great Wall begin?
    Answer: In the Qin dynasty

Level 3

14. For how many years did the Dalai Lamas use the Potala Palace as their winter home?
    Answer: 311 years
15. Where can the Sarawak Chamber be found?
    Answer: In Borneo, Malaysia
16. If Mount Fuji is 12,385 ft. (3,776m) high, how much higher is Mount Everest than Mount Fuji?
    Answer: 16,636 ft. (5,072m)
17. If the Petronas Twin Towers' skybridge is 558 ft. (170m) high, how much taller are the towers themselves?
    Answer: 925 ft. (282m) taller
18. How long is the Great Wall of China?
    Answer: Around 3,900 mi. (6,300km)

ANSWERS:
Europe

Level 1

1. Where is Red Square: in Paris, France, or Moscow, Russia?
   Answer: In Moscow, Russia
2. Does the Channel Tunnel go under or over the English Channel?
   Answer: Under
3. The Leaning Tower of Pisa was designed to lean. True or false?
   Answer: False (but it began leaning during construction)
4. How many tracks are in the Channel Tunnel: one, two, or three?
   Answer: Three

Level 2

5. The Eisriesenwelt ice cave is the largest ice cave in the world. True or false?
   Answer: True
6. Is the Guggenheim Museum in Paris, Bilbao, or Salzburg?
   Answer: Bilbao
7. Was the Eiffel Tower built in Paris, France, to celebrate Bastille Day, the end of the Hundred Years' War, or the Universal Exhibition?
   Answer: The Universal Exhibition
8. Who commissioned the building of Saint Basil's Cathedral: Ivan the Terrible, Rasputin, or Catherine the Great?
   Answer: Ivan the Terrible
9. What does "Eisriesenwelt" mean: tiny ice world, giant cave, or giant ice world?
   Answer: Giant ice world
10. Which famous Alpine mountain is pyramid-shaped?
    Answer: The Matterhorn
11. What features appear on the top of Saint Basil's Cathedral?
    Answer: Onion domes
12. How high is Mont Blanc: 15,770 ft. (4,808m), 19,050 ft. (5,808m), or 25,610 ft. (7,808m)?
    Answer: 15,770 ft. (4,808m)
13. What is a campanile: a bell tower, dome, or steeple?
    Answer: A bell tower
14. How much does the Eiffel Tower's structure weigh: around 5,330, 7,300, or 10,300 tons?
    Answer: Around 7,300 tons

Level 3

15. How long is the Channel Tunnel?
    Answer: 31 mi. (50km)
16. How long did it take to construct the Leaning Tower of Pisa?
    Answer: 197 years
17. What forms the bottom of the Eiffel Tower?
    Answer: A base held by four pillars
18. What material covers the curved panels of the Guggenheim Museum?
    Answer: Titanium

ANSWERS: North America

Level 1

1. The Statue of Liberty is in Washington, D.C. True or false?
   Answer: False (it is in New York Harbor)
2. How many waterfalls make up Niagara Falls?
   Answer: Three
3. The Grand Canyon is in Arizona. True or false?
   Answer: True
4. Which is the world's tallest tree: the coast redwood or the Scots pine?
   Answer: The coast redwood
5. Does the Golden Gate Bridge cross the San Francisco Bay?
   Answer: Yes

Level 2

6. Which U.S. president's face is not carved on Mount Rushmore: Lincoln, Kennedy, or Theodore Roosevelt?
   Answer: Kennedy
7. How many main sections make up the Grand Canyon: three, five, or seven?
   Answer: Three (the South Rim, the North Rim, and the Inner Canyon)
8. How many faces of U.S. presidents were carved into Mount Rushmore: three, four, or five?
   Answer: Four
9. How high is the Statue of Liberty: 271 ft. (82.5m), 307 ft. (93.5m), or 312 ft. (95m)?
   Answer: 307 ft. (93.5m)
10. How old is the oldest giant sequoia: 1,000, 3,200, or 5,500 years old?
    Answer: 3,200 years old
11. Do the vertical ribs on the Golden Gate Bridge stand out on a sunny day?
    Answer: Yes
12. What "S" on the Statue of Liberty's crown represent the world's seven seas and continents?
    Answer: Spikes
13. Rearrange COWES TOAST to name where redwoods grow.
    Answer: West coast

Level 3

14. Why do the towers on the Golden Gate Bridge appear taller than they are?
    Answer: The top of the towers are smaller than the base of the towers
15. How do the plants change as you go farther down into the Grand Canyon?
    Answer: They become shorter and sparser
16. How much wider is Horseshoe Falls than American Falls?
    Answer: 1,538 ft. (469m) wider
17. How long did it take to carve the monument at Mount Rushmore?
    Answer: 14 years
18. How long is the Golden Gate Bridge?
    Answer: 8,977 ft. (2,737m)

ANSWERS: South America

Level 1

1. Did the Incas build Machu Picchu in the Andes?
   Answer: Yes
2. Angel Falls is the highest waterfall in the world. True or false?
   Answer: True
3. The Amazon is the world's largest river, but not the longest. True or false?
   Answer: True
4. Which city is famous for its beaches: Lima or Rio de Janeiro?
   Answer: Rio de Janeiro
5. The llama is a type of wild cat. True or false?
   Answer: False (it is a camelid)

Level 2

6. Can a statue of Jesus be found at the top or the base of Sugar Loaf Mountain in Brazil?
   Answer: At the top
7. What percentage of Earth's oxygen does the Amazon rain forest produce: two percent, ten percent, or 20 percent?
   Answer: 20 percent
8. Angel Falls is named after which American pilot?
   Answer: James Crawford Angel
9. Machu Picchu was built in which century: the 1200s, 1300s, or 1400s?
   Answer: The 1400s
10. Is Lake Titicaca a freshwater lake or a saltwater lake?
    Answer: A freshwater lake
11. How many structures made up Machu Picchu: around ten, 100, or 200?
    Answer: Around 200
12. What "A" in Argentina has fine fleece?
    Answer: Alpaca
13. In the Quechua language does Machu Picchu mean "high mountain," "old mountain," or "young mountain"?
    Answer: "Old mountain"
14. Can the source for the Amazon river be found in the Andes, Himalayas, or Rocky Mountains?
    Answer: The Andes

Level 3

15. How long is the Amazon river?
    Answer: 3,960 mi. (6,387km)
16. Where can most of the remaining rain forests be found?
    Answer: The Amazon basin
17. What are the artificial islands in Lake Titicaca made from?
    Answer: Reeds (totora reeds)
18. What material did the Incas use to build their structures?
    Answer: Ashlar blocks

ANSWERS: Australia and Oceania

Level 1

1. Is Sydney Australia's largest city or one of its smaller cities?
   Answer: It is Australia's largest city
2. Easter Island (or Rapa Nui) is the home of statues that were carved by Polynesian settlers. True or false?
   Answer: True
3. Does the kangaroo live in Australia?
   Answer: Yes
4. Road trains are really trucks that pull trailers. True or false?
   Answer: True

Level 2

5. Uluru in Australia is also called Ayers Rock. True or false?
   Answer: True
6. How many statues are there on Easter Island (or Rapa Nui): six, 60, or 600?
   Answer: 600
7. Uluru is sacred to: British convicts, Australian Aborigines, or marsupials?
   Answer: Australian Aborigines
8. What is attached to the front of an Australian road train: a roo bar, bull bar, or marsupial bar?
   Answer: A roo bar
9. What can be found on New Zealand's North Island: volcanoes, geysers, hot springs, or all of the above?
   Answer: All of the above
10. How long was the longest road train: 13 trailers, 33 trailers, or 113 trailers?
    Answer: 113 trailers
11. What "F" are the Naracoorte Caves in Australia known for?
    Answer: Fossils
12. Was Sydney founded as a new colony for sheep farmers, for sugar plantations, or as a convict settlement?
    Answer: As a convict settlement

Level 3

13. What is the name for the Easter Island (or Rapa Nui) statues?
    Answer: Moai
14. What "M" is a type of animal group, with the largest one living in Australia?
    Answer: Marsupial
15. In what year did paleontologists first visit Victoria Fossil Cave—one of the Naracoorte Caves in Australia?
    Answer: 1969
16. Where was the Sydney Opera House built?
    Answer: On Bennelong Point in Sydney Harbour, Australia
17. What is the Maori name for New Zealand?
    Answer: Aotearoa
18. How far is Easter Island from South America?
    Answer: Around 2,480 mi. (4,000km)

ANSWERS: Antarctica

Level 1

1. Penguins live in Antarctica. True or false?
   Answer: True
2. How do people travel on the ice in Antarctica: by snowmobile, car, or bus?
   Answer: By snowmobile
3. There are permanent research stations in Antarctica. True or false?
   Answer: True
4. What are groups of elephant seals called: harems or groupies?
   Answer: Harems
5. A penguin is a bird. True or false?
   Answer: True

Level 2

6. How many scientists live and work in Anatarctica during the summer: 400, 4,000, or 40,000?
   Answer: 4,000
7. What does the Global Positioning System link to: the Internet, cell phones, or satellites?
   Answer: Satellites
8. Is the Lambert Glacier Antarctica's largest, smallest, or youngest glacier?
   Answer: Its largest glacier
9. How deep can an elephant seal dive: down to 50 ft. (15m), 500 ft. (150m), or 5,000 ft. (1,500m)?
   Answer: Down to 5,000 ft. (1,500m)
10. Why do whales migrate north: to breed, feed, or follow ships?
    Answer: To breed
11. When do whales migrate south: in the spring, summer, fall, or winter?
    Answer: In the summer
12. What is a Dornier 228: a plane, snowmobile, or bulldozer?
    Answer: A plane
13. Ranulph Fiennes and Mike Stroud pulled their own sleds as they crossed Antarctica in 1993. True or false?
    Answer: True

Level 3

14. What are rookeries?
    Answer: Large penguin colonies
15. What is the name of Earth's most southern point?
    Answer: The South Pole
16. Which vehicle has tracks like a bulldozer?
    Answer: The Hagglund
17. What might a beachmaster have in his harem?
    Answer: Up to 50 cows
18. Why are special tents used by scientists?
    Answer: To resist the strong, icy winds

ANSWERS:

The Sun

Level 1

1. The Sun has a core. True or false?
   Answer: True
2. While it is daytime in one part of Earth, can it be nighttime in another part of Earth?
   Answer: Yes
3. What "S" is the name that we give to the different times of the year?
   Answer: Seasons
4. Rearrange RINSE US to spell the time of day when Earth turns toward the Sun and the Sun first appears above the horizon.
   Answer: Sunrise

Level 2

5. Energy released from the Sun affects electronic systems, such as telephone networks, on Earth. True or false?
   Answer: True
6. At sunset is Earth turning toward or away from the Sun?
   Answer: Away from the Sun
7. Bright patches that appear in the Sun's corona are called solar prominences. True or false?
   Answer: False (they are called solar flares)
8. How long does a sunspot cycle usually last?
   Answer: 11 years
9. What comes between Earth and the Sun in a solar eclipse: the Moon, Mars, or Venus?
   Answer: The Moon
10. What "R" does Earth do as it orbits around the Sun?
    Answer: Rotates
11. What are magnetic storms on the Sun called: coronas, sunspots, or eclipses?
    Answer: Sunspots
12. What "H" does the Sun seem to sink below at sunset?
    Answer: Horizon
13. What is visible during a solar eclipse: sunspots, the Sun's corona, or neither?
    Answer: The Sun's corona
14. Do solstices occur when Earth is most or least tilted on its axis?
    Answer: When it is most tilted

Level 3

15. How hot is the hottest part of the Sun?
    Answer: 59,000,000°F (15,000,000°C) at the core
16. What "T" is the dividing line between daytime and nighttime?
    Answer: Terminator
17. How large can sunspots be?
    Answer: 31,000 mi. (50,000km) in diameter
18. Name three things that are released from a buildup of energy in the Sun's corona.
    Answer: Radio waves, ultraviolet light, and X-rays

ANSWERS:

The Moon

Level 1

1. Does the Sun or Earth light up the Moon?
   Answer: The Sun
2. The Moon doesn't have any gravity. True or false?
   Answer: False (it has one sixth of the gravity produced by Earth)
3. Does the Moon orbit around Earth or the Sun?
   Answer: Earth
4. When the sea falls back from the shore it is low tide. True or false?
   Answer: True

Level 2

5. The new moon is sunny on the side that we cannot see. True or false?
   Answer: True
6. There is a face of the Moon that we never see. True or false?
   Answer: True
7. What "G" causes tides?
   Answer: Gravity (the Moon's gravity)
8. Which type of tide occurs when the Moon is overhead: high tide or low tide?
   Answer: High tide
9. How long does the Moon take to orbit Earth: 24 hours, 27.3 days, or 39.5 days?
   Answer: 27.3 days
10. Who was the first astronaut to set foot on the Moon: Al Shepard, Buzz Aldrin, or Neil Armstrong?
    Answer: Neil Armstrong
11. Does Earth's or the Sun's shadow pass over the Moon during a lunar eclipse?
    Answer: Earth's shadow
12. Which "W" means that the Moon is getting thinner?
    Answer: Waning
13. Are high tides higher or lower during spring tides?
    Answer: Higher
14. Do neap tides occur when Earth, the Moon, and the Sun are in line?
    Answer: No, they occur when Earth, the Moon, and the Sun move apart

Level 3

15. What is the diameter of the Moon?
    Answer: 2,155 mi. (3,476km)
16. How long does the Moon take to pass through all of its phases?
    Answer: 29.3 days
17. Where are the Sun and the Moon when there is a full moon?
    Answer: On opposite sides of Earth
18. When does a lunar eclipse occur?
    Answer: When the full moon passes exactly behind Earth
19. What was the date of the first U.S. Moon landing?
    Answer: July 21, 1969

ANSWERS: Constellations

Level 1

1. You must always use binoculars or a telescope to see stars. True or false?
   Answer: False (some stars can be seen with just your eyes)
2. The constellation Scorpius is also known as Scorpio. True or false?
   Answer: True
3. How many halves can the celestial sky be split into: two or three?
   Answer: Two
4. Can the Southern Cross be seen in the Northern Hemisphere?
   Answer: No
5. Centaurus is a constellation named after a creature from Greek mythology. True or false?
   Answer: True

Level 2

6. Pegasus is named after which animal from Greek mythology: a winged horse, bull, or goat?
   Answer: A winged horse
7. Columba is named after which bird sent from the Ark by Noah to look for land: a dove, pigeon, or eagle?
   Answer: A dove
8. Which constellation did sailors use to navigate in the Southern Hemisphere?
   Answer: The Southern Cross
9. Rearrange BRUIN COLAS to name an instrument that is used for stargazing.
   Answer: Binoculars
10. Which star is the brightest: Sirius, Orion, or Cygnus?
    Answer: Sirius, (a star in the constellation of Canis Major)
11. Which "O" is the constellation with the largest number of bright stars?
    Answer: Orion
12. Rearrange BEE GLUE SET to spell the name of the bright red star that marks Orion's shoulder.
    Answer: Betelgeuse
13. Which "C" is a southern constellation that can be seen in the Northern Hemisphere in February?
    Answer: Columba

Level 3

14. What object does the constellation Libra depict?
    Answer: A set of scales
15. What is the name of the 13th-brightest star in the sky?
    Answer: Antares (a star in the constellation of Scorpius)
16. When in history do we know that the Southern Cross could be seen from the Middle East?
    Answer: In biblical times
17. Name the bright star that marks the tail of Cygnus.
    Answer: Deneb

ANSWERS: Outer space

Level 1

1. Which can you find in outer space: a green hole, black hole, or orange hole?
   Answer: A black hole
2. Who was a famous astronomer: Rubble, Bubble, or Hubble?
   Answer: Hubble
3. The galaxy that contains Earth is called the Creamy Way. True or false?
   Answer: False (it is called the Milky Way)
4. Does a star begin life in a nest or in a nebula?
   Answer: In a nebula

Level 2

5. A galaxy is a large group of black holes. True or false?
   Answer: False (it is a huge group of stars)
6. Stars usually last for billions of years. True or false?
   Answer: True
7. Which is an American space agency: LASA, MASA, or NASA?
   Answer: NASA
8. When a nebula shrinks and condenses, does it heat up or cool down?
   Answer: It heats up
9. Does the Milky Way appear to be pale, colorful, or dark in the night sky?
   Answer: Pale
10. Rearrange RAVEN SOUP to name a type of space explosion.
    Answer: Supernova
11. How many galaxies are in the Local Group: around three, around 30, or around 300?
    Answer: Around 30
12. A nebula is a large star. True or false?
    Answer: False (it is a cloud of dust and gas)
13. Is the Milky Way a large galaxy or a small galaxy?
    Answer: A large galaxy
14. How many types of galaxies are there: four, five, or seven?
    Answer: Four
15. Which forms first: a red giant or a white dwarf?
    Answer: A red giant

Level 3

16. In which part of the Milky Way is Earth's solar system?
    Answer: In one of its arms
17. What do some scientists believe lies in the center of our galaxy?
    Answer: A giant black hole
18. What is the main gas that is found in the Eagle Nebula?
    Answer: Hydrogen

ANSWERS: Gold

Level 1

1. What "Y" color is gold?
   Answer: Yellow
2. Where was there a famous gold rush that began in 1848: California or Ohio?
   Answer: California
3. Gold is a hard metal. True or false?
   Answer: False (it is soft)
4. What is gold dust: chunks of gold or tiny particles of gold?
   Answer: Tiny particles of gold

Level 2

5. Rearrange GET GUNS to name the gold pieces that are found by mining.
   Answer: Nuggets
6. Were there gold rushes in the 1800s in South Africa, Russia, or Japan?
   Answer: In South Africa
7. Which "O" is the word for rock that contains metals such as gold?
   Answer: Ore
8. Rearrange ANN PING to name a way of searching for gold in rivers using a wide pan.
   Answer: Panning
9. What "G" do we call a person who can make jewelry out of gold?
   Answer: Goldsmith
10. What "I" is the word for the bars of gold that countries keep as part of their money reserves?
    Answer: Ingot
11. Exposing gold to air can make it dull. True or false?
    Answer: False
12. What "P" is the name for someone who searches for gold?
    Answer: Prospector
13. Gold can be pulled out to make thin wire. True or false?
    Answer: True

Level 3

14. Which country is the world's largest gold producer?
    Answer: South Africa
15. What were used to wash gold pieces from riverbeds?
    Answer: Shallow metal pans
16. Where is the largest gold mine?
    Answer: In West Papua, Indonesia
17. For how long has gold been used as money?
    Answer: 4,000 years
18. What "E" is a substance that cannot be broken down such as gold?
    Answer: Element

ANSWERS: Caves

Level 1

1. Worms sometimes live in caves. True or false?
   Answer: True
2. Do bats or eagles roost in the roofs of caves?
   Answer: Bats
3. Do bacteria and insects feed on fungi or potatoes growing in caves?
   Answer: Fungi
4. Plants, such as ferns and mosses, cannot grow in a cave entrance. True or false?
   Answer: False

Level 2

5. Rearrange NOODLE WRAPS to name a big cat that shelters in caves during the winter.
   Answer: Snow leopard
6. What is volcanic lava when it is red-hot, soft, and runny: molten, malted, or molded?
   Answer: Molten
7. Name one of two "S" birds that nest on ledges in the ceiling of a cave's entrance.
   Answer: Swallows or swiftlets
8. Rearrange LEAST STIGMA to name the rock formations that grow up from the floors of caves.
   Answer: Stalagmites
9. Fungi growing in caves need little light, water, or nutrients. True or false?
   Answer: False (fungi need little light, but they do need moisture and nutrients)
10. Do cockroaches or swallows feed on bat droppings in caves?
    Answer: Cockroaches
11. Which is the name of a zone of a cave system: the sunrise zone, twilight zone, or midnight zone?
    Answer: Twilight zone
12. Which rock formations hang like icicles from the roofs of caves: stalagmites or stalactites?
    Answer: Stalactites
13. Name two "S" types of creatures that can live in caves.
    Answer: Spiders and scorpions

Level 3

14. Which "C" is a mineral that is formed when limestone is dissolved?
    Answer: Calcite
15. Temperatures remain constant in which cave zone?
    Answer: The dark zone
16. Underground rivers carve out what features?
    Answer: Tunnels and caves
17. What happened to the soft lava that once filled a lava tube?
    Answer: It drained or flowed away
18. Rearrange BLAME EMPIRE to form another word meaning "watertight."
    Answer: Impermeable

ANSWERS: Climate

Level 1

1. During a drought, is there less or more rainfall than usual?
Answer: Less rainfall

2. What are clouds made of: water vapor or icy water?
Answer: Water vapor

3. Cirrus is the name for a type of cloud. True or false?
Answer: True

Level 2

4. Which "S" is the largest desert in the world?
Answer: Sahara

5. Which is a greenhouse gas: oxygen or carbon dioxide?
Answer: Carbon dioxide

6. In how many years do meteorologists think that all of the glaciers could melt away: ten, 20, or 30?
Answer: 30 years

7. Is an arid climate hot and wet, hot and dry, or cold and icy?
Answer: Hot and dry

8. Where did scientists find a hole in the ozone layer: over Antarctica, the Arctic, or both?
Answer: Both

9. How much rainfall do deserts receive in a year: less than 10 in. (25cm), less than 20 in. (50cm), or more than 3 ft. (1m)?
Answer: Less than 10 in. (25cm)

10. Which of these two cloud types brings rain: cirrus or cumulonimbus?
Answer: Cumulonimbus

11. Rearrange ACE GIRL to name a source of water entering rivers.
Answer: Glaciers

12. What "L"s have been drying up in recent years?
Answer: Lakes

13. Are cumulus clouds wispy or puffy clouds?
Answer: Puffy

14. How much of the land on Earth is desert: one third, one quarter, or one fifth?
Answer: One third

Level 3

15. During a drought, why do crops die?
Answer: Because water supplies dry up

16. The ozone layer shields Earth from what type of harmful rays?
Answer: Ultraviolet

17. What never thaws in the tundra?
Answer: The soil

18. When did the recent drought in the Sahel, northern Africa, begin?
Answer: 1968

19. How high up in the atmosphere is the ozone layer?
Answer: 14 mi. (22km)

ANSWERS: Storms

Level 1

1. Lightning is a spark of electricity in a cloud. True or false?
Answer: True

2. Is a blizzard a snowstorm or a dust storm with strong winds?
Answer: A snowstorm with strong winds

3. Where do sandstorms happen: in deserts or rain forests?
Answer: In deserts

4. What time of year do thunderstorms usually happen: in the summer or winter?
Answer: In the summer

Level 2

5. If a wave tips over a lifeboat, does it always sink?
Answer: No (modern lifeboats can flip upright)

6. Rearrange FIND LOGO into a word that describes what happens when seawater spills over onto dry land.
Answer: Flooding

7. How many people are killed by lightning in the U.S. every year: around ten, 100, or 1,000?
Answer: Around 100

8. How many thunderstorms take place on Earth at any one time: around 20, 200, or 2,000?
Answer: Around 2,000

9. Electricity is made in what type of cloud: nimbostratus, cumulonimbus, or cumulus?
Answer: Cumulonimbus

10. Lightning always takes the form of a long, bright streak that follows a zigzag path. True or false?
Answer: False (lightning can be ball-shaped)

11. What "M" is the word for a weather expert?
Answer: Meteorologist

12. What happens to a tree that is struck by lightning: does it get soggy, glow in the dark, or is it blown apart?
Answer: It is blown apart

13. What type of "G" system can be found on lifeboats?
Answer: Global Positioning System

Level 3

14. A huge North Sea storm surge in 1953 hit which countries?
Answer: The U.K. and the Netherlands

15. What is thunder?
Answer: The vibrations that are made by heated air

16. What is the effect of warm air from the ground rising quickly into the cold atmosphere?
Answer: It can cause wind, rain, and thunderstorms

17. What is a lightning rod?
Answer: A metal rod that directs lightning to the ground

18. How high can wind blow sand during a sandstorm?
Answer: 4,920 ft. (1,500m) high

ANSWERS: Hurricanes and tornadoes

Level 1

1. Are planes ever flown into the center of a hurricane?
   Answer: Yes (in order to take measurements)
2. There is torrential rain during a hurricane. True or false?
   Answer: True
3. Do hurricanes usually happen during the warmer or colder months?
   Answer: The warmer months
4. Are hurricanes strong enough to lift up boats and trucks?
   Answer: Yes
5. What is the term for studying storms close up: storm chasing, storm checking, or storm charting?
   Answer: Storm chasing

Level 2

6. Tornadoes are not much more than 30 ft. (10m) in diameter. True or false?
   Answer: False (they can be up to 1 mi., or 1.5km, wide)
7. What is the name of the truck that is used for studying storms close up?
   Answer: Doppler on wheels
8. Do hurricanes form over land or water?
   Answer: Over water (but they move to land)
9. Where is Tornado Alley: in China, India, or the U.S.?
   Answer: The U.S.
10. What "D" is a type of radar that is used to investigate storms?
    Answer: Doppler
11. How many tornadoes can the U.S. have in a year: ten, 100, or more than 1,000?
    Answer: More than 1,000
12. What is the minimum water temperature needed for a hurricane to form: 72°F (22°C), 81°F (27°C), or 86°F (30°C)?
    Answer: 81°F (27°C)
13. What "R" equipment can be found on a weather-tracking plane?
    Answer: Radar
14. Do hurricanes move faster or slower as they get close to land?
    Answer: Faster

Level 3

15. What two things do weather-tracking planes measure about a hurricane?
    Answer: Wind speed and pressure
16. Inside what type of cloud do tornadoes form?
    Answer: Cumulonimbus (thunderclouds)
17. What are hurricane surges?
    Answer: Huge waves that flood coasts

ANSWERS: Tsunamis

Level 1

1. A tsunami can travel thousands of miles. True or false?
   Answer: True
2. A tsunami is only around 3 ft. (1m) high when it is traveling across the ocean. True or false?
   Answer: True
3. Can ships pass over tsunamis before they reach the coast?
   Answer: Yes (the waves are small until they reach the coast)
4. A tsunami is one massive wave. True or false?
   Answer: False (a tsunami is a train, or series, of waves)
5. Does a tsunami start on land or at sea?
   Answer: At sea

Level 2

6. Rearrange HE ATE QUARK to name an undersea event that can cause a tsunami.
   Answer: Earthquake
7. What "A" is a rock hurtling through space, which may crash into the sea and set off a tsunami?
   Answer: Asteroid
8. Tsunamis can be formed by rock slides. True or false?
   Answer: True
9. What is the average height above sea level of a tsunami wave as it hits a coast: 10 ft. (3m), 150 ft. (45m), or 1,640 ft. (500m)?
   Answer: 10 ft. (3m)
10. There are usually two to four hours between two tsunami waves in a train. True or false?
    Answer: False (it is usually 15–60 minutes between two waves)
11. How fast can a train of waves travel: 43 mph (70km/h), 105 mph (170km/h), or 434 mph (700km/h)?
    Answer: 434 mph (700km/h)
12. Do waves from tsunamis look curved or square when they are seen from the side?
    Answer: Square (hurricane waves are curved)
13. Are megatsunami waves less than 13 ft. (4m), 46 ft. (14m), or more than 130 ft. (40m) high?
    Answer: More than 130 ft. (40m) high

Level 3

14. Name the parts of Earth's crust that move, causing an earthquake.
    Answer: Tectonic plates
15. Why do tsunamis slow down as they approach a shore?
    Answer: The seabed rising up toward a coast slows it down
16. How many people were killed in the Indian Ocean tsunami?
    Answer: Around 230,000
17. Which volcano in Indonesia erupted in 1883, causing massive waves that killed 36,000 people?
    Answer: Krakatoa
18. What does the word "wavelength" mean?
    Answer: The distance between one wave and the next

ANSWERS: The senses

Level 1

1. Which "T" is the part of the mouth that you use to taste food?
   Answer: Tongue
2. To smell something, you have to breathe in the smell through your nose. True or false?
   Answer: True
3. Do sensors in the ear send information about sound to the other ear or to the brain?
   Answer: To the brain
4. If a person needs glasses, are the objects that he or she sees without them focused or blurry?
   Answer: Blurry

Level 2

5. Rearrange FINEST GRIP to name a part of the body that is sensitive to touch.
   Answer: Fingertips
6. Does light enter the eye through the pupil, lens, or retina?
   Answer: The pupil
7. Do sound waves first enter the ear through the outer ear, middle ear, or inner ear?
   Answer: The outer ear
8. Rearrange LIBERAL to name a method that people can use to read with their fingertips.
   Answer: Braille
9. Is the middle ear made up of tiny bones, cilia, or sensor cells?
   Answer: Tiny bones
10. Name four basic types of tastes that your tongue can detect.
    Answer: Sweet, salty, sour, and bitter
11. Which "C" is the word for the tiny hairs in the nose?
    Answer: Cilia
12. How many taste buds can be found on your tongue and throat: less than 100, 1,000, or up to 10,000?
    Answer: Up to 10,000
13. What "G" would you wear to correct blurry vision?
    Answer: Glasses
14. Which part of the ear vibrates: the eardrum, middle ear, or cochlea?
    Answer: Eardrum

Level 3

15. Where on your body are the sensors that detect temperature?
    Answer: All over your body, in the skin
16. Upside-down images form on which part of the eye?
    Answer: The retina
17. Rearrange CHEER TOP TROOPS into a word for cells that are found in the retina.
    Answer: Photoreceptors
18. Do the sounds made by flutes have long wavelengths?
    Answer: No (they are high-pitched instruments so make sounds with short wavelengths)

ANSWERS: Digestion

Level 1

1. Waste passes from the large intestine to the anus. True or false?
   Answer: True
2. What should you do when you feel thirsty: eat ice cream or drink water?
   Answer: Drink water
3. Where is saliva produced: in the mouth or the liver?
   Answer: In the mouth
4. What "T" rolls food into a ball before swallowing?
   Answer: Tongue

Level 2

5. Most sugars and fats are broken down in the large intestine. True or false?
   Answer: False (they are broken down in the small intestine)
6. Are finger-shaped villi found in the small intestine?
   Answer: Yes
7. Why do we need proteins: to prevent heart disease, provide energy, or for bodybuilding?
   Answer: For bodybuilding (for strong bones and to build muscles)
8. Rearrange BOTCHED ARRAYS to name something that is found in food.
   Answer: Carbohydrates
9. Is urine held in the stomach, bladder, or lungs?
   Answer: In the bladder
10. Where is bile stored: in the small intestine, stomach, or gallbladder?
    Answer: In the gallbladder
11. Does digestion in the stomach take one, two, or four hours?
    Answer: Four hours
12. What "B" is the name of the ball of food that is pushed down to the stomach when you swallow?
    Answer: Bolus
13. How long does digestion usually take in the intestines: eight, 20, or 30 hours?
    Answer: 20 hours
14. How much of our bodies is water: one third, two thirds, or four fifths?
    Answer: Two thirds

Level 3

15. What role does saliva play in digestion?
    Answer: It starts the digestion of sugars
16. What are enzymes?
    Answer: Digestive chemicals that help break down proteins
17. What does bile do?
    Answer: Digests fats
18. What "P" is the name for the muscle movements that push food down the esophagus?
    Answer: Peristalsis

ANSWERS: Inventors

Level 1

1. Is a telescope or a microscope used to see planets?
   Answer: A telescope
2. Are microscopes used by scientists or musicians to carry out experiments?
   Answer: Scientists
3. The Greek philosopher and scientist Aristotle studied plants and animals. True or false?
   Answer: True
4. What is believed to have been the first writing instrument: a stylus made from reed or a pencil?
   Answer: A stylus made from reed

Level 2

5. The other planets in the solar system orbit Earth. True or false?
   Answer: False (all the planets orbit the Sun)
6. Rearrange MARINES US to name the ancient people who are believed to have invented the first writing system.
   Answer: Sumerians
7. Which "O" is a building where astronomers study the sky?
   Answer: Observatory
8. When did Aristotle begin to study nature: around 3000 B.C., 350 B.C., or A.D. 1350?
   Answer: 350 B.C.
9. Who built the first telescope: Galileo Galilei or Isaac Newton?
   Answer: Galileo Galilei
10. Rearrange REMOTE BAR to name a scientific instrument.
    Answer: Barometer
11. Which scientist figured out the movement of the planets: Aristotle, Galileo Galilei, or Isaac Newton?
    Answer: Isaac Newton
12. Which scientist studied plants and animals: Aristotle, Galileo Galilei, or Isaac Newton?
    Answer: Aristotle
13. Benjamin Franklin installed a lightning rod on his house. True or false?
    Answer: True
14. Were the first writings made on clay, paper, or plant leaves?
    Answer: Clay

Level 3

15. In which year did Alexander Graham Bell first successfully try his telephone?
    Answer: 1876
16. Who discovered that electricity has positive and negative charges?
    Answer: Benjamin Franklin
17. Who made the first star maps?
    Answer: Chinese astronomers
18. What shapes form the letters in cuneiform writing?
    Answer: Triangles and lines

ANSWERS: Cars

Level 1

1. What "G" do most cars run on?
   Answer: Gasoline
2. The Ford Model-T was the first affordable car. True or false?
   Answer: True
3. The Mini was originally designed for driving where: in the city or in the countryside?
   Answer: In the city
4. From where do solar-powered cars get their energy?
   Answer: The sun

Level 2

5. How many wheels did Karl Benz's Motorwagen have: two, three, or four?
   Answer: Three
6. Rearrange ARE RELAX to name a part that is found in a car.
   Answer: Rear axle
7. What nationality was Henry Ford: British, American, or Australian?
   Answer: American
8. How many doors did the original Mini have?
   Answer: Two
9. Which type of car is better for the environment: a gasoline-powered car or a solar-powered car?
   Answer: A solar-powered car
10. What "E" drives a car forward?
    Answer: Engine
11. Was the Ford Model-T also known as "Thin Lizzie," "Tin Lizzie," or "Tin Dizzy"?
    Answer: "Tin Lizzie"
12. Which was the first vehicle to use a gasoline-powered engine?
    Answer: Karl Benz's Motorwagen
13. In which decade was the Mini introduced: the 1950s, 1960s, or 1970s?
    Answer: The 1950s
14. In 1914 a Ford Model-T could be assembled in 93 minutes. True or false?
    Answer: True
15. Solar-powered cars can run all of the time. True or false?
    Answer: False (they may not run in bad weather)

Level 3

16. Is a propeller shaft a type of long rod, a series of gears, or a type of steering mechanism?
    Answer: A type of long rod
17. What "A" means the way that air flows over a moving car?
    Answer: Aerodynamics
18. What "T" helps control the engine's speed?
    Answer: Transmission

ANSWERS: Motorcycles

Level 1

1. Is the Lambretta a scooter?
   Answer: Yes
2. A "chopper" is a motorcycle that was changed by chopping off parts from its frame. True or false?
   Answer: True
3. Rearrange EMPOD to name a very small type of motorcycle.
   Answer: Moped
4. The first motorcycle was made in Germany. True or false?
   Answer: True

Level 2

5. In racing do motorcycles have the same or different engine capacities?
   Answer: The same
6. Are the handlebars on choppers higher or lower than on other motorcycles?
   Answer: Higher
7. What "S" is a bike that motocross racers use?
   Answer: Scrambler
8. Was the Vespa introduced in 1946, 1956, or 1966?
   Answer: In 1946
9. What "S" is the name for a motorcycle carriage with only one wheel?
   Answer: Sidecar
10. Did the Hildebrand brothers' 1889 trial motorcycle have a steam-driven or a gasoline-driven engine?
    Answer: A steam-driven engine
11. Superbikes are not road bikes. True or false?
    Answer: False (they are specially adapted road bikes)
12. Scramblers race for how long: 10 to 40 minutes or one to two hours?
    Answer: 10 to 40 minutes
13. Is Harley Davidson known for scooters or choppers?
    Answer: Choppers

Level 3

14. Name two of the three engine classes for Grand Prix motorcycle circuit racing.
    Answer: 125cc, 250cc, and MotoGP (up to 800cc)
15. In what year did Eric Oliver first win the World Motorcycle Sidecar Championship?
    Answer: In 1949
16. What "P" is another word for a trial model?
    Answer: Prototype
17. What was the top speed of the motorcycle that was made by the Hildebrand brothers and Alois Wolfmuller?
    Answer: 25 mph (40km/h)
18. What is the name of the largest sidecar maker?
    Answer: Watsonian-Squire

ANSWERS: Airplanes

Level 1

1. Are the economy-class seats in an airplane usually in the back of the cabin or in the front?
   Answer: In the back of the cabin
2. Do aircraft taxi or train as they move along the ground?
   Answer: Taxi
3. Is cargo packed into huge containers before being loaded onto a plane?
   Answer: Yes
4. Rearrange NICER SOUPS to name a really fast aircraft.
   Answer: Supersonic

Level 2

5. At an airport passengers might be driven in a shuttle to aircraft that are parked on the runway. True or false?
   Answer: True
6. Which "T" is the name of a building in an airport?
   Answer: Terminal
7. What "F" is the name of the part of an airplane where digital screens provide flight information?
   Answer: Flight deck
8. Cargo decks can be found under the cabins. True or false?
   Answer: True
9. What was the first wide-body jet plane: the Boeing 747 or the Airbus A380?
   Answer: The Boeing 747
10. Do scissor trucks lift cargo containers into the cargo hold or lift passengers to the passenger cabins?
    Answer: They lift cargo containers
11. Did Concorde fly from London, Paris, New York City, or all of the above?
    Answer: All of the above
12. Which one is quieter: the Boeing 747 or the Airbus A380?
    Answer: The Airbus A380
13. What "B" is the term used when a plane turns left or right in the air?
    Answer: Bank
14. Where in an airport do passengers go when they want to board a plane?
    Answer: The departure lounge (in the terminal building)

Level 3

15. What do flaps on the wings do when they are open?
    Answer: They act like brakes
16. In which year did Concorde begin its passenger service?
    Answer: In 1976
17. What are the metal strips on the wings called that make the plane turn?
    Answer: Ailerons
18. What is Mach 2.2 expressed in miles per hour?
    Answer: 1,364 mph (2,200km/h)

ANSWERS: Ancient Egyptian daily life

Level 1

1. What animals did the Egyptians hunt: hippopotamuses, horses, or hamsters?
   Answer: Hippopotamuses
2. Out of what material did Egyptians build boats: plastic, plywood, or papyrus?
   Answer: Papyrus
3. Egyptians did not farm the land next to the Nile river. True or false?
   Answer: False
4. Egyptians built houses out of mud bricks. True or false?
   Answer: True

Level 2

5. Were Egyptian peasants ever beaten?
   Answer: Yes
6. OH APRON can be rearranged to name what weapon that was used in hunting?
   Answer: Harpoon
7. At what age did Egyptian children begin going to school: three, four, or five?
   Answer: Four
8. Egyptians drank beer. True or false?
   Answer: True
9. When did the Nile river flood: in the spring, summer, or winter?
   Answer: In the summer
10. Who baked bread in ancient Egypt: the men or the women?
    Answer: The women
11. Only Egyptian boys went to school. True or false?
    Answer: False
12. In what season did the Egyptian harvest take place?
    Answer: Spring
13. What was a mertu: a type of person, type of food, or type of house?
    Answer: A type of person
14. What animals did the Egyptians use to help plow the land?
    Answer: Oxen
15. What "F" is used to make linen clothing?
    Answer: Flax

Level 3

16. What did Egyptians call a team of five laborers?
    Answer: A hand
17. What "S" was an Egyptian hairstyle worn by children?
    Answer: Side locks
18. What "B" is a crop that was used by Egyptians to make a popular drink?
    Answer: Barley

ANSWERS: Ancient Egyptian gods and goddesses

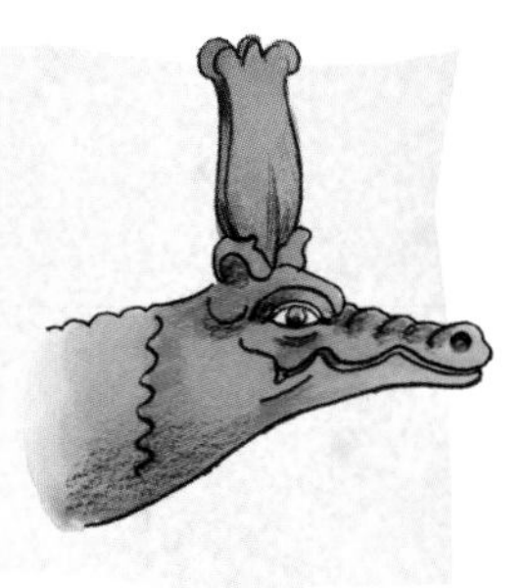

Level 1

1. The ancient Egyptians believed in magic. True or false?
   Answer: True
2. Who was a ruler of the gods: Ma, Ra, or Pa?
   Answer: Ra
3. What name is given to evil magic: red, black, or blue?
   Answer: Black
4. Egyptians made statues of their gods. True or false?
   Answer: True

Level 2

5. What was a "coming forth": a birth, death, or type of procession?
   Answer: A type of procession
6. Only priests took part in daily rituals at the great temples. True or false?
   Answer: True
7. ALE TUM can be rearranged to give the name of what item that was supposed to protect people against magic?
   Answer: Amulet
8. What type of animal bit the god Ra: a tiger, cobra, or spider?
   Answer: A cobra
9. Anubis had the head of which animal: a snake, jackal or rhino?
   Answer: A jackal
10. Was Amun a god of fire or air?
    Answer: Air
11. On what item of jewelry would an Egyptian wear a model of a hand?
    Answer: A bracelet
12. Which god was the guardian of the underworld?
    Answer: Anubis
13. Who was the husband of Isis?
    Answer: Osiris

Level 3

14. Who learned Ra's secret name?
    Answer: Isis
15. What mask would priests wear when preparing a body for burial?
    Answer: A jackal mask
16. Which Egyptian god had a name that meant "The Hidden One"?
    Answer: Amun
17. What "K" is the location of a great temple to Amun?
    Answer: Karnak
18. In which city was Amun originally worshiped?
    Answer: Thebes

ANSWERS: Ancient Greek warfare

Level 1

1. What were Greek shields made out of: linen, paper, or wood?
   Answer: Wood
2. REAPS can be rearranged to name what weapon that was used by the Greeks?
   Answer: Spear
3. Where did the battle of Salamis take place: on land or at sea?
   Answer: At sea
4. What did Greeks make helmets out of: bronze, copper, or aluminum?
   Answer: Bronze

Level 2

5. The main tactic of Greek warships was to ram the enemy. True or false?
   Answer: True
6. What was a phalanx: a weapon, formation, or oar?
   Answer: A formation
7. RIM TREE can be rearranged to name what Greek warship?
   Answer: Trireme
8. Spartans were Greeks. True or false?
   Answer: True
9. At what age did boys start training in Sparta: seven, nine, or 11?
   Answer: Seven
10. What color did Spartans paint on their shields: red or yellow?
    Answer: Red
11. Who won the battle of Salamis: the Greeks or the Persians?
    Answer: The Greeks
12. Rearrange I PASS to name a Greek shield.
    Answer: Aspis
13. What "H" was the most common type of soldier in ancient Greece?
    Answer: Hoplite (a foot soldier)
14. What part of the human body did a greave protect?
    Answer: The shin
15. Who was Xerxes: a Persian king, Spartan general, or Theban god?
    Answer: A Persian king

Level 3

16. What letter did Spartans paint on their shields?
    Answer: The letter "L"
17. What did Spartans call their country?
    Answer: Lacedaemonia
18. From what city were the Greeks who fought in Salamis?
    Answer: Athens
19. What type of weapon was a xiphos?
    Answer: A type of sword

ANSWERS: Ancient Greek gods and goddesses

Level 1

1. What "Z" was the king of the gods?
   Answer: Zeus
2. The Greeks sacrificed bulls to the gods. True or false?
   Answer: True
3. Was Aphrodite the goddess of love and beauty or of hatred and ugliness?
   Answer: Love and beauty

Level 2

4. What "A" was the Greek god of war?
   Answer: Ares
5. What was the symbol of Athene: the owl, eagle, or crow?
   Answer: The owl
6. WORN RUDDLE can be rearranged to give the name of what place Greeks went to after death?
   Answer: Underworld
7. Was Asclepius the god of law or medicine?
   Answer: Medicine
8. Who was the Greek god of the Sun: Artemis, Poseidon, or Apollo?
   Answer: Apollo
9. Who went to the Elysian Fields: those who had led good lives or those who had led bad lives?
   Answer: Those who had led good lives
10. What "L" was a gift of wine poured onto an altar?
    Answer: Libation
11. What "S" was the river that the Greeks crossed when they died?
    Answer: Styx
12. Athene was the goddess of hunting. True or false?
    Answer: False
13. Where was the Panathenaea held?
    Answer: In Athens
14. Rearrange STAR RUT to name a burning pit.
    Answer: Tartarus
15. What animal appeared in the symbol of Asclepius: a snake, spider, or scorpion?
    Answer: A snake
16. What "O" was a temple in which people could ask questions about the future?
    Answer: Oracle

Level 3

17. What gift did Athene give Athens?
    Answer: The first olive tree
18. Who was the husband of Aphrodite?
    Answer: The ugly god Hephaestos
19. Which temple in Athens contained a huge gold and ivory statue of Athene?
    Answer: The Parthenon

ANSWERS: The Roman Empire

Level 1

1. What could no one wear except for the emperor: polka dots, purple, or hats?
   Answer: Purple
2. The Romans built winding roads. True or false?
   Answer: False
3. SEA NET can be rearranged to name what group of citizens?
   Answer: Senate

Level 2

4. What were aqueducts used to transport: water, people, or food?
   Answer: Water
5. Was Rome founded by a pair of twins or a pair of lovers?
   Answer: A pair of twins
6. Which famous Roman was murdered: Hadrian, Augustus, or Julius Caesar?
   Answer: Julius Caesar
7. What "V" looted Rome?
   Answer: Vandals
8. The name Augustulus meant "father of Augustus." True or false?
   Answer: False
9. Augustus conquered the Dacians. True or false?
   Answer: False (Trajan did)
10. What was a toga: a crown, shoe, or robe?
    Answer: A robe
11. How long is Zaghouan Aqueduct: more than 46 mi. (74km), more than 57 mi. (92km), or more than 68 mi. (109km)?
    Answer: More than 57 mi. (92km)
12. Was Odoacer a German or a Greek?
    Answer: A German
13. SOUL RUM can be rearranged to give the name of what founder of Rome?
    Answer: Romulus
14. Julius Caesar was the first emperor. True or false?
    Answer: False (Augustus was the first emperor)
15. Augustus was the son of Julius Caesar. True or false?
    Answer: False
16. Under which emperor was the empire at its largest: Nero, Trajan, or Vespasian?
    Answer: Trajan

Level 3

17. Who was the first Christian emperor?
    Answer: Constantine
18. Who said "I found Rome brick and left it marble"?
    Answer: Augustus
19. Who killed himself so that Trajan would not capture him?
    Answer: The Dacian king, Decebalus

ANSWERS: Roman warfare

Level 1

1. Roman soldiers fought together in formations. True or false?
   Answer: True
2. What was the symbol of the Roman army: a mouse, eagle, or giraffe?
   Answer: An eagle
3. Would Roman soldiers be more likely to form a tiger, tortoise, or toad?
   Answer: A tortoise

Level 2

4. What was an aquilifer: a general, doctor, or standard bearer?
   Answer: A standard bearer
5. What "L" was the name for a Roman foot soldier?
   Answer: Legionary
6. Was a ballista used to throw spears or rocks?
   Answer: Spears
7. COIN TUNER can be rearranged to give the name of what army officer?
   Answer: Centurion
8. What was an onager: a war machine, soldier, or shield?
   Answer: A war machine
9. The Romans conquered the German tribes. True or false?
   Answer: False
10. What "G" was a land conquered by Julius Caesar?
    Answer: Gaul
11. What name was given to soldiers from the provinces?
    Answer: Auxiliaries
12. TOE STUD can be rearranged to give the name of what formation?
    Answer: Testudo
13. Roughly how many men were there in a legion: 50, 500, or 5,000?
    Answer: 5,000
14. What "P" was an empire to the east of Rome?
    Answer: Parthian Empire
15. How many years did an auxiliary have to spend in the army before they were given citizenship?
    Answer: 25 years

Level 3

16. How many soldiers were there in a century?
    Answer: 100
17. Who fought Julius Caesar in a great civil war?
    Answer: Pompey
18. Which Roman general was killed in the battle of Carrhae?
    Answer: Crassus

ANSWERS: The Aztecs

Level 1

1. The Aztecs sometimes demanded prisoners for human sacrifices. True or false?
   Answer: True
2. What did scribes do: write things down or fight in battles?
   Answer: Write things down
3. Most Aztec houses were made out of concrete. True or false?
   Answer: False

Level 2

4. The Aztecs had a team of men who collected household garbage. True or false?
   Answer: True
5. What does the name "tlatoani" mean: speaker or listener?
   Answer: Speaker
6. I BUTTER can be rearranged to name what type of payment made to the Aztecs?
   Answer: Tribute
7. Where was the Aztec capital built: on Lake Texcoco, Mount Texcoco, or the Texcoco river?
   Answer: Lake Texcoco
8. The Aztec capital had no streets. True or false?
   Answer: True
9. Who conquered the Aztecs: the Spanish, French, or Portuguese?
   Answer: The Spanish
10. The Aztec word "hueyi" means "small." True or false?
    Answer: False (it means "great")
11. Aztec houses had no toilets. True or false?
    Answer: False
12. A chinampa was a type of floating house. True or false?
    Answer: False (it was a floating garden)
13. What was a "snake woman": a warrior, doctor, or adviser?
    Answer: An adviser
14. What "G" did Aztecs use in writing?
    Answer: Glyphs
15. How many days were there in the Aztec sacred calendar: 160, 260, or 360?
    Answer: 260

Level 3

16. How many types of calendars did the Aztecs have?
    Answer: Two
17. What was the Aztec capital city?
    Answer: Tenochtitlán

ANSWERS: Aztec religion

Level 1

1. The Aztecs only sacrificed animals. True or false?
   Answer: False
2. What did Aztecs use to make the balls used in tlachtli: rubber, iron, or wood?
   Answer: Rubber
3. Was Huitzilopochtli the god of the Sun or the god of the night?
   Answer: The god of the Sun

Level 2

4. Where did Aztecs perform sacrifices: on top of a temple, inside of a temple, or in front of a temple?
   Answer: On top of a temple
5. What was the Aztec color of sacrifice: red, yellow, or blue?
   Answer: Blue
6. Aztec priests shaved off their hair. True or false?
   Answer: False (they grew it long)
7. What was cut out during a sacrifice: the tongue, liver, or heart?
   Answer: The heart
8. Was Tlaloc the god of rain or the god of the Moon?
   Answer: The god of rain
9. Where did Huitzilopochtli have a shrine: in all temples or at the Great Temple in the capital city?
   Answer: At the Great Temple in the capital city
10. Which Aztecs filed their teeth into points: warriors, priests, or rulers?
    Answer: Priests
11. How often did the Aztecs make sacrifices to Huitzilopochtli: every hour, every day, or every five years?
    Answer: Every day
12. What was the penalty for losing a game of tlachtli?
    Answer: Being offered as a sacrifice
13. How long did the Aztecs claim it took to sacrifice 84,400 victims: four days, four months, or four years?
    Answer: Four days

Level 3

14. BISON AID can be rearranged to name what volcanic rock, used by the Aztecs to make knives?
    Answer: Obsidian
15. Players in tlachtli could only use their hands. True or false?
    Answer: False (they could not use their hands)
16. Which animal eating a snake was a sign to the Aztecs to build a city?
    Answer: The eagle
17. What did Aztec priests use to paint their skin black?
    Answer: Soot

ANSWERS: Fairy tales

Level 1

1. Cinderella marries a prince. True or false?
   Answer: True
2. Are Hansel and Gretel abandoned in the woods or in a town?
   Answer: In the woods
3. Is Gretel, Cinderella, or Sleeping Beauty woken up by a kiss from a prince?
   Answer: Sleeping Beauty
4. Does the Pied Piper lure children away from town or get them to return to town?
   Answer: He lures them away from town

Level 2

5. For how long does Sleeping Beauty sleep: ten years, 50 years, or 100 years?
   Answer: 100 years
6. In *Rumpelstiltskin* is straw, palm leaves, or sheep's wool spun into gold?
   Answer: Straw
7. What "G" is the witch's house made of in later versions of *Hansel & Gretel?*
   Answer: Gingerbread
8. What "F" does the Pied Piper play to lure away the children?
   Answer: Flute
9. Are there more than 30, 340, or 560 versions of Cinderella?
   Answer: More than 340
10. What are mermaids: half men and half goat, half men and half fish, or half women and half fish?
    Answer: Half women and half fish
11. Is Hamelin a German, French, or Austrian town?
    Answer: A German town
12. Are Hansel and Gretel the children of a miller, prince, or woodcutter?
    Answer: A woodcutter
13. Who told the king that it was possible to spin gold: Rumpelstiltskin, the miller, or his daughter?
    Answer: The miller

Level 3

14. In the Chinese version of *Cinderella* which "W" finds the slipper?
    Answer: Warlord
15. Who wrote *The Little Mermaid?*
    Answer: Hans Christian Andersen
16. In which story does a fairy cast a spell?
    Answer: Sleeping Beauty
17. In what year did the children really leave Hamelin?
    Answer: 1284
18. When was the earliest version of *Cinderella* written?
    Answer: Around A.D. 850

ANSWERS: Theater

Level 1

1. Stage carpenters work with wood. True or false?
   Answer: True
2. Stagehands are normally in charge of the actors' costumes. True or false?
   Answer: False (dressers are in charge of the costumes)
3. Does a costume designer or a set designer plan the layout of the stage?
   Answer: A set designer
4. Set builders build theater scenery. True or false?
   Answer: True
5. Is stage smoke a type of special effect?
   Answer: Yes

Level 2

6. What "C" is the name for the clothing that performers wear?
   Answer: Costume
7. Does a costume designer work with a set designer?
   Answer: Yes
8. Which "D" cleans and fixes the costumes?
   Answer: Dresser
9. Does New York's Metropolitan Opera House require 200, 500, or 1,000 staff to put on a performance?
   Answer: 1,000
10. Is the place where the audience sits called the wings, backstage, or the auditorium?
    Answer: The auditorium
11. On stage what would a suitcase be considered: a set, costume, or prop?
    Answer: A prop
12. Are the sides of a stage that are out of the audience's view called the wings, upstage, or front of house?
    Answer: The wings
13. New York's Metropolitan Opera House is also known as what: the Op House, the Met, or the Big Stage?
    Answer: The Met
14. Rearrange AT BELL to name a type of performance that may need a dresser.
    Answer: Ballet

Level 3

15. Where are sets often assembled?
    Answer: On the stage
16. What is the largest number of people that can watch a single performance at New York's Metropolitan Opera House?
    Answer: 3,800
17. Which theater staff sometimes help actors make quick costume changes?
    Answer: Dressers
18. Who uses scale models of the stage in their work?
    Answer: The set designer

ANSWERS: William Shakespeare

Level 1

1. *Macbeth* is a play about a figure from Scottish history. True or false?
   Answer: True
2. Was Shakespeare's theater called the Swan or the Globe?
   Answer: The Globe
3. *Hamlet* is a comedy. True or false?
   Answer: False (it is a tragedy)
4. Did Shakespeare write a play called *Romeo and Juliet* or *Verona and Juliet?*
   Answer: Romeo and Juliet

Level 2

5. Were people who watched a play from the pit called pitlings, groundlings, or watchlings?
   Answer: Groundlings
6. Was Shakespeare born in London, Stratford-upon-Avon, or Paris?
   Answer: Stratford-upon-Avon
7. What was the name of the uncovered part of the theater where people stood to watch plays?
   Answer: The pit
8. Richer people watched plays in the Globe in a covered area. True or false?
   Answer: True
9. Could the Globe hold 500, 1,500, or 3,000 people?
   Answer: 3,000
10. Which "M" is Shakespeare's bloodiest tragedy?
    Answer: Macbeth
11. Is the line "To be, or not to be" from *Macbeth, Hamlet,* or *Romeo and Juliet?*
    Answer: Hamlet
12. Is *Romeo and Juliet* based on real lovers or a made-up tale?
    Answer: Real lovers
13. The Globe was built close to which river in London, England?
    Answer: The Thames river
14. Was *Hamlet* first performed around 1550, 1600, or 1625?
    Answer: Around 1600

Level 3

15. Where was the home of the real couple on whose story Shakespeare based *Romeo and Juliet?*
    Answer: Verona, Italy
16. Which British king had a friendship with Shakespeare?
    Answer: King James I
17. In what year was the Globe rebuilt after it had burned down?
    Answer: 1614
18. By which year was Shakespeare recognized as a playwright?
    Answer: 1592

ANSWERS: Famous ballets

Level 1

1. *The Nutcracker* features a nutcracker turned into a prince. True or false?
   Answer: True
2. Is *Swan Lake* a difficult ballet to perform?
   Answer: Yes
3. Was *Giselle* first performed in London, England, or Paris, France?
   Answer: Paris, France
4. Junior ballet dancers sometimes do solo performances. True or false?
   Answer: True

Level 2

5. Is *The Firebird* based on a Shakespeare play or on Russian folk tales?
   Answer: On Russian folk tales
6. Who composed the music for the ballet *The Sleeping Beauty*: Tchaikovsky or Petipa?
   Answer: Tchaikovsky
7. Is *Giselle* still performed the same way it was in the first production?
   Answer: No (changes have been made since then)
8. In *The Firebird* the dancer performing the part of the firebird often wears a plain costume. True or false?
   Answer: False (the costume is usually elaborate)
9. Odile in *Swan Lake* is what type of creature?
   Answer: A black swan maiden
10. Which "P" roles are unsuitable for junior soloists?
    Answer: Principal roles
11. Was the composer for *The Sleeping Beauty* Russian, French, or American?
    Answer: Russian
12. *The Nutcracker* is a popular production at what time of year?
    Answer: Christmastime
13. Aside from Odile, who is one of the other characters seen in *Swan Lake?*
    Answer: A prince or an evil sorcerer

Level 3

14. What is the first name of the composer of the music for *The Firebird?*
    Answer: Igor (Stravinsky)
15. In which year was the first production of *The Nutcracker?*
    Answer: 1892
16. Puss in Boots makes an appearance in which ballet?
    Answer: The Sleeping Beauty
17. In which year was *Giselle* first performed?
    Answer: 1841
18. Who choreographed the ballet *The Sleeping Beauty?*
    Answer: Marius Petipa

ANSWERS: Basketball

Level 1

1. Children can play basketball. True or false?
   Answer: True
2. Is Michael Jordan British or American?
   Answer: American
3. A regular shot in basketball scores two points. True or false?
   Answer: True
4. Are competition basketballs orange, yellow, or green?
   Answer: Orange

Level 2

5. How many feet off the ground is the basket:
   7 ft. (2m), 10 ft. (3m), or 16 ft. (5m)?
   Answer: 10 ft. (3m)
6. In which year was basketball invented: 1891, 1911, or 1931?
   Answer: 1891
7. Does a basketball weigh 21–23 oz. (600–650g),
   24–26 oz. (700–750g), or 28–30 oz. (800–850g)?
   Answer: 21–23 oz. (600–650g)
8. What "H" is the line across the middle of a basketball court?
   Answer: Halfway line
9. Rearrange CHAIN to spell the country that basketball player Yao Ming is from.
   Answer: China
10. In which part of the basketball court can players only stay with the ball for three seconds: the key, the center of the court, or in the corners of the court?
    Answer: The key
11. How many panels make up a basketball: three, six, or eight?
    Answer: Eight
12. Are the balls used by children smaller, bigger, or the same size as the balls that are used by adults?
    Answer: Smaller
13. What type of basket was first used to play basketball: a basket for peaches, blueberries, or tomatoes?
    Answer: A basket for peaches

Level 3

14. How many feet wide is a basketball court?
    Answer: 50 ft. (15m)
15. How many inches taller is Yao Ming than Michael Jordan?
    Answer: 1 ft. and 1 in. (31cm)
16. Who invented basketball?
    Answer: James Naismith
17. In basketball what is the highest number of points that a single shot can score?
    Answer: Three points are awarded for a long-distance shot
18. How much is a foul shot worth?
    Answer: *One point*

ANSWERS: Horse and pony care

Level 1

1. Horses and ponies do not like being groomed. True or false?
   Answer: False
2. Are horses and ponies sometimes massaged?
   Answer: Yes
3. Is the seat that a rider sits on called a bridle or a saddle?
   Answer: A saddle
4. Horses and ponies mostly eat hay and grass. True or false?
   Answer: True
5. Horses and ponies are kept in buildings called what: stables or pastures?
   Answer: Stables

Level 2

6. What is the cloth that is used after grooming called: a rubber glove, stable glove, or stable cloth?
   Answer: A stable cloth
7. Is braiding done before or after clipping and grooming?
   Answer: After
8. What type of "C" comb can remove dried mud from a horse's or pony's body?
   Answer: Curry comb
9. What "M" name is the hair on a horse's or pony's neck?
   Answer: Mane
10. Rearrange DIG BEND to give the name of something that is replaced in the stable every day.
    Answer: Bedding
11. How many times a day must a horse or pony be fed: once, twice, or three times?
    Answer: Twice
12. Name one of two "B" grains that are used in concentrated feeds for horses and ponies.
    Answer: Barley and bran
13. Is a sponge, tack, or saddle soap used to clean around a horse's or pony's eyes?
    Answer: A sponge
14. Can horses and ponies eat only small amounts of grains or large amounts?
    Answer: Small amounts (they have small stomachs)

Level 3

15. How much manure can an adult horse produce in a week?
    Answer: More than 300 lbs. (140kg)
16. What is the term that is used for putting a saddle and bridle on a horse or pony?
    Answer: Tacking up
17. What object containing horse and pony food is hung up in the stall?
    Answer: A haynet
18. How many pounds of hay can an adult horse eat in a day?
    Answer: 22 lbs. (10kg)

ANSWERS: Martial arts

Level 1

1. Are martial artists often trained to use their skills to defend or to fight?
   Answer: To defend
2. Tai chi movements are sharp and sudden. True or false?
   Answer: False (they are flowing and slow)
3. Is karate a type of striking martial art?
   Answer: Yes
4. Are throwing techniques and armlocks part of judo or kung fu?
   Answer: Judo

Level 2

5. Does kickboxing, tai chi, or karate combine boxing with kicking moves?
   Answer: Kickboxing
6. Does a kickboxer score points by striking with their hands, feet, or both?
   Answer: Both
7. Training for karate is divided into three parts: basics, forms, and sparring. True or false?
   Answer: True
8. Which "J" country does kendo come from?
   Answer: Japan
9. Which color is usually the highest in the colored belt system used in many martial arts: brown, black, or purple?
   Answer: Black
10. Which qualities are required for success in martial arts: discipline and self-control or taking your own lead and being quick to respond?
    Answer: Discipline and self-control
11. Which "K" is a form of martial art that is known for its kicks and open-hand techniques?
    Answer: Karate
12. Which martial art is based on animal poses: tai chi, karate, or kendo?
    Answer: Tai chi
13. Which European country does the form of kickboxing called "savate" come from: Italy, Spain, or France?
    Answer: France

Level 3

14. Why does the color of a belt worn by a judo or karate student change?
    Answer: To indicate a student's progress
15. What is the name of the sword that is used in kendo?
    Answer: Shinai
16. The teachings of which Buddhist led to the beginning of many martial arts?
    Answer: Bodhidharma
17. Which martial art is based on jujitsu?
    Answer: Judo

ANSWERS: Motorsports

Level 1

1. A driver's helmet protects them against what: ice, wind, or fire?
   Answer: Fire
2. Rearrange GEE INN to spell the name of a part of a car.
   Answer: Engine
3. Formula One cars are low and streamlined. True or false?
   Answer: True
4. Does the team decide on a plan in order to win the race?
   Answer: Yes

Level 2

5. Which "M" is the name of the stewards who are in charge of fire safety?
   Answer: Marshals
6. How fast can an F1 pit crew change four wheels: seven, 17, or 37 seconds?
   Answer: Seven seconds
7. Many F1 drivers consider Silverstone to be one of the fastest F1 racetracks. True or false?
   Answer: True
8. How many gallons of gasoline does an F1 car normally use to drive 60 mi. (100km): seven, 13, or 20?
   Answer: Around 20 gallons
9. What was the world land speed record for an F1 car set in 2006: 22 mph (35km/h), 220 mph (355km/h), or 960 mph (1,550km/h)?
   Answer: 220 mph (355km/h)
10. What are the top three NASCAR championships?
    Answer: The Busch Series, the Craftsman Truck Series, and the Nextel Cup
11. What is the important difference between ordinary tracksuits and the race suits that are worn by racecar drivers?
    Answer: Race suits are fireproof
12. What is the strong frame that makes up a NASCAR's structure made out of?
    Answer: Steel
13. The average speed over the entire racetrack of the Talladega Superspeedway is what: 100 mph (160km/h), 188 mph (303km/h), or 220 mph (354km/h)?
    Answer: 188 mph (303km/h)

Level 3

14. What must a driver do at a pit stop?
    Answer: Stop the car in the exact spot and wait for a signal before going
15. What are g-forces?
    Answer: Acceleration forces that are caused by gravity
16. What does the pit crew do to a race car during a pit stop?
    Answer: Change the wheels, refuel, and make repairs
17. What is the advantage of starting a Formula One race with tanks that are half full?
    Answer: The car is lighter, so it will go faster

Index

M

N

O

P

R

S

T

U

V

W

X

Y

Z

Acknowledgments

The publisher would like to thank the following for permission to reproduce their material. Every care has been taken to trace copyright holders. However, if there have been unintentional omissions or failure to trace copyright holders, we apologize and will, if informed, endeavor to make corrections in any future edition.

b = bottom, c = center, l = left, r = right, t = top

PHOTOGRAPHS

10*cl* Corbis/Michael Weber/zefa; 34*br* Kingfisher; 45*b* Corbis/John Hicks;
47*t* Corbis/Jose Fuste Raga; 49*tl* Corbis/Tibor Bognar; 54*tr* Corbis/L. Clarke; 63*tr* Corbis/Jeff Taflan/zefa;
63*c* Roger Ressmeyer/Corbis; 66*bl* NASA/ESA; 66*br* NASA; 75*cr* Corbis/Hulton-Deutsch Collection;
81*b* Corbis/Simon Marcus; 83*c* Corbis/Mark Seelen/zefa; 85*tl* Michael Freeman/Corbis;
87*t* Corbis/Fiat; 87*b* Fiat/Reuters/Corbis; 116*l* Lenfilm/The Kobal Collection;
116*b* 20th Century Fox/The Kobal Collection/Morton, Merrick; 126*b* Sutton